NEW MEXICO
BIRD FINDING GUIDE

Revised Edition

EDITORS

Dale A. Zimmerm[illegible]

Marian A. Zir[illegible]

John N. D[illegible]

ILLUSTRATIONS

Dale A Zimmerman

MAPS

James Karo

Published by the New Mexico Ornithological Society 1992
First Printing 1992

To Boyd Brown McLeod (1921-1988),
founder of the New Mexico Ornithological Society in 1962,
this publication is dedicated with affection and thanks.

The New Mexico Ornithological Society
Post Office Box 3068
Albuquerque, New Mexico 87190

CONTENTS

ACKNOWLEDGMENTS

Some of the information on the central Rio Grande was provided with the permission of the Army Corps of Engineers and the Middle Rio Grande Conservancy District.

The nine geographical sections of this publication were authored, in whole or in part, by the following local birders: Pat Basham, Sherry Bixler, James Black, Warren Bloys, David Cleary, Wesley Cook, Karen Copeland, Nancy Cox, Steven Cox, Nancy Dobbins, John Durrie, Robert Edens, Jr., John Egbert, William Felten, Ralph Fisher, Jr., Paul Fitzsimmons, Roland Goodman, Larry Gorbet, Stephen Hoffman, William Howe, John Hubbard, Charles Hundertmark, Dustin Huntington, Sue Huntington, Nancy Hutto, Glen Hvennegaard, Kay Jenness, Robert Jenness, Adolph Krehbiel, Arch McCallum, Alan Nelson, John Parmeter, Christopher Rustay, Catherine Sandell, Hart Schwarz, Jerri Smith, Patricia Snider, Peter Stacey, Dale Stahlecker, Jackie Talley, Ross Teuber, James Travis, Steve West. Barry Zimmer, Kevin Zimmer, Marian Zimmerman, and Dale Zimmerman.

Patricia Snider assumed the all-important responsibility of securing authors, as detailed above.

James Travis provided helpful editorial assistance.

Wade Douglas has generously shared several Zimmerman drawings used in this publication.

Mary Alice Root, president of the NMOS (1989-1992), has given leadership and encouragement during the entire revision process and with the help of Bo West has done the final word processing of the manuscript.

The use of the equipment and the help of the personnel (especially Ray Granillo) in the Computer Pods of The University of New Mexico made this project possible.

THE EDITORS

INTRODUCTION

"New Mexico is certainly the greatest center of rare birds in the United States" wrote Spencer Baird, Secretary of the Smithsonian Institution, 120 years ago. This honor now clearly belongs to Alaska, but New Mexico still boasts a varied and extensive bird population comprising 460 verified species. The State is thus surpassed only by Texas, California and Arizona, and is equal to Colorado, Oregon and Florida, in its number of bird species. This results in part from New Mexico's size and great habitat diversity as well as from its geographic position at the range limits of numerous species. The latter factor tends to produce relatively small (and perhaps fluctuating) populations of certain birds which are easier to locate elsewhere (especially Arizona). This is doubtless responsible for New Mexico receiving less attention from the birding community in general, and is reflected in the comparatively few organized professional birding tours visiting the State. Nevertheless, seeing many birds of special interest here is relatively simple and straightforward provided one knows where to find them.

The New Mexico chapter in O. S. Pettingill's A GUIDE TO BIRD FINDING WEST, 2nd Ed. (1981) and the first edition of the NEW MEXICO BIRD FINDING GUIDE (1984) remain useful but are now outdated. Habitats and highways constantly change, and the past few years have seen increased interest in New Mexican birds resulting in considerable new available information. Thus the need for an updated guide has become apparent.

The nomenclature used herein is essentially that of the 6th edition of the American Ornithologists' Union CHECK-LIST OF NORTH AMERICAN BIRDS (1983). Many persons still use older identification guides and are not familiar with English name changes during the past decade. To avoid confusion, we have shown parenthetically the earlier (and often better-known) name the first time a species is referred to in a given section. This procedure is employed only where names are confusingly dissimilar to those heretofore used. Parenthetical names are also used for certain distinctive subspecies until recently considered to be of specific rank.

New Mexico's still comparatively sparse human population is concentrated in a few urban areas, and many of the more remote places are seldom visited by bird students, resulting in substantial gaps in our knowledge of bird distribution in the State. Users of this publication can materially add to our understanding of migration and distribution by submitting their bird records -- with supporting documentation for rarities -- to The Regional Editor of American Birds or to the New Mexico Ornithological Society, P. O. Box 3068, Albuquerque, New Mexico 87190.

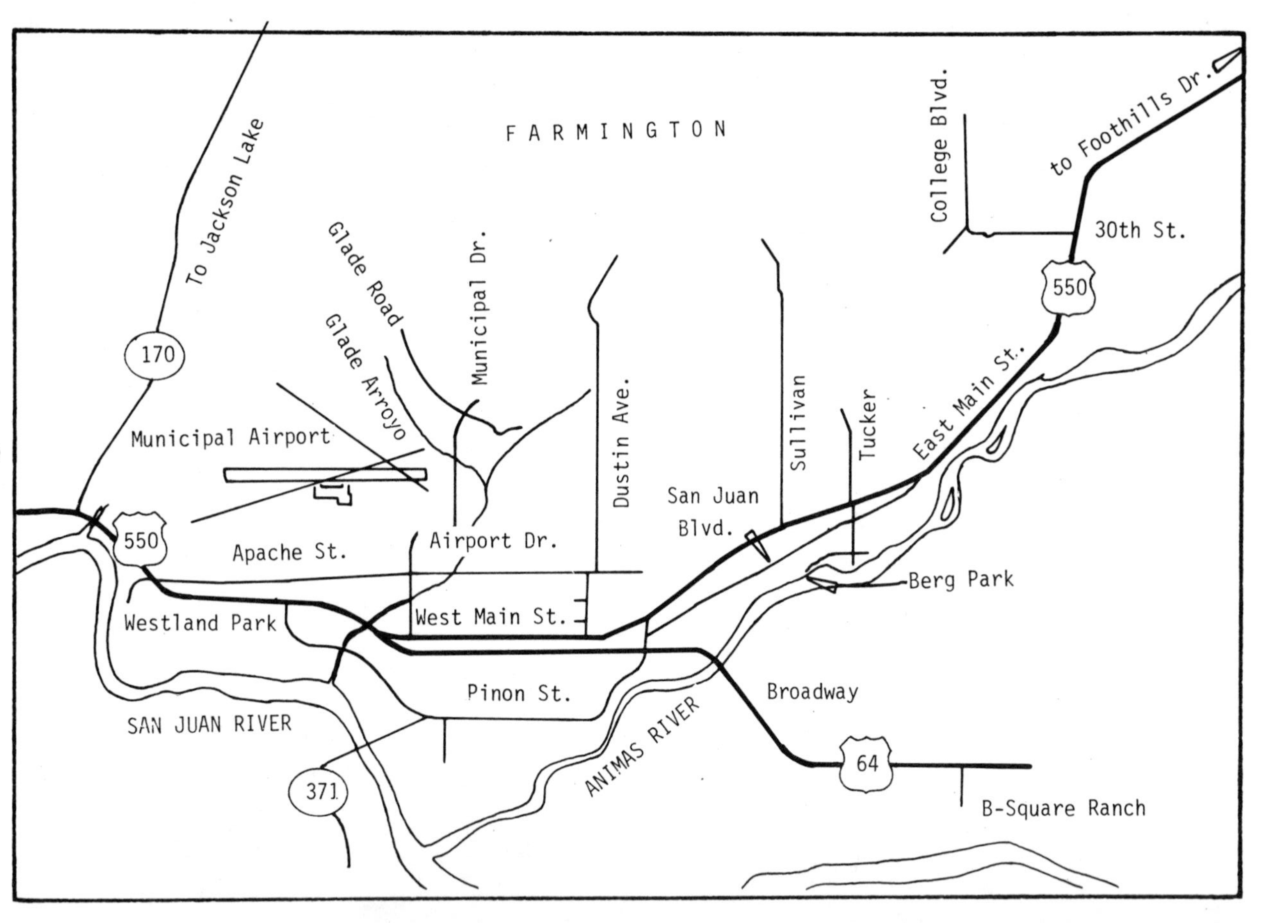

FARMINGTON
College Blvd.
to Foothills Dr.
30th St.
550
To Jackson Lake
Glade Road
Municipal Dr.
Glade Arroyo
170
Dustin Ave.
Sullivan
Tucker
East Main St.
Municipal Airport
San Juan
Blvd.
550
Apache St.
Airport Dr.
Berg Park
West Main St.
Westland Park
Pinon St.
Broadway
SAN JUAN RIVER
ANIMAS RIVER
64
371
B-Square Ranch

NORTHWEST

Alan Nelson

The San Juan River, New Mexico's largest in water volume, enters the State from Colorado and is immediately impounded by Navajo Dam. It then flows westward to Shiprock and turns northwest into Utah near Four Corners. Along both sides of the river are riparian woodland and irrigated farmland, providing an oasis in an otherwise xeric environment. Two tributaries, the Animas and La Plata rivers, also possessing reasonable riparian growth, join the San Juan at Farmington. Both public and private lands offer limited access. West of Shiprock, the San Juan River Valley can be reached by following an unmarked but well-traveled road immediately south of the USPHS hospital on the west side of US 666 north of Shiprock. There are several good stops during the first 12 miles.

FARMINGTON

Farmington, the largest city in northwestern New Mexico, offers many motels and restaurants, making it a good base for day trips to areas described in this section.

In the city, riparian habitat is accessible at the following three locations: Westland Park, beside the San Juan River at the west side of Westland Park subdivision, off West Main at the Apache Street intersection; along Glade Arroyo where it crosses Municipal Drive; and at Berg Park, south of San Juan Boulevard, between Sullivan and Tucker, along the bank of the Animas River. The city is developing a system of trails along seven miles of the Animas and San Juan rivers, mostly for passive recreation. Access points will include East Main near 20th Street and along Browning Parkway at Animas River Park. Browning Parkway connects East Main Street with US 64 just east of the B-Square Ranch entrance.

Special birds to look for in the Farmington area include Lewis's Woodpeckers, which can often be found along West Apache Street, west of Municipal Drive, and in large trees on Wall Avenue, two blocks north of Main; and Rosy Finches which have been seen in winter along Glade Road as it follows Glade Arroyo on the northwest side of town. Species such as Pinyon Jay, Common Bushtit and Rock Wren can be found in the pinyon-juniper areas which are reached by following Foothills Drive north off East Main or by going north on Dustin and College Boulevard.

B-SQUARE RANCH

This land on the southeast edge of Farmington's city limits borders the San Juan River for nearly six miles and hosts a variety of bird life. Access is from

Rock Wren

US 64, about 1.5 miles east of the Animas River bridge on East Broadway. The entrance is just east of a large grove of evergreen trees on the south side of the highway. Permission can be obtained before going there by calling (505) 325-7873. (Tom Bolack, a former State governor, is the owner.) A map is available at the headquarters, a ranch house straight south on the entrance road, bordered by spruce trees. Two artificial lakes, grain fields, and supplemental feeding attract about 50,000 wintering waterfowl, numerous shorebirds, and many raptors.

Birds of particular interest here include: Green-backed (Green) Heron, Snow and Ross's geese, Wood Duck, Osprey, numerous wintering hawks, both eagles, Prairie Falcon, Sora, Virginia Rail, Bewick's Wren, migrating warblers (including Black-throated Gray, Townsend's, Black-and-White, and MacGillivray's), Rose-breasted Grosbeak (occasional), Indigo and Lazuli buntings, and Great-tailed Grackle.

A museum in the headquarters displays mounted specimens of many local birds, especially raptors and waterbirds. There is no charge for admission to the grounds or museum.

LION'S PARK

Proceed 3.5 miles west of the US 550-NM 170 junction in Farmington to County Road 489 (the old Kirtland Highway). One mile west on this road, a wooden sign directs birders to Lion's Park on the banks of the San Juan River where there are considerable riparian growth and a few picnic tables. Roads are poorly marked, but the one beside the river can be traveled for about 0.25 mile westward.

Summer birds of note here include American and Least bitterns, Northern Shoveler, Virginia Rail, Sora, Common Moorhen (Gallinule), Yellow-billed Cuckoo, Eastern Kingbird, Marsh Wren, and Great-tailed Grackle.

MORGAN LAKE

Just north of the Fruitland Post Office on County Road 489, a paved road leads southwest to 1,200-acre Morgan Lake and the Four Corners Power Plant, south of the San Juan River. The lake, used for cooling water and to create steam at the power plant, is edged with tules, tamarisk (salt-cedar), cottonwood, and Russian olive.

Birding is best in the delta, created by the inflow of water pumped from the river and expanding at the rate of several feet per year (In 1990 it covered about five acres). Sedges, marsh grass, other wet-ground forbs and shrubs grow in the lower sites. This area is reached by turning right (west) at the northern lake shore on either of two dirt roads and traveling west about 0.5

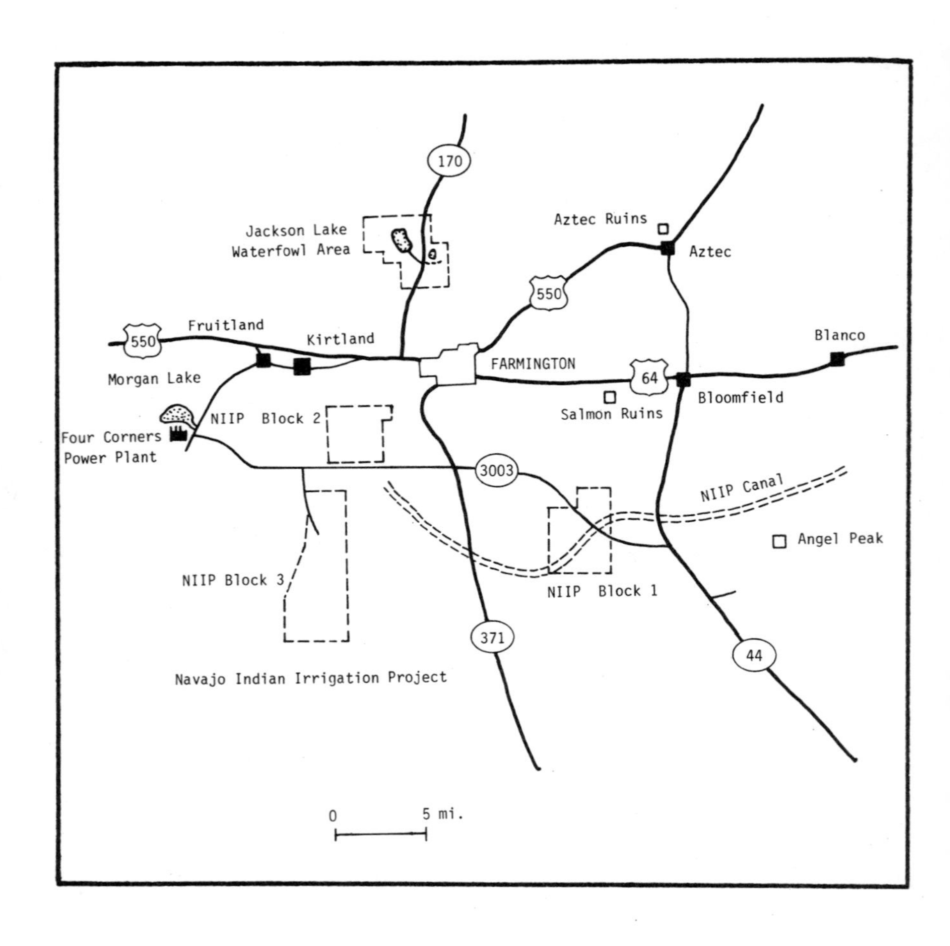
170
Jackson Lake
Waterfowl Area
Aztec Ruins
Aztec
550
550
Fruitland
Kirtland
Blanco
Morgan Lake
FARMINGTON
64
Bloomfield
Salmon Ruins
NIIP Block 2
Four Corners
Power Plant
3003
NIIP Canal
Angel Peak
NIIP Block 3
NIIP Block 1
371
44
Navajo Indian Irrigation Project
0
5 mi.

mile. (The road nearer the lake can be impassible if the water level is high.) The road along the northern edge, the dam on the west end, and the paved road east of the lake provide the best birding areas and offer nearly unbroken views of the lake. The southern shore can be reached from the paved road by turning right near the southeastern edge of the lake.

This lake provides a haven for the greatest variety of shorebirds and waterfowl in northwestern New Mexico. Most of San Juan County's wader records have come from here. April-May and late August-November provide the greatest diversity. Horned Grebes are occasional from November to April. American White Pelicans are most likely in September, and Double-crested Cormorants have wintered (1981, 1982). White-faced Ibis may rest here in large numbers in April-May and again in September. Ospreys visit in April and September, and Prairie Falcons are possible all year.

Migrating plovers include Semipalmated, Snowy (not regular), Lesser Golden (rare), and Black-bellied. Long-billed Curlews stop occasionally, especially in fall. To be expected are both yellowlegs, Willet, Marbled Godwit, occasional Sanderling, and Western, Least and Pectoral sandpipers. American Avocets are regular migrants. Black-necked Stilts are occasional, as are Red-necked (Northern) Phalaropes. The most common gull is Ring-billed. Herring Gulls typically appear in fall, and California Gulls have become regular in recent springs. Franklin's and Bonaparte's gulls are present spring and fall, and there is one recent record of Sabine's Gull. Caspian and Common terns are occasional.

American (Water) Pipits are regular in winter, Yellow-headed Blackbirds nest during May and June in the tules, and Lincoln's and Savannah sparrows are here from March to May.

Heading directly south from Fruitland Post Office, one takes a private road 0.25 mile to a small lake, ringed by trees and shrubs; a small marsh on the north side has attracted Wood Duck and Hooded Merganser in winter.

JACKSON LAKE REFUGE

Along both sides of NM 170, 5 miles north of its intersection with US 550 near the west edge of Farmington, is the Jackson Lake State Game Refuge. The headquarters consist of an old farmhouse and a trailer complex on the west side of NM 170. The parking lot is located 0.25 mile north of headquarters, and the lake is a quarter-mile walk from there. Permission to bird the refuge on the east side of the highway may be obtained at the farmhouse headquarters or by calling (505) 325-4122.

Grain and alfalfa fields, brush and riparian thickets beside the La Plata River attract many birds. The lake, with varying water levels, has tules and some trees on the west bank. Pied-billed Grebes and American Bitterns nest in the tules, while other summer visitors have included Yellow-billed Cuckoo, Ash-throated Flycatcher, Lazuli Bunting, and Blue Grosbeak, The lake serves as a winter resting area for many waterfowl, especially Common Goldeneye, Redhead, and Canvasback. At this season, look, too, for Tundra (Whistling) Swan and American Tree and Harris's sparrows (rare). Year-round residents include Cooper's Hawk, Golden Eagle, Gambel's Quail, Great Horned Owl, Pinyon Jay, Black-capped Chickadee, White-breasted Nuthatch, and Bewick's Wren.

NAVAJO INDIAN IRRIGATION PROJECT

The Navajo Indian Irrigation Project (NIIP) is located south of Farmington in a gently rolling plain. About 60,000 acres were under cultivation in 1990, producing enormous fields of grain, alfalfa, and a few other crops. Most alfalfa fields are literally covered with rodent mounds, and this abundance of rodents attracts raptors. The area is best reached from Farmington on NM 371 at South Lake and Pinyon streets. The road leads south, climbing a rocky cliff known as "Shannon Bluffs." After about 6 miles, a right turn on Navajo Road 3003 will take one to blocks 3 and 4 of the project. A left turn leads to blocks 1 and 2, about 8 miles distant. In this area where Navajo 3003 crosses the Main Canal (there is a sign), turn right (south), about 1.5 miles to headquarters (homes and offices). From 1 to 3 miles south and west from headquarters is one of the best raptor areas. As many as 100 raptors of six species may be found here in an hour or less from November through March. Caution: The paved roads here are generally not marked and are confusingly similar.

Raptors in the NIIP include Red-tailed and Ferruginous hawks year-round, Swainson's in spring; Rough-legged Hawk, Golden Eagle, Northern Harrier, Prairie Falcon, and Short-eared Owl in winter. Scaled Quail, Lark Bunting (in migration), and Savannah, Vesper, Lark, and Chipping sparrows also may be seen. Wintering geese feed morning and evening in the fields, flying the several miles from the San Juan Valley each time, easily visible as they fly over Navajo 3003, especially just east of Gallegos Arroyo on the project's west side. Navajo 3003 continues east and intersects NM 44 about 5 miles from the Main Canal. Continuing south on NM 44 for 5 miles, one comes to a road leading 0.5 mile east to Angel Peak Recreation Site. There are picnic tables (no water) and camping sites overlooking spectacular Kutz Canyon and Angel Peak. Birds include Golden Eagle, Scaled Quail, and in winter, Rosy Finches.

FARMINGTON TO BLANCO

Along US 64, public birding areas are limited to three places: McGee Park is 7 miles east of Farmington at the San Juan County Fairgrounds. Access is available to several salt-cedar-skirted ponds created from gravel-pit operations. Ask the attendant south of the largest building for permission to bird areas to the west and south of the race track. Two miles east of McGee Park is Salmon Ruins, owned by the San Juan Archeological Association. Picnicking is allowed on the property fronting the river, which possesses wooded riparian habitat. A San Juan County bird checklist is also available. In Bloomfield City Park, Green-backed Heron and Mississippi Kite have been seen. If entering Bloomfield from the west on US 64, continue past the junction with NM 44 which leads south. US 64/NM 44 continues east and curves to the north. Exactly at the end of the curve, First Street enters from the south (right). Turn onto First Street and follow it south to the park beside the river.

Marshes border the part of NM 44 which leads south from Bloomfield. The marsh on the west can be productive, and a small dike pushes through its center from the highway after a short jump over a ditch. Year-round open water, tules and cattails are attractive to numerous marsh birds, including American Bittern, Snowy Egret, White-faced Ibis, several dabbling duck species, Virginia Rail and Sora, wintering Long-billed Dowitcher, Marsh Wren, and Common Yellowthroat.

On US 64, 2.5 miles east of the Bloomfield intersection of US 64 and NM 44, County Road 4901 runs south 0.5 mile to NM Game and Fish Department land called the Rutherford Tract. This riparian area along the San Juan River is good for the following summer birds: Great Blue Heron, Cooper's Hawk, Spotted Sandpiper, Black-chinned Hummingbird, Western Wood-Pewee, Black-capped Chickadee, Bewick's Wren, Yellow-breasted Chat, Black-headed and Blue grosbeaks, Lazuli Bunting, and Song Sparrow. Wintering birds include Bald Eagles and many waterfowl. Camping is allowed but the only facility is a boat-launching ramp.

NAVAJO DAM

Navajo Dam was built to control the flow of the San Juan River. The lake, when full, is over 30 miles long, extending into Colorado along the San Juan, Piedra, and Los Pinos rivers. Excellent campgrounds are available near the dam and in Colorado at state parks. Follow the signs in the park.

To reach the dam from Bloomfield, follow US 64/NM 44 north 0.5 mile to just past the Bloomfield High School grounds. At the first street-light, turn right on US 64. Follow this road 8.5 miles to Blanco, then beyond (same highway) another 2.3 miles. Here NM 511 branches northeast (left) 14 miles to the dam. The site also may be reached from Aztec's northern city limits off NM 550, following NM 173. In 18 miles, this road meets NM 511. Turn east (left) to reach the dam.

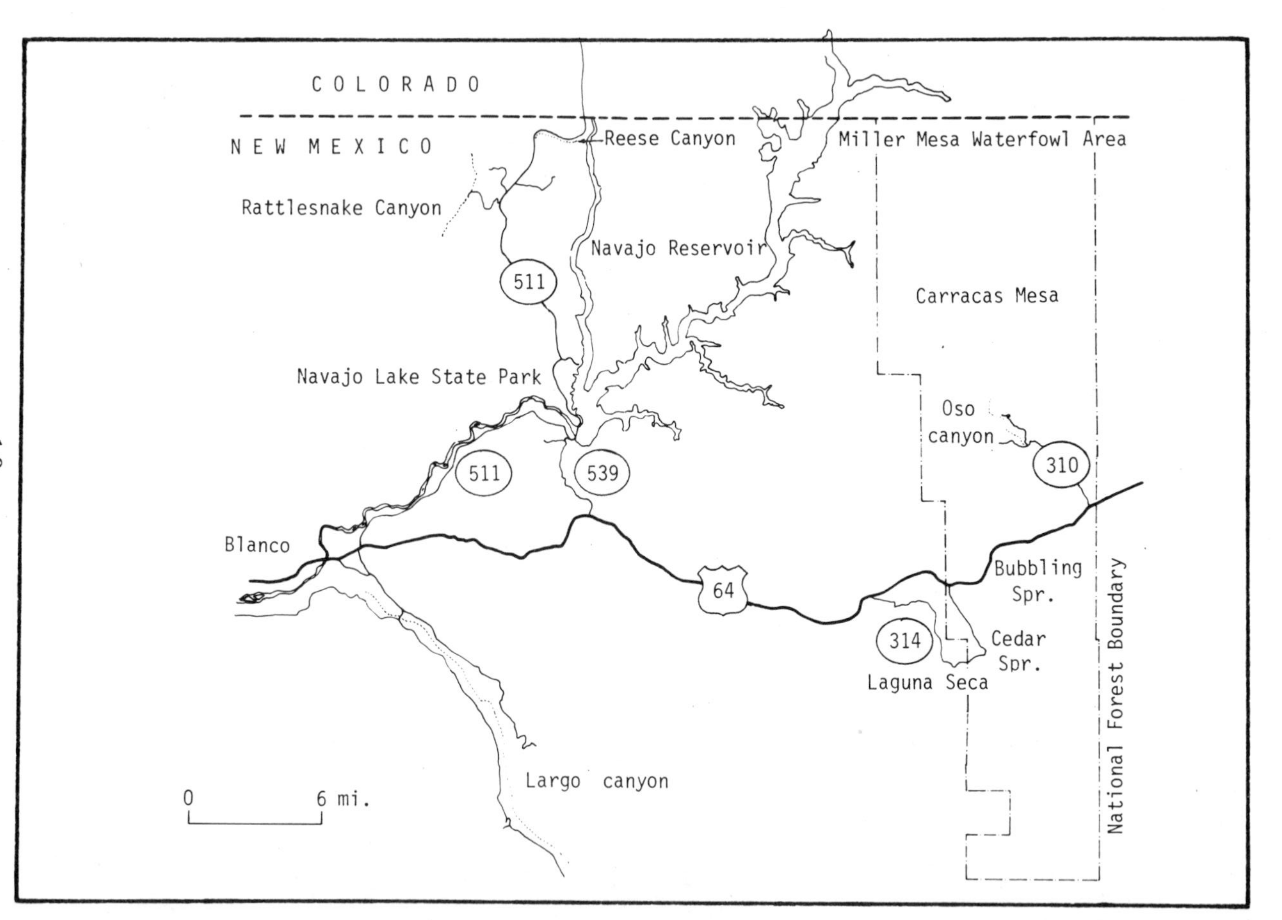

COLORADO
NEW MEXICO
Reese Canyon
Miller Mesa Waterfowl Area
Rattlesnake Canyon
Navajo Reservoir
511
Carracas Mesa
Navajo Lake State Park
Oso canyon
511
539
310
Blanco
64
Bubbling Spr.
314
Cedar Spr.
Laguna Seca
National Forest Boundary
Largo canyon
0
6 mi.

At 0.25 mile west of the San Juan River crossing on NM 173, a dirt road turns north. Good signs direct one to the Cottonwood Campground (all facilities) along the river, and to Simon Canyon (a BLM natural area). Parking for Simon Canyon is 3 miles from NM 173. Birding is good at the mouth and along the stream in the canyon for about 0.5 mile upstream. Summer birds include White-throated Swift, Western Wood-Pewee, Violet-green and Cliff swallows, White-breasted Nuthatch, Rock and Canyon wrens, Solitary Vireo, Western Tanager, Black-headed Grosbeak, and Lesser Goldfinch.

The river below the dam is deep and wide for about 4 miles, its banks covered with willow, salt-cedar, and cottonwood. Song Sparrows sing here in June, and Mallard and teal nest along the river.

The numerous wintering waterfowl include Tundra Swan (occasional). Greater White-fronted Goose, Gadwall, Lesser Scaup, Common Goldeneye, Barrow's Goldeneye (occasional), and Hooded Merganser. In the winter of 1989-1990, Barrow's Goldeneyes were along the river near the NM 173 bridge and behind the nearby Sportsmens Inn.

Bald Eagles (common) and American Dippers are also on the lake and river in winter. Ospreys appear in September and April. Horned Grebes have wintered at the Pine River Marina. The campgrounds are favored by Pinyon Jay, Plain Titmouse, and Black-headed Grosbeak during the breeding season.

A state game refuge at the north end of the lake at Miller Mesa can be reached by road from Allison, Colorado. Turn south from Colorado Highway 151, 1.5 miles to the refuge (and the New Mexico state line), or travel 2 miles east of Allison and turn south (right) at a rock-faced store, proceeding 3 miles to the refuge. Waterfowl and wintering Bald Eagles are the main birds of interest.

LARGO CANYON

One of the country's longest "dry" watercourses, Largo Canyon is reached from US 64, 1 mile east of Blanco. It is easy to get lost in this area, and the available maps do not seem adequate. The roads are all dirt and should be traveled only in dry weather. Several side roads used mostly by oil and gas crews serving pipelines and wells lead up secondary canyons. Most workmen will stop to help with directions or if assistance is needed. Birds of this area include nesting Cooper's Hawk in cottonwood groves, Red-tailed Hawk, Golden Eagle, occasional Peregrine Falcon, Northern Pygmy and Long-eared owls, Common Poorwill, Gray Flycatcher, Cassin's Kingbird, Western and Mountain bluebirds, Sage Thrasher, Blue Grosbeak, Canyon (Brown) Towhee, and Black-throated Sparrow.

RATTLESNAKE-REESE CANYONS

North of Navajo Dam, along NM 511, the country is mostly pinyon-juniper-covered mesas interspersed with sage-chamisa vegetation in the valleys and arroyos. About 15 miles north of Navajo Dam, the highway abruptly descends into Reese Canyon, following it to the Pine River into Colorado. Summer birds of the canyon include: Sharp-shinned, Cooper's and Red-tailed hawks, Common Poorwill, Gray Flycatcher, Scrub and Pinyon jays, Clark's Nutcracker, Mountain Chickadee, Plain Titmouse, Common Bushtit, Blue-gray Gnatcatcher, Gray Vireo (in pinyons), Solitary Vireo (in ponderosa pine-oak growth in the canyon bottom), Black-throated Gray Warbler, Black-headed Grosbeak, Rufous-sided Towhee, and Chipping Sparrow.

Rattlesnake Canyon is reached from NM 511, 15 miles north of Navajo Dam, just before NM 511 drops into Reese Canyon. Following an unmarked dirt road west (left) from the highway brings one to ponderosa pines after 2 miles, where birds are similar to those in Reese Canyon.

ANIMAS RIVER VALLEY

The Animas River, which enters the State from Colorado and flows into the San Juan River at Farmington, is fairly well bordered with trees, shrubs, and farms. However, the once largely agricultural valley is giving way to subdivisions and separate homesites along most of US 550 between Farmington and Aztec. This latter town now has the only public birding areas in the Animas Valley outside Farmington. At Aztec Ruins National Monument (there is a sign at the highway) a picnic ground is in an area shaded by elm and cottonwood trees, and at 0.25 mile west of the Animas River bridge, a city street leads south to Riverside Park with picnic tables and a nature trail through a riparian area.

There are two roads offering less traveled alternatives to US 550. Flora Vista Road along the north bank begins at the eastern city limits of Farmington (at the east end of the cemetery) and extends nearly to Aztec. Ruins Road begins in Aztec at the west end of the Animas River bridge on US 550. At Aztec Ruins, turn right and follow the paving. There are many good river viewpoints, ponds, and groves of trees. This road is particularly good for wintering Bald Eagles.

CARSON NATIONAL FOREST

The Jicarilla Apache Reservation portion of Carson National Forest, on both sides of US 64, begins about 32 miles east of Blanco. A ranger station, about 4 miles west of the forest boundary, is open weekdays. There, one should obtain maps, which are essential for effective birding.

The forest is an area of high mesas, deep canyons, and rocky cliffs, covered by pinyon-juniper and Gambel's oak on the hills, with sagebrush and some cottonwoods in the valleys and along stream beds. The highest elevations and northern exposures contain fairly extensive stands of ponderosa pine with some Douglas-fir and aspen. Such a diversity of habitats explains why over 100 species of birds have been found here.

US 64 is the area's only paved highway. Bubbling Springs is about 1.5 miles into the forest if traveling east. Birds here include: Red-tailed Hawk, Golden Eagle, Broad-tailed Hummingbird, Cassin's Kingbird, Pinyon Jay, Rock Wren, Green-tailed and Rufous-sided towhees, and Chipping Sparrow.

Near the eastern forest boundary on US 64, a sign indicates FR 310 turning north into the forest leading toward Carracas Mesa. Take this road about 5.5 miles north of US 64 to Oso Canyon to a pond which attracts birds from miles around. To reach the water, turn left at a pipeline structure very close to the road. Then take a foot trail past the pond and down into a meadow with an old corral and second smaller pond.

Breeding birds to watch for include: Northern Goshawk, Golden Eagle, Northern Pygmy and Saw-whet owls, Common Poorwill, Broad-tailed Hummingbird, Williamson's Sapsucker, Purple Martin, Steller's, Scrub and Pinyon jays, Clark's Nutcracker, all three nuthatches, House Wren, Blue-gray Gnatcatcher, Western Bluebird, Gray Vireo, Virginia's, Black-throated Gray, and Grace's warblers, Western Tanager, Rufous-sided Towhee, Chipping Sparrow, Cassin's Finch, and Red Crossbill.

Another area with similar birds and a small campground is Cedar Spring, reached from US 64 at about 2 miles east of the west boundary of the forest. FR 314 turns south and leads up a rather steep mesa into forest land after about 7 miles. Sitting quietly at the spring can be an excellent way to see the local birds.

Beyond Cedar Spring, the road goes to Laguna Seca, largest of the ponds in this forest, sometimes covering about five acres. Here watch for all three teal, Willet, Wilson's Phalarope, Purple Martin, Clark's Nutcracker, Brewer's Blackbird, and Vesper Sparrow. Spotted Owls have summered in this general area.

TOADLENA

The greenery at Toadlena, west of US 666 at the west end of Navajo 19, 25 miles south of Shiprock, provides an oasis at the base of the Chuska Mountains (which themselves offer little to the birder). There is a combination of highland and lowland vegetation, plus orchards, fields, and streams. Numerous birds come for water here, especially during migration.

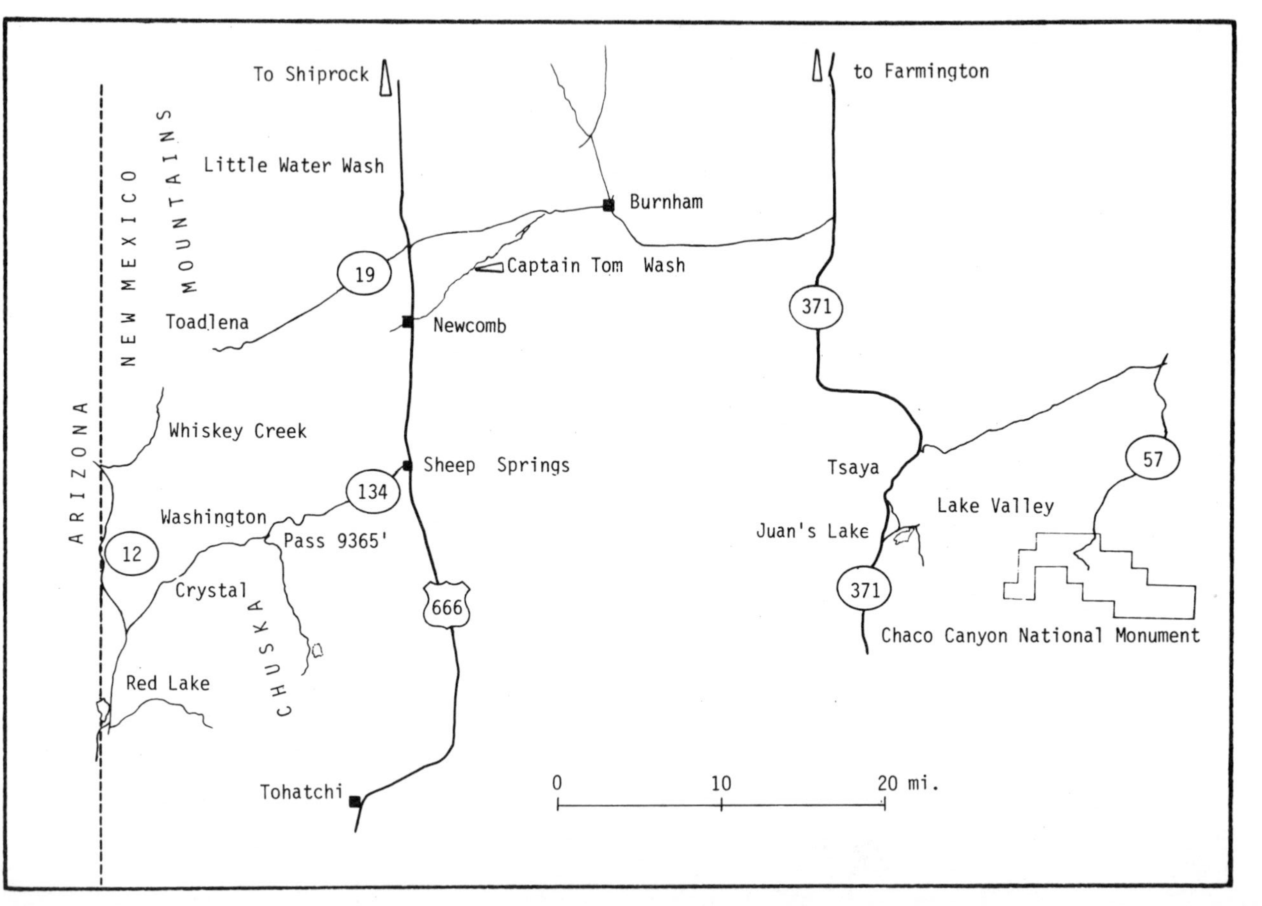
To Shiprock
to Farmington
Little Water Wash
Burnham
Captain Tom Wash
19
Toadlena
Newcomb
371
NEW MEXICO
MOUNTAINS
ARIZONA
Whiskey Creek
Sheep Springs
134
Washington
Pass 9365'
12
Crystal
CHUSKA
666
Red Lake
Tohatchi
Tsaya
57
Lake Valley
Juan's Lake
371
Chaco Canyon National Monument
0
10
20 mi.

Likely species are waterfowl at the ponds, Lewis's and Acorn woodpeckers, Williamson's Sapsucker, Pinyon Jay, Rock and Canyon wrens, Western and Mountain bluebirds, and Townsend's Solitaire. Fall birds include Townsend's Warbler, Western Tanager, Black-headed Grosbeak, Green-tailed Towhee, and Lincoln's Sparrow.

About 1 mile west of Toadlena, up steep, rocky Navajo NR 7172, the pinyons give way to ponderosa pine and oak. The first road to the left, Navajo FR 7180, leads to a capped spring after 0.1 mile. Birds of interest here are Wild Turkey, Band-tailed Pigeon, Lewis's and Acorn woodpeckers, Williamson's Sapsucker, Clark's Nutcracker, Grace's Warbler, Western Tanager, Green-tailed Towhee, Cassin's Finch, and Red Crossbill.

Owl Spring Picnic Ground on the east side of Washington Pass, on NM 134, 11 miles west of Sheep Springs, has similar birds, as does the campground on the west side of Washington Pass.

Large lakes on the mountain top attract breeding Western and Eared grebes and waterfowl, including Mallard, Pintail, and Ruddy Duck.

Navajo FR 8000, going south at Washington Pass, leads through Douglas-fir, aspen and grasslands to several lakes on both sides of the road. Long Lake, about 8 miles in length along its west side, has ponderosa pines to the west and grassland to the east. This is a good place for waterfowl, a breeding spot for Eared Grebe and possibly Western Grebe, Mallard, Pintail, and Ruddy Duck. Various migrating shorebirds stop here beginning in July.

About 4 miles farther is Whiskey Lake, which has similar birds but is less scenic. There is fair fishing here, but both a Navajo tribal permit and a State license are required.

At about 0.25 mile west of Washington Pass, Navajo FR 7170 heads north toward Todacheenie (3.5 miles) and Berland lakes (2.6 miles farther) as well as several unnamed lakes. Except for the grebes, birds here are similar to those in the lakes south of Washington Pass, but the scenery is better. Around these lakes one may also find many ducks during migration (especially September-October), as well as Red-naped and Williamson's sapsuckers, Olive-sided Flycatcher, Purple Martin, Clark's Nutcracker, all three nuthatches, Western and Mountain bluebirds, Townsend's Solitaire (August-September), many warbler species, including Orange-crowned, Nashville, Virginia's, Townsend's, Grace's, and MacGillivray's; also Western Tanager, Cassin's Finch, Red Crossbill, and Pine Siskin.

South of Crystal, 5 miles south of the intersection of NM 134 and Navajo Route 12, is Red Lake, astride the Arizona border. Roads to the shore are on the north and south ends of the lake, which is about 1.5 miles long and a mile wide. Birds present here include many ducks (some of which nest), Sora, Sandhill Crane, and Yellow-headed Blackbird. Just south of the lake, on NM 134, is the community of Navajo, with a food store and gas station.

Whiskey Creek crosses Navajo Route 12 less than 10 miles north of its junction with NM 134 and just inside the Arizona border. South of this crossing 1.1 miles, Navajo FR 7300 goes eastward, soon paralleling Whiskey Creek. At 1.6 miles, before turning sharply to the right (Navajo FR 7330) and leaving the stream bed, a poor road (still NFR 7300) turns to the left. Passing through at least three gates (be sure to reclose them), this road follows Whiskey Creek for several miles. Good, undeveloped campsites are located along the stream. Vegetation is a combination of lowland riparian and high-elevation plants, creating diverse habitats. Summer birds include Acorn Woodpecker, Solitary and Warbling vireos, Virginia's Warbler, Green-tailed Towhee, and Red Crossbill. From the junction with NFR 7300, NFR 7330 goes south for several miles through pinyon-ponderosa pine habitat. Half a mile south of 7300 is a small (dry) campground on the west side of the road.

NEWCOMB OASIS

At Newcomb, on US 550, 30 miles south of Shiprock, the riparian growth of eastward-flowing Captain Tom Wash attracts migrants. The wash is just north of the store and easily identified by the tree-lined banks. Access is gained from a road turning west from US 666 at the bridge. It is best not to go farther than 2 miles, as the road soon deteriorates.

TAMARISK OASIS

From Burnham (12.3 miles east of US 666 on Navajo Route 5), travel north 4 miles on a dirt road. (Do not take the fork heading northeast from Burnham marked "Farmington.") At Tamarisk Oasis the road crosses an earthern dam, which contains an intermittent pond largely surrounded by salt-cedar growth. Below the dam is more salt-cedar mixed with greasewood. Fall birds here include Northern Harrier, Prairie Falcon, Scaled Quail, Great Horned and Long-eared owls, Red-naped Sapsucker, Willow and Cordilleran (Western) flycatchers, Say's Phoebe, Blue-gray Gnatcatcher, Warbling Vireo, Townsend's Warbler (August-September), Western Tanager, and Chestnut-collared Longspur. The raptors listed also winter here.

MIDDLE CHACO OASIS

On the south end of the dam at Tamarisk Oasis, an unmaintained road leads northwestward, following the arroyo 2.8 miles, turning left 0.7 mile at a fork, then 0.2 mile north to the oasis. On the left, a pond of an acre or more is fed by an artesian well which spills over an earthern dam on the right. This permanent water supply has allowed growth of cattails, tules, and a few meadow grasses among the numerous salt-cedars.

Waterfowl and shorebirds stopping here during migration include all three teals, American Avocet, Least and Western sandpipers, Common Snipe, and Long-billed Dowitcher. Other birds sighted here include Great Egret, Northern Harrier, Prairie Falcon, Scaled Quail, Pinyon Jay, Bewick's Wren, Blue Grosbeak, Savannah Sparrow, and Yellow-headed Blackbird.

Common Poorwill

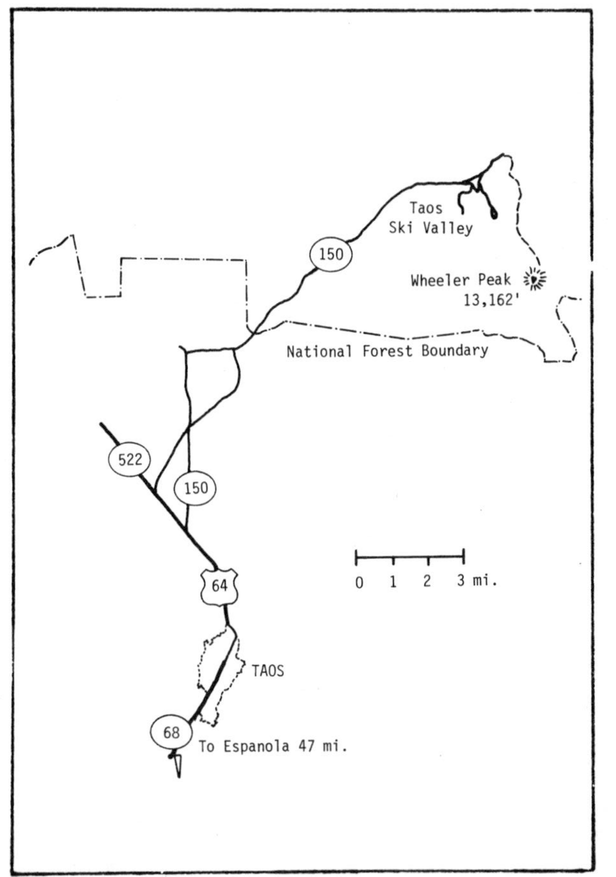
Taos
Ski Valley
150
Wheeler Peak
13,162'
National Forest Boundary
522
150
64
0 1 2 3 mi.
TAOS
68
To Espanola 47 mi.

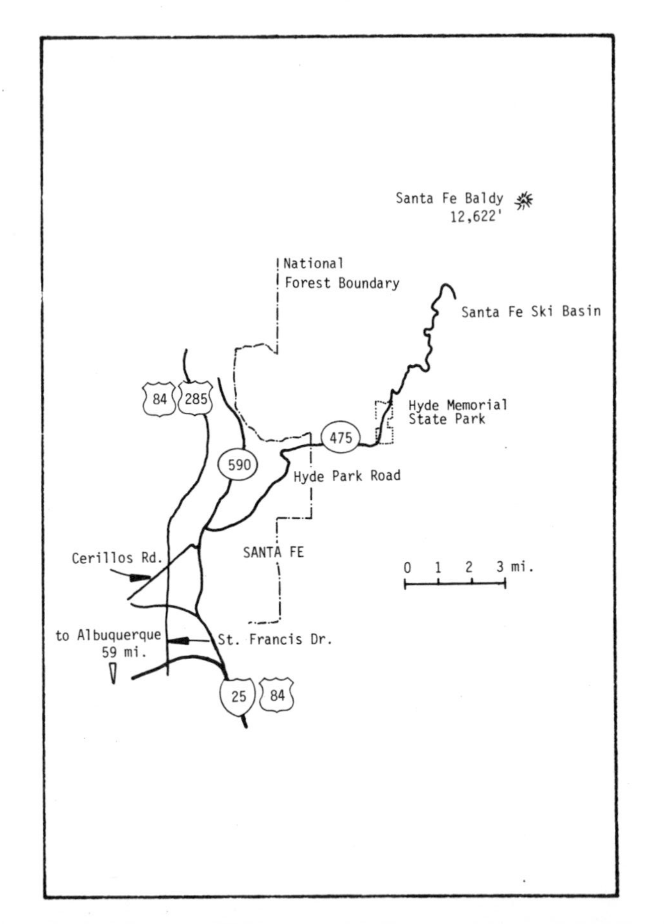
Santa Fe Baldy
12,622'
National
Forest Boundary
Santa Fe Ski Basin
84
285
Hyde Memorial
State Park
475
590
Hyde Park Road
SANTA FE
Cerillos Rd.
0 1 2 3 mi.
to Albuquerque
59 mi.
St. Francis Dr.
25
84

NORTH CENTRAL

Patricia Snider, Karen Copeland, John Durrie,
John Egbert, Charles Hundertmark, Dustin Huntington,
Dale Stahlecker, James Travis

The largely mountainous north-central section of New Mexico offers some of the most varied breeding birdlife in the State. The upper elevations contain high-altitude species such as Three-toed Woodpecker, Gray Jay, Clark's Nutcracker, Rosy Finch, Pine Grosbeak, and Red Crossbill. In addition, the high-country lakes are excellent for waterbirds, both during migration and in the breeding season. Although some choice areas are accessible by vehicle, others are within wilderness areas and require substantial hiking. It is advisable to obtain maps from the Forest Service office in Santa Fe for excursions on National Forest lands. Elevations in this region range from 5,500 feet along the Rio Grande near Española to 12,000 feet on the highest peaks.

SANTA FE

The State capital has excellent accommodations and is particularly noted for its fine restaurants. It is located on I-25 and US Highways 285/84. At 7,000 feet, its breeding birds include Northern (Red-shafted) Flicker, Say's Phoebe, Scrub and Pinyon jays, American Crow, Common Raven, Plain Titmouse, White-breasted Nuthatch, American Robin, Northern Mockingbird, Solitary Vireo, Canyon (Brown) Towhee, Chipping Sparrow, Western Meadowlark, House Finch, and Lesser Goldfinch.

Migrants include various waterfowl, Red-tailed Hawk, American Kestrel, swallows, flycatchers, Western and Mountain bluebirds, vireos, warblers, Green-tailed Towhee, and many sparrows.

Winter visitants include Hairy and Downy woodpeckers, Mountain Chickadee, Townsend's Solitaire, Western and Mountain bluebirds (most winters), Cedar Waxwing, Dark-eyed Junco, Song and White-crowned sparrows, Cassin's Finch, Pine Siskin, and Evening Grosbeak.

On the city's outskirts are the Santa Fe Ski Basin and Hyde State Park, both reached by turning right (east) at Paseo de Peralta (NM 589) from US 285/84 (St. Francis Drive) and driving to the rose-colored Masonic Temple on the left. Just past the Temple (where there is a traffic light) turn left (north) onto Bishop's Lodge Road (NM 590). Follow this a short distance to Artists Road (where signs point to the Ski Basin) and turn right (east). This becomes Hyde Park Road (NM 475) which leads to the park along Little Tesuque River at an elevation of about 8,000 feet. In winter, at the upper picnic areas enroute to the ski basin, Gray Jays are often rather tame. Also here are Clark's

Nutcracker and Steller's Jay, and Blue Grouse are present in the aspen-spruce forests.

Proceed nearly to the ski area (10,000 feet) and park on the left, where a trail leads to Santa Fe Baldy, a 12,623-foot peak extending above tree-line. The summit is about 7.5 miles from the trail-head. Hikers who persist on this rather rugged trail may find Rosy Finch or even White-tailed Ptarmigan, re-introduced by the New Mexico Department of Game and Fish and present in small numbers. Blue Grouse display along the trail in spring.

The forest along the route is largely aspen, and in early October the color is spectacular. For those failing to reach timberline, even a short walk along the trail can be productive for typical montane species, especially in August. Here are Red-naped and Williamson's sapsuckers, Three-toed and Downy woodpeckers, Western Wood-Pewee, Dusky Flycatcher, Violet-green Swallow, Gray Jay, Clark's Nutcracker, Mountain Chickadee, White-breasted, Red-breasted and Pygmy nuthatches, Brown Creeper, House Wren, Ruby-crowned Kinglet, Townsend's Solitaire, Hermit Thrush, Warbling Vireo, Yellow-rumped Warbler, Western Tanager, Green-tailed Towhee, White-crowned Sparrow, Dark-eyed (Gray-headed) Junco, Cassin's Finch, Red Crossbill, and Pine Siskin. Pine Grosbeaks have been seen in the scattered spruces by the picnic grounds at the end of the road near the lower ski lift, and an occasional American Dipper visits the stream at the upper ski area. Wilson's Warbler and Lincoln's Sparrow may be present in the low willows edging the water.

Another interesting route is the continuation of Bishop's Lodge Road past the lodge into Tesuque, where in summer one may expect the following species in the orchards: Mourning Dove, Hairy and Lewis's woodpeckers, Western Wood-Pewee, Say's Phoebe, Barn Swallow, Scrub and Steller's jays, Black-billed Magpie, Plain Titmouse, Western Bluebird, Solitary Vireo, Western Tanager, Black-headed and Blue grosbeaks, Rufous-sided and Canyon towhees, Chipping Sparrow, Brown-headed Cowbird, and House Finch. In winter the trees may attract large numbers of Cedar Waxwings.

At the north edge of Tesuque are two ponds which attract migrant waterfowl. They are on Tesuque Pueblo land, so do not enter the fenced area. The ponds are visible as one reaches NM 591 and heads right (north) thereon back toward the main highway (US 285/84).

RANDALL DAVEY AUDUBON CENTER

The Randall Davey Audubon Center in Santa Fe is the State office for the National Audubon Society and one of its six education centers. The property, at the mouth of Santa Fe Canyon, encompasses 135 acres of primarily pinyon-juniper woodland with ponderosa pine at the upper elevations, and a small side canyon which provides access to the Santa Fe National Forest. Nearby Two Mile Reservoir attracts migratory birds such as Osprey and waterfowl, while the cultivated grounds surrounding the buildings draw many passerines.

The Center is situated three miles from Santa Fe's central plaza and is accessible to all vehicles throughout most of the year. From I-25, take the Old Pecos Trail exit and follow Old Pecos Trail/Old Santa Fe Trail to the stoplight at Alameda Avenue. Turn right and follow this road, which parallels the Santa Fe River, until it curves and crosses the river (usually dry but nevertheless good for birds; a vagrant Varied Thrush was present in the area for several weeks in early 1990). Opposite the large adobe church, Cristo Rey, turn left onto Upper Canyon Road and follow it to the "Y." Keeping right at the "Y," continue on the dirt road for 0.6 mile to the Randall Davey Center parking lot. From US 285 (St. Francis Drive in Santa Fe), turn east at the stoplight on Alameda Avenue and follow the same directions as above.

The grounds and trails are accessible daily from 9 a.m. to 5 p.m., but birders are welcome to park on the road-side and enter the grounds on foot outside of these hours. The office and an excellent natural history bookstore are open on weekdays year-round, as well as Sundays in June, July and August. A small admission fee is requested from non-Audubon members. Bird walks, natural history workshops, and children's programs are offered all year, and the Center's staff conducts birding tours to other prime locations in the State. For further information, call (505) 983-4609 or write Randall Davey Audubon Center, P. O. Box 9314, Santa Fe, NM 87504-9314.

Available at the office is an interpretive guide to a half-mile loop trail as well as bird checklists for the State and for 147 species of birds documented in the immediate area.

THE TURQUOISE TRAIL

The scenic route to Albuquerque, State Road 14, winds south from Santa Fe for 45 miles through the old gold-mining towns of Cerrillos, Madrid, and Golden to I-40 at Tijeras. The route traverses mixed grassland and pinyon-juniper woodland. For birding, exit I-25 ten miles southwest of Santa Fe onto SR 14. Beyond the New Mexico State Penitentiary, 3 miles from I-25 (signs along the roadway caution about stopping in this area), the road enters grassland at the upper end of the Estancia Valley. Here, near the northern extremity of its range in central New Mexico, Cassin's Sparrows can be found in the summer. The most reliable place for them is west of the road in a two-mile stretch of relatively undisturbed grassland from about 3 miles south of the penitentiary to the small community of San Marcos (at SR 586). They are most easily detected near dawn in June when their characteristic flight song

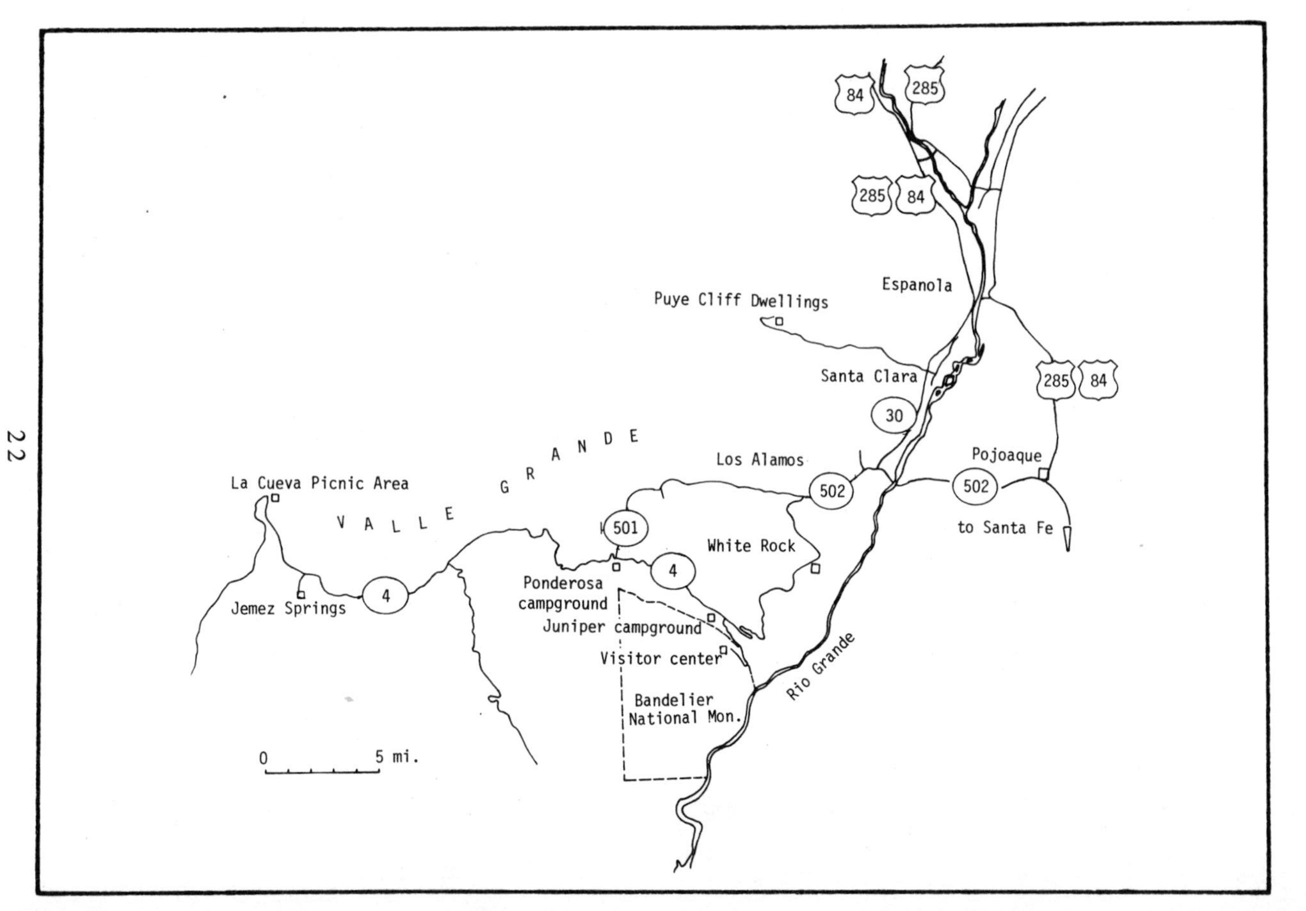

84
285
285
84
285
84
Espanola
Pojoaque
502
to Santa Fe
Santa Clara
30
Puye Cliff Dwellings
502
Los Alamos
White Rock
Rio Grande
4
501
Ponderosa campground
Juniper campground
Visitor center
Bandelier National Mon.
V A L L E G R A N D E
La Cueva Picnic Area
4
Jemez Springs
0
5 mi.

can be heard from the roadside. Horned Lark and Western Meadowlark summer in this area as well.

South of San Marcos, the road winds through pinyon-juniper woodland, with picturesque rock formations on the hillsides (expect Rock Wrens in summer), as well as areas of grassland. The most abundant summering bird is Northern Mockingbird which can be heard at almost any stop along the road. Typical birds of the wooded sections at this season are Mourning Dove, Common Nighthawk, Ladder-backed Woodpecker (irregular), Ash-throated Flycatcher, Cassin's Kingbird, Scrub Jay, Pinyon Jay (usually in small flocks), Plain Titmouse, Bewick's Wren, Canyon Towhee, Lark and Chipping sparrows. Scott's Oriole and Black-throated Sparrow, southwestern species near the northern edge of their breeding range in central New Mexico, summer regularly between Madrid and Golden. Just south of San Marcos and in Cerrillos, the road crosses streams where there are Black-headed and Blue grosbeaks and Northern Oriole. There is also a Cliff Swallow colony in Cerrillos, and Say's Phoebe and House Finch are likely around settlements.

In winter, Mountain and Western bluebirds, American Robin and, occasionally, Townsend's Solitaire frequent the woodlands, feeding on juniper berries.

SAN ILDEFONSO, LOS ALAMOS, BANDELIER NATIONAL MONUMENT

This part of the north-central region spans elevations from 5,500 feet between Pojoaque and San Ildefonso in the Rio Grande Valley to 7,500 feet at Los Alamos. It embraces pinyon-juniper woodland, grassland, and ponderosa pine forests on the Pajarito Plateau, the remnant of ancient lava flows from the volcanoes that formed the Jemez Mountains. Much of this plateau was covered by ash to depths of hundreds of feet, and many of the mesas were created by lava flows. A few streams, as in Frijoles and Los Alamos canyons, are lined with alder, ash, narrowleaf cottonwood, and boxelder along their descent to the Rio Grande. The mesas are covered by open ponderosa pine forests, in places with an understory of scrub oak, locust, Apache plume, and squawbush.

Follow US 285/84 north from Santa Fe, exiting left (west) at Pojoaque on NM 502 which leads to Los Alamos. Take the first right turn (0.5 mile from the intersection), proceed 0.1 mile, and then turn left (west) onto a dirt road toward the San Ildefonso Pueblo, following the usually dry Tesuque River. Among the summering species to be expected in this area of pastures, orchards, and riparian growth are American Kestrel, Scaled and Gambel's quail, Greater Roadrunner, Lewis's Woodpecker, Western Kingbird, Northern Rough-winged and Barn swallows, Scrub and Pinyon (occasional) jays, Black-billed Magpie, American Robin, Northern Mockingbird, Loggerhead Shrike, Black-headed and Blue grosbeaks, Canyon Towhee, various sparrows, Red-winged Blackbird, Western Meadowlark, Brown-headed Cowbird, and Northern (Bullock's) Oriole.

After about three miles, proceed on the right fork to the productive San Ildefonso Pueblo irrigation pond;, where summering birds may include Pied-billed Grebe, American Coot, Ladder-backed Woodpecker (rare), and Great-tailed Grackle.

Past the pond, continue through the pueblo to NM 502, turning right (west) to Los Alamos and Bandelier National Monument, the area's prime birding site. To reach the Monument, exit from NM 502 after 12.1 miles onto NM 4 heading south toward the community of White Rock. One mile farther, near the intersection with Pajarito Road, is the Monument's disjunct Tsankawi section, an easily accessible area for birds of pinyon-juniper woodland. A 2-mile self-guiding trail leads from the highway on a circular route through a large unexcavated Indian ruin. Another entry into the fenced park is from a pull-off on the southeast side of the road, 0.5 mile back on NM 4. Breeding here are Black-chinned Hummingbird, Gray Flycatcher, Say's Phoebe, Ash-throated Flycatcher, Cassin's Kingbird, Scrub and Pinyon jays, Plain Titmouse, Bushtit, Bewick's Wren, Blue-gray Gnatcatcher, Black-throated Gray Warbler, Canyon Towhee, and House Finch.

From here the highway winds for 11 miles through similar habitat, dipping into shallow wooded canyons, past White Rock to the main entrance to Bandelier National Monument. Most of the land bordering the north side of the road is restricted property of the Los Alamos National Laboratory, but at pull-offs along the road, and on trails into the woodland to the left side of the road, one can expect to see characteristic birds.

Juniper Campground, 0.2 mile from the entrance, is a rewarding spot to start birding in the main section of the Monument. The open pinyon-juniper woodland with scattered ponderosa pines around the campground is an excellent site for Gray Flycatcher. From late May through early July they are particularly vocal just before dawn.

From the park entrance, a 3-mile drive to the Visitor Center takes one into Frijoles Canyon. The Center has interpretive programs and a bird list. Some of the best birding can be done from the loop trail up the canyon, which is designed to exhibit a complete sample of the Indian ruins of the area. In summer, the steep cliffs are frequented by Rock and Canyon wrens, and White-throated Swift and Violet-green Swallow fly overhead. Breeding birds typical of the ponderosa pine forest can be observed along the trail to the Ceremonial Cave. These include Northern Pygmy Owl (irregular), Broad-tailed Hummingbird, Hairy Woodpecker, Northern Flicker, Hammond's Flycatcher, Western Wood-Pewee, Steller's Jay, Mountain Chickadee, Pygmy Nuthatch, Western Bluebird, Hermit Thrush, American Robin, Warbling and Solitary vireos, Grace's and Virginia's warblers, Western Tanager, Black-headed Grosbeak, Rufous-sided Towhee, Chipping Sparrow, Brown-headed Cowbird, and Lesser Goldfinch. Watch for Hepatic Tanager in pines in the lower canyons of Los Alamos. Common Raven and Great Horned Owl nest in the cliffs, while Cooper's Hawk breeds regularly within the canyon.

Turkey Vultures roost nightly in the cottonwoods near the Visitor Center from spring to fall. Careful observation of the vultures soaring overhead may reveal a Zone-tailed Hawk which occasionally has nested in nearby inaccessible canyons.

A 2.5-mile trail from the Visitor Center winds downstream to the waterfalls and to the Rio Grande. American Dipper can be found in the stream below the falls, and where the trail descends into pinyon pine and oak growth watch for Ladder-backed Woodpecker. In summer, Blue Grosbeak, Lazuli and (occasionally) Indigo buntings inhabit riparian vegetation near the canyon mouth.

To reach the higher portions of Bandelier, drive to Ponderosa Campground, 6 miles west of the Visitor Center on NM 4. The route passes through areas burned in the major La Mesa fire of 1977. Lewis's and Acorn woodpeckers and Mountain Bluebirds can be seen from the road on snags left from the fire.

Ponderosa Campground is situated in open pine forest at the edge of the old burn. The trail through the pines just west of the campground provides an exceptional opportunity to see Hammond's Flycatcher in a traditional nesting area for the species. Other birds of the ponderosa forest are easily observed from this trail as it continues south 1.3 miles to Upper Frijoles Crossing. On June evenings along here, one is likely to hear territorial Flammulated Owls, as well as Common Poorwills calling from the burned area to the east.

Easiest access to the high montane species is via the road to the Pajarito Mountain Ski Area. Take Route 501 north from Ponderosa Campground for 6 miles to the Y-intersection where 501 turns right and downhill to Los Alamos. Continue straight for 0.5 mile to Camp May Road, which branches west, going uphill. Here one leaves the pines of the mesa and enters a montane mixed-conifer zone. The road climbs 4.2 miles to the Ski Area. Coniferous forest birds to be expected, along with many of the species found in the ponderosas, are Band-tailed Pigeon, Red-naped and Williamson's sapsuckers (in aspens), Three-toed Woodpecker (occasional), Olive-sided and Cordilleran flycatchers, Clark's Nutcracker, Red-breasted Nuthatch, Brown Creeper, Golden and Ruby-crowned kinglets (in spruce-fir forest near the mountian crests), Orange-crowned and MacGillivray's warblers, Dark-eyed Junco (Gray-headed form), Cassin's Finch, and Red Crossbill.

Gray Jays summer on the highest peaks and occasionally are seen in winter at the ski area. On the ascent, several forest roads branch to the south through areas inhabited by Wild Turkey; the gobblers are vocal in early spring. Trails heading north and west from the ski area lead through conifers and aspens to productive mountain meadows where Blue Grouse, Green-tailed Towhee and Lincoln's Sparrow may be found.

Several areas near the Los Alamos townsite offer a variety of birds. For example, the well-landscaped Community Center at Central and 14th Street is productive throughout the year. A typical sample of the area's birds can be found in Los Alamos Canyon, which has most breeding species of the ponderosa pine and mixed conifer forests, including three of the four *Empidonax* flycatchers. To reach this site, go north from downtown on Trinity Drive and turn left onto Diamond Drive at the traffic light. Turn right onto West Road just before the Los Alamos Bridge, then immediately left onto a road that descends into the canyon. This road follows the canyon upstream 0.7 mile before it turns sharply uphill, continuing, with a dirt surface, for 1.5 miles to the reservoir. Along this route MacGillivray's Warbler nests in riparian shrubbery, and Cordilleran Flycatcher is common along the stream. A second route is via a paved road up the hill and around a switchback to the drier mesa-top forest. Park in one of the pull-offs and walk west along the upper edge of the canyon. Breeding here are Dusky Flycatcher and Grace's Warbler in the open ponderosa pine woods, and Virginia's Warbler in the scrub oaks. Hammond's Flycatcher is found a half-mile farther west in the denser, more uniform stands of ponderosa pine.

One may also take Diamond Drive north from the bridge to the Los Alamos Golf Course, turning right (south) on 35th Street, left after one block onto Villa, then right on 34th Street. The canyon here has a resident colony of Acorn Woodpeckers. Continue on Diamond Drive 0.3 mile to the Guaje Pines Cemetery where a mixture of deciduous trees and conifers provides an attractive birding site. Several trails lead from the cemetery into the relatively undisturbed forests and canyons of the northern portion of the county.

The lower ends of the major canyons that cut through the Pajarito Plateau are of particular interest, although most of them are not readily accessible. Lower Los Alamos Canyon has a public trail, the entrance to which is from the northwest side of Route 4, 0.6 mile from the intersection of NM 4 and Route 502. It follows a streambed (usually dry) through pinyon-juniper and ponderosa pine woods, ending at the Laboratory boundary. Here are some breeding birds more typical of lower habitats: Cooper's and Red-tailed hawks, Mourning Dove, Common Poorwill, and Hepatic Tanager.

The lower canyons and eastern parts of the county are particularly productive during migration. In late summer, an influx of migrating northern humingbirds begins. The Rufous arrives in late July, as does the less numerous Calliope. These, along with Broad-tailed, are present until mid-September. In fall, Western and Cassin's kingbirds, Sage Thrasher, Northern Oriole, Brewer's, Lincoln's and other sparrows, and Pine Siskin are seen. Another excellent place for birds in migration is Frijoles Canyon in Bandelier National Monument. It is especially good for warblers, often with Yellow-rumped and Wilson's in abundance and Townsend's regular in autumn.

The appearance of nomadic finches highlights winter birding in Los Alamos. In most years, flocks of Pine Siskins, Cassin's Finches, Red Crossbills, and Evening Grosbeaks move around the townsite, often feeding in the vicinity of the Community Center. Winter also brings other montane species, such as Clark's Nutcracker and Red-breasted Nuthatch into the lower forests.

JEMEZ MOUNTAINS

To explore the higher montane country, take NM 4 west from the junction with Route 501 in Los Alamos. The road immediately begins a steep, curving climb along the edge of Water Canyon, with a spectacular view of the entire Bandelier region south to the the Sandia Mountains. At 6.3 miles, turn left (south) on the Dome Road (FR 289) and thence to Dome Meadow after another 4.2 miles. From here a network of dirt roads winds through high montane mixed conifer and aspen forests leading to streams, intermittent ponds, and wet canyons. Summering birds typical of these habitats are Blue Grouse, Wild Turkey, Broad-tailed Hummingbird, Williamson's and Red-naped sapsuckers, Downy, Hairy, and Three-toed (irregular) woodpeckers, Northern Flicker, Violet-green Swallow, Western Wood-Pewee, Hammond's, Dusky, Cordilleran and Olive-sided flycatchers, Steller's Jay, Clark's Nutcracker, Common Raven, Mountain Chickadee, White-breasted, Red-breasted and Pygmy nuthatches, Brown Creeper, Hermit Thrush, Townsend's Solitaire, Golden-crowned and Ruby-crowned kinglets, American Robin, House Wren, Warbling Vireo, Orange-crowned and Yellow-rumped warblers, Western Tanager, Black-headed Grosbeak, Chipping Sparrow, Gray-headed Junco, Pine Siskin, Red Crossbill (irregular), and Evening Grosbeak. Logging has created large open areas, now overgrown with brush and grass, providing different habitats which are particularly rewarding in late summer when hummingbirds (Broad-tailed, Rufous, and Calliope) and other migrants are present. Green-tailed Towhee breeds around the edges of these clearings.

Forest Road 287 to the east follows Obsidian Ridge to an intermittent stream and Alamo Canyon. FR 289 continues to St. Peter's Dome and into Cochiti Canyon. A likely place for Three-toed Woodpecker is the aspen-covered hillside accessible via FR 36, which branches from FR 289 2.5 miles beyond Dome Meadow.

NM 4 continues west from the junction with Dome Road, descending into Valle Grande, a large volcanic caldera measuring 13 by 18 miles. The floor of the caldera is fenced, but there are several pull-offs for viewing birds which include Red-tailed Hawk, American Crow, Mountain Bluebird, and Brewer's Blackbird. Leaving the southern rim of the Valle Grande, NM 4 continues through montane forest to Jemez Springs, 30 miles from Los Alamos. En route there are several campgrounds (off the highway) where birding is good. About 8 miles from the western edge of Valle Grande, the highway crosses the East Fork of the Jemez River. Shortly thereafter, one may take FR 233 south, following the river to Jemez Falls Campground. Black Swifts have been seen overhead from this road and American Dippers reside along the stream.

HIGH ROAD FROM ESPAÑOLA TO TAOS

From the junction with NM 68 (the northern extension of US 285) take NM 76 east through residential areas, orchards (which may yield Lewis's Woodpecker), and juniper woodland to Truchas, a total of 16 miles. For the next 13.5 miles, toward Peñasco, the route alternates between pinyon-juniper woodland and ponderosa pine forest, dipping into a succession of valleys. An interesting variety of birds exists in this mix of habitats. Summering are Say's Phoebe, Northern Rough-winged, Cliff, and Barn swallows, Black-billed Magpie, American Crow, Common Raven, Mountain Bluebird, American Robin, Red-winged Blackbird, Western Meadowlark, Brewer's Blackbird, Brown-headed Cowbird, and House Finch; also look for Yellow Warbler, Song Sparrow, and Northern Oriole in the willows and cottonwoods where the road crosses the stream.

Breeding birds of the pinyon-juniper woodland include Gray and Ash-throated flycatchers, Cassin's Kingbird, Scrub and Pinyon jays, Plain Titmouse, Bushtit, Bewick's Wren, Blue-gray Gnatcatcher, Black-throated Gray Warbler, and Canyon Towhee. Nesting in the ponderosa pine forest are Mourning Dove, Common Nighthawk, Common Poorwill, Broad-tailed Hummingbird, Hairy Woodpecker, Northern Flicker, Western Wood-Pewee, Hammond's Flycatcher, Violet-green Swallow, Steller's Jay, Mountain Chickadee, White-breasted and Pygmy nuthatches, Western Bluebird, Townsend's Solitaire, Hermit Thrush, Solitary Vireo, Yellow-rumped and Grace's warblers, Western Tanager. Black-headed Grosbeak, Rufous-sided Towhee, Chipping Sparrow, Dark-eyed Junco, Pine Siskin, and Lesser Goldfinch.

Turn right (northeast) onto NM 75 at Peñasco, which then bends north at the eastern edge of the town. Vadito and the Rio Pueblo are 2.2 miles farther. After another 3.5 miles, NM 75 joins NM 518. The left (north) branch goes to Taos through habitats similar to those previously traversed. Continuing straight ahead, NM 518 follows the Rio Pueblo valley into higher coniferous forests where expected breeding birds include Cordilleran Flycatcher, Warbling Vireo, Virginia's Warbler (on hillsides with scrub oak), MacGillivray's Warbler, Blue Grosbeak, and Green-tailed Towhee. The willow thickets along the stream in the first five miles east of Vadito are worthy of careful search for Lazuli Bunting (regular in summer), Gray Catbird, Veery (rare but regular since 1987), and Common Yellowthroat. American Dipper and, irregularly, Spotted Sandpiper frequent the stream.

In the mixed coniferous forest, look for Band-tailed Pigeon, Red-naped Sapsucker, Olive-sided Flycatcher, Clark's Nutcracker, House Wren, Ruby-crowned Kinglet. Orange-crowned Warbler, Red Crossbill (irregular), and Evening Grosbeak. Near the crest (14.5 miles from the NM 75/518 Junction), where the valley levels and broadens, Lincoln's and White-crowned sparrows may be sought in the meadows.

COCHITI RESERVOIR

Cochiti Reservoir is the only large body of water in central New Mexico. It is reached by going north from Albuquerque on I-25 for about 40 miles to the second Cochiti exit (exit 264, NM 16). Proceed west on NM 16 for several miles and turn right (north) at a sign reading, "Welcome, Cochiti Lake." This road leads across the dam, providing an excellent view of the lake, as well as of a large pond on the right, often good for shorebirds and ducks. Parking is not permitted on the dam, but one can usually pause long enough for binocular viewing or brief scope use.

Turn right at the end of the dam road and go a few hundred yards to a booth where someone may collect a fee. Just after passing the booth, turn right onto a dirt/gravel road that leads to a swimming area, a good spot from which to scope the lake for migrant waterfowl and gulls. Tundra (Whistling) Swan, Oldsquaw, and California Gull have been seen here, and during spring and fall migration, flocks of longspurs visit the area near the water.

Return to the paved road, turn left past the booth, and proceed to the road's end, turning left there on NM 22. On the right, at the bottom of a long hill, there are a grove of large cottonwoods and a small stream flanked by shrubbery. Pull off to the right of the road and look for ducks and very likely a Black Phoebe. On the hillside to the left of the road, one may find American (Water) Pipit and Western Bluebird. It should be noted that this area below the dam is Cochiti Pueblo land, and although the pueblo does not seem to object to birders, cameras are NOT allowed and should not be used, even for bird photography.

Two-tenths of a mile farther, the road passes over the Rio Grande Outlet Channel, the dam spillway being on the left. Pause here or pull off the road just beyond the bridge to watch the Cliff Swallows in spring and summer and,

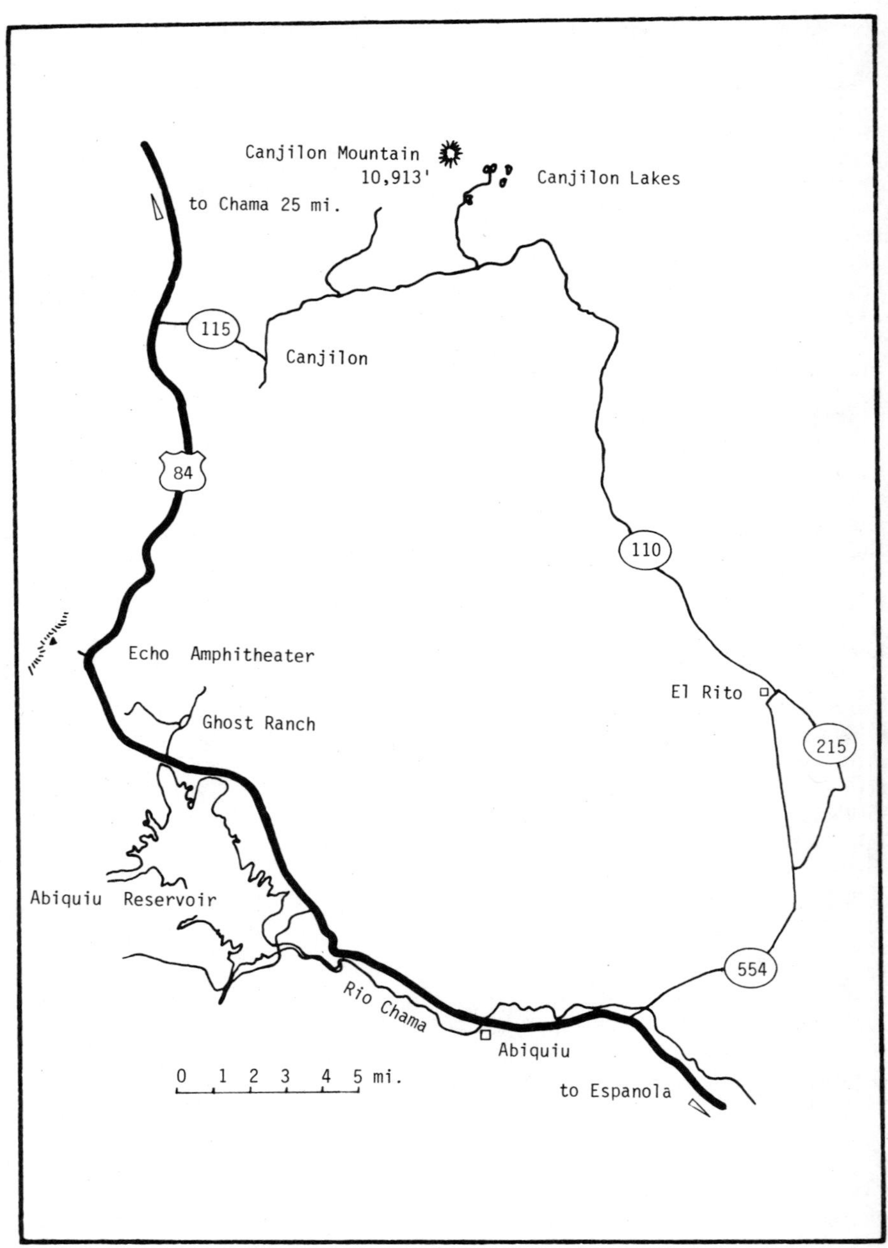
Canjilon Mountain
10,913'
Canjilon Lakes
to Chama 25 mi.
115
Canjilon
84
110
Echo Amphitheater
Ghost Ranch
El Rito
215
Abiquiu Reservoir
554
Rio Chama
Abiquiu
0 1 2 3 4 5 mi.
to Espanola

in winter, Ring-billed Gull, Great Blue Heron, and occasional Common Snipe flying by. A pleasing variety of dabbling and diving ducks may also be seen on the river. During the winter, up to a dozen Bald Eagles may often be seen in the cottonwoods below the outlet where they feed on injured, stunned or dead fish floating down the channel.

For those wishing to go to Santa Fe, there is a sign to the left a mile or so beyond the spillway, indicating a junction with NM 16 which leads to I-25. For those returning to Albuquerque, continue on NM 22, through Peña Blanca, to I-25, about 5 miles distant.

Five miles south on I-25, a road heads east, immediately opposite the westbound exit for Santo Domingo Pueblo. Just south of this road and within a half mile of I-25, is an extensive flat field, for a number of years one of the most reliable sites in central New Mexico for nesting Mountain Plover. Unfortunately, recent disturbance from highway construction proved to be a deterrent, and the plovers have not been seen there for the past two years.

ABIQUIU - CHAMA

On the scenic drive from Española to Chama, US 84 parallels the Rio Chama as far as Abiquiu. An excellent place to see wintering Bald Eagles, which often perch in riverside cottonwoods, is at a large bend in the river 2 miles beyond the junction of NM 110 and US 84 (or about 0.25 mile past Trujillo's store). Common Mergansers, Common Goldeneyes and other ducks as well as Canada Geese and Great Blue Herons may be seen on the water. Golden Eagles may perch on the high cliff north of the bridge, just west of Abiquiu. Other good overlooks are located near the Abiquiu Elementary School, one mile west of town, and at a point 4 miles beyond Abiquiu where the highway climbs away from the river. Scanning the trees and cliffs may disclose a Bald Eagle. This section of water is also favored by wintering waterfowl.

About 6.3 miles beyond Abiquiu one may take NM 96 to the left (west) to reach picnic sites and overlooks for Abiquiu Reservoir. A spotting scope is needed to adequately see species such as Bald Eagle and Common Merganser, which may congregate on or near open water when the surface is partly frozen. Summer recreational activity, especially boating, severely limits waterbird use in that season.

As one heads north again on US 84, the highway crosses open grasslands interspersed with pinyon-juniper woodlands. In winter, Red-tailed and Ferruginous hawks, Prairie Falcon, or Golden Eagle may perch on power poles and fence posts. Rough-legged Hawk and Merlin are rare but regular winter visitors. Brilliant sandstone cliffs, made famous by Georgia O'Keefe, come into view as one proceeds north. Seven miles beyond NM 96 is the turnoff for the Ghost Ranch Conference Center. Park off the highway opposite the Center's entrance and scan the dead cottonwoods in the lake for Bald Eagle in winter, Osprey in migration, and nesting Double-crested Cormorants in summer. One may drive to the Conference Center for hikes to Kitchen Mesa or Chimney Rock, which offer outstanding views and reasonable birding. However, expect the grounds to be busy in summer.

Echo Amphitheater is 3.6 miles north along US 84 from the Ghost Ranch turnoff. In summer the cliffs are inhabited by White-throated Swifts, American Kestrels, Violet-green Swallows, and Canyon Wrens. A walk through the pinyon-juniper woodland should reveal Cassin's Kingbird, Ash-throated Flycatcher, Scrub and Pinyon jays (the latter often in large, noisy flocks), Plain Titmouse, and Bushtit.

At 11.3 miles beyond Echo Amphitheater, NM 115 turns east from US 84, beginning a route which will take the birder through a variety of montane habitats and eventually back to Abiquiu, Española, and Santa Fe. It is important to take adequate supplies of food, water, and gasoline. In the small town of Canjilon, 3.4 miles from US 84, inquire at the Forest Service Ranger Station (on the right as one enters the village) about road conditions, especially if seeking to pursue Boreal Owls. Turn sharply left (north) near a small gas station/store (the last service for 30 miles) 0.25 mile past the Ranger Station, and follow NM 110 for 7.8 miles. There, take the paved road which turns left (north) and climbs 5 miles to Canjilon Lakes, several small bodies of water (ca. 10,000-feet elevation) visited by fishermen and a few waterfowl. (There are three campgrounds in the area.) Spruce-fir forests surround the lakes and harbor numerous birds, including the possibility of Blue Grouse hens with broods, Olive-sided Flycatchers and other montane species. Boreal Owl has been found on Canjilon Mountain, about 3 miles north of the end of the road, but it involves an arduous climb or a circuitous drive in a four-wheel-drive vehicle to reach suitable habitat.

Returning to NM 110, turn left (east) again and follow this rough dirt road over Mogote Ridge at 9,500 feet and down into the next valley. A breeding bird survey along here from the lakes to the town of El Rito has produced 78 species in June, including six warblers, four Empidonax flycatchers, Williamson's Sapsucker, and Three-toed Woodpecker. At 7.8 miles from the Canjilon Lakes turnoff, NM 110 leading to El Rito turns sharply right (south). Continuing straight ahead (east) on Forest Service Road 106 will eventually take one to Vallecitos and NM 111 and thus to US 285 south to Española. Highway NM 110 connects with NM 554 in El Rito and finally back to US 84 near Abiquiu. Sage Sparrow has been found on this latter route about 6 miles south of El Rito.

Choosing to omit the Canjilon Lakes loop, one may instead continue north on US 84 toward Chama through pinyon-juniper woodlands, sagebrush flats, and farmland. Wintering raptors may include more Bald Eagles, which sometimes feed on elk and deer carcasses near the highway. This route has especially good birding in spring and summer. Near Tierra Amarilla, 16 miles north of NM 115, Brewer's Blackbirds become increasingly common in the meadows adjacent to the highway. Culverts in this area may have nesting Barn Swallows, and the fields near the Parkview Fish Hatchery at Los Ojos sometimes support a few breeding Bobolinks. To reach the hatchery, drive 2.5 miles north of the blinking light in Tierra Amarilla. Take an inconspicuous left turn immediately south of the more obvious junction with NM 95 (to Heron Lake). Once on this road, turn right (south) in the middle of the village of Los Ojos, and at 1.5 miles from US 84 turn left toward the hatchery.

Willow Flycatchers nest in the thickets along the irrigation ditches, and Black-capped Chickadees have also been seen here. Swallows, Common Ravens and Black-billed Magpies are regular near the hatchery in summer, as are Ospreys in migration. Returning to the hatchery turnoff, go left 0.7 mile to a sign marking a left turn to Burns Canyon Lake. The lake is especially good for migrating waterfowl, while surrounding thickets and pastures have a variety of songbirds. Both the hatchery and lake are managed by the New Mexico Department of Game and Fish.

Heron and El Vado reservoirs to the west of Tierra Amarilla are heavily used by recreationists during the summer. California Gull, Western Grebe, and an occasional White Pelican summer here but do not breed. During other seasons these lakes are attractive to a variety of migrating and wintering waterbirds such as Common Loon, Eared Grebe, and many ducks. Bald Eagles remain all winter if the water is open. To reach Heron Lake, drive 7 miles west from US 84 on NM 95. Numerous pullouts and campsites along the southern shore provide unobstructed views. Check tall trees and snags along the shore for wintering Bald Eagles or migrant Ospreys. By continuing past Heron Lake on NM 95 one can view the north end of El Vado Reservoir as well, but the road becomes dirt and is treacherous when wet.

To reach El Vado Dam, turn west at the blinking light in Tierra Amarilla and drive 1.6 miles, past the high school to a stop sign. Turn left onto NM 112 and proceed 11.5 miles to the dam. A dirt road along the west shore of El Vado Reservoir connects NM 95 and NM 112 but should not be traveled when wet except with four-wheel drive. In summer, a stop at El Vado Ranch, 0.5 mile below the dam, will provide views of Barn and Cliff swallows over the river, numerous nesting Brewer's Blackbirds, Yellow Warblers, and often Northern (Bullock's) Orioles.

At Chama, 8.8 miles north of the intersection of NM 95 and US 84, food, lodging, and gas are available, making the town a good base for exploring this portion of New Mexico.

JICARILLA LAKES

If one plans to explore the Jicarilla Apache Reservation, utilization of Reservation businesses helps to show them the economic value of their abundant wildlife. A fine motel/restaurant and gas stations are available in Dulce, 25 miles west of Chama on NM 64. Camping is also possible at Dulce, Mundo, Enbom, and Stone lakes.

The Jicarilla Reservation covers more than 800,000 acres and includes sagebrush-grasslands, pinyon-juniper woodlands, and ponderosa pine and mixed conifer forests. A birder could profitably spend days exploring and enjoying this area. However, the jewels of the reservation are its lakes, most of which can be reached by a loop drive beginning at Dulce. Four miles south of this town on US 64 is Dulce Lake, and during the summer the marsh at its south end provides the best birding. Unfortunately, the shoulder is narrow and there are few safe parking places. In May and June, Pied-billed Grebe and American Coot nest here, and Common Yellowthroat and an occasional Song Sparrow sing from the bulrushes. Mallards and other waterfowl are usually found in the shallows, and Sora or Virginia Rail may be seen at times, all near the road. Migration can bring surprises, such as six Ospreys seen on an April morning and a pair of courting Hooded Mergansers in early May.

At 10.8 miles south of Dulce on US 64, turn left (south) onto NM 537 to visit La Jara Lake. At 5.3 miles, take road J-33 which turns left (east) with no warning. (If missed, one will pass below the dam on the left, then reach a junction with a paved road (J-15) at mile 5.7.) The marsh is at the upper end of the lake, about a mile along J-33. Western Grebe has nested here, and Wood Duck has been seen. Return to NM 537, turn left (east) on J-15 and continue 11.4 miles to reach Stone Lake where Western Grebes also have nested.

Stinking (Burford) Lake, one of the best sites for waterfowl in the State, is farther south on J-8. From Stone Lake, the road is dirt and after heavy rains becomes nearly impassable. There are extensive stands of sagebrush where Brewer's and Vesper sparrows are abundant and Sage Thrashers and Sage and Lark sparrows can also be found. At 5.3 miles the road forks, and the right branch goes around the lake (make left turns that keep the lake on the left even if it is out of sight) to South Bay. Sometimes one may have close views of American Avocets and Savannah Sparrows, both of which nest along the shore; be careful not to disturb them when breeding. In July there is likely to be an Eared Grebe colony of several hundred floating nests in the open water of the bay.

Returning to the road fork, turn left and check the lake at intervals. During wet years, over 2,000 pairs of Eared Grebes have nested here (rarely, the lake has been totally dry). July is the best month to view grebes as well as White-

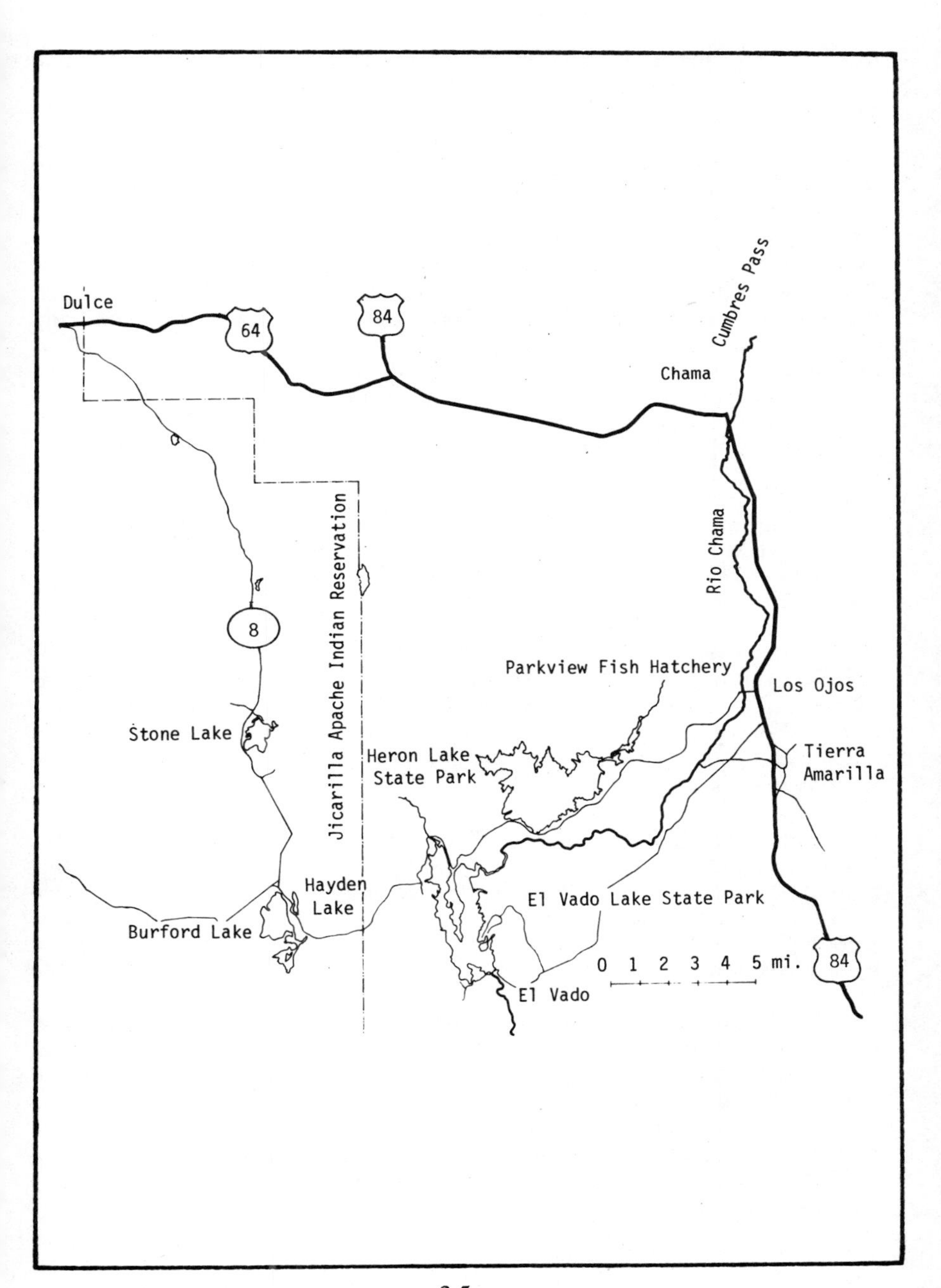
Dulce
64
84
Cumbres Pass
Chama
Rio Chama
Jicarilla Apache Indian Reservation
8
Parkview Fish Hatchery
Los Ojos
Tierra
Amarilla
Stone Lake
Heron Lake
State Park
Hayden
Lake
Burford Lake
El Vado Lake State Park
0 1 2 3 4 5 mi.
84
El Vado

faced Ibis and Black-crowned Night-Heron which nest in the bulrushes and forage along the shore. Yellow-headed Blackbirds sing from the rushes edging the lake, and American Coots are found in the open water. Ducks of 10 to 15 species also can be seen by scanning with binocular or scope. In July and August over 5,000 ducks may be present, but identification is difficult because they are molting.

At 1.1 miles from the road fork, Hayden Lake is visible on the left, and 0.1 mile farther a pullout on the right permits an overview of Stinking Lake. The viewing distance is great, however, and a scope is essential. Continue on for another 0.1 mile to the dam on Hayden Lake for close views of Eared and Pied-billed grebes, numerous species of ducks and shorebirds, as well as nesting Yellow-headed and Red-winged blackbirds. A mile farther along, in a gap between two mesas, is another bay of Stinking Lake, as well as two smaller lakes. All possess large numbers of breeding birds in good years, but during drought, lakes of this sort with small drainage basins may completely disappear. In this area, also, look for breeding Lazuli Bunting.

Continuing through the gap, around the north end of El Vado Reservoir, and following NM 95 past Heron Lake will take one back to US 84. (Camping is available at both reservoirs.) Or one can return to Dulce via J-8, checking Enbom, Horse, and Mundo lakes enroute.

For those wishing to explore more of the high country, NM 17 heads northeast out of Chama to Cumbres Pass just across the Colorado border. At the edge of town, the highway crosses a bridge over the Chama River where a dirt road descends to the streamside on the left. One may follow the stream for 0.4 mile with frequent pulloffs for parking to observe high country riparian species.

In summer, Lewis's Woodpecker, Dusky Flycatcher, Yellow Warbler and Yellow-rumped Warbler nest there. From the bridge to the narrow-gauge railroad station at Cumbres Pass, the distance is 11.5 miles. It is a scenic drive with side roads into the National Forest. The railroad station, at 10,022 feet, is a good place for higher-elevation birds. Be warned that here snow can persist well into summer.

For those who wish to return to Albuquerque or Santa Fe by a different route, US 64 goes east from US 84 to Hopewell Lake at 13.3 miles south of Chama. As it ascends from juniper woodland up to mixed conifer and aspen forest, the road offers many spectacular vistas. The turnoff to Hopewell Lake, in the Carson National Forest, is 44.9 miles from Chama. At a fork only 0.1 mile from US 64, a right turn leads to the lake, and the left turn continues into the National Forest. During winter and spring, the roads here may be impassable, but in summer they provide access to high-country breeding birds.

Continue on US 64 to the junction with US 285 in Tres Piedras at 19.7 miles beyond the Hopewell Lake turnoff. Heading south on 285, one may proceed to Española and Santa Fe or turn left on NM 96 about 20.8 miles south of Tres Piedras. This route leads into the Rio Grande gorge for a return to Santa Fe via NM 68. At 10.1 miles from the turn, the surface becomes gravel and the road descends steeply into the gorge. Despite its sharp curves, the road is in reasonable condition. Along NM 68, in the gorge, there are several picnic areas and pulloffs where the road parallels the river on the east side. In summer, expect White-throated Swift, Rock and Canyon wrens, and Yellow Warbler.

VALLE VIDAL AND LATIR LAKES

About 24 miles north of Taos on NM 522 is the town of Questa. There, at the Questa Ranger District headquarters of the Carson National Forest, one may obtain an up-to-date map and other information about the Valle Vidal, an important 100,000-acre montane tract of national forest in the Sangre de Cristo Mountains. The turnoff to Valle Vidal (NM 196) is located at the town of Costilla, 20 miles beyond Questa and just south of the Colorado line. Supplies are available in Costilla or in Amalia, 6 miles to the east.

The area provides access to the varied habitats of typical montane breeding birds, and the chance to find White-tailed Ptarmigan, Rosy Finch, and other high-country species. The dominant habitats include mixed conifer and spruce-fir forests, subalpine forest/shrubland, and alpine tundra.

The public lands at Valle Vidal provide two campgrounds, an extensive parkland of montane grasses and bristlecone pine forest, Costilla and Comanche creeks, and the Shuree Ponds. One can most easily reach the highest areas through the Rio Costilla Cattle and Land Association property. These lands are part of the original Sangre de Cristo Land Grant and include the Latir Lakes which can be reached by driving east 6 miles to Amalia from Costilla, then heading toward Valle Vidal on Forest Road 1950. For birding fishermen, Valle Vidal special use permits are available from the New Mexico Department of Game and Fish or from tackle shops in Taos and at the Amalia store.

About 10 miles east of Amalia, turn right (south) on the Association's four-wheel-drive road. Count on a two-hour drive to the eight lakes from Costilla, and stop at the self-service fee station on the entrance road. Camping, day use, and fishing permits are available at the station for a small fee. This is the only road in the State that provides access to true alpine habitats. Recommended times to look for ptarmigan and Rosy Finches are early July through late September.

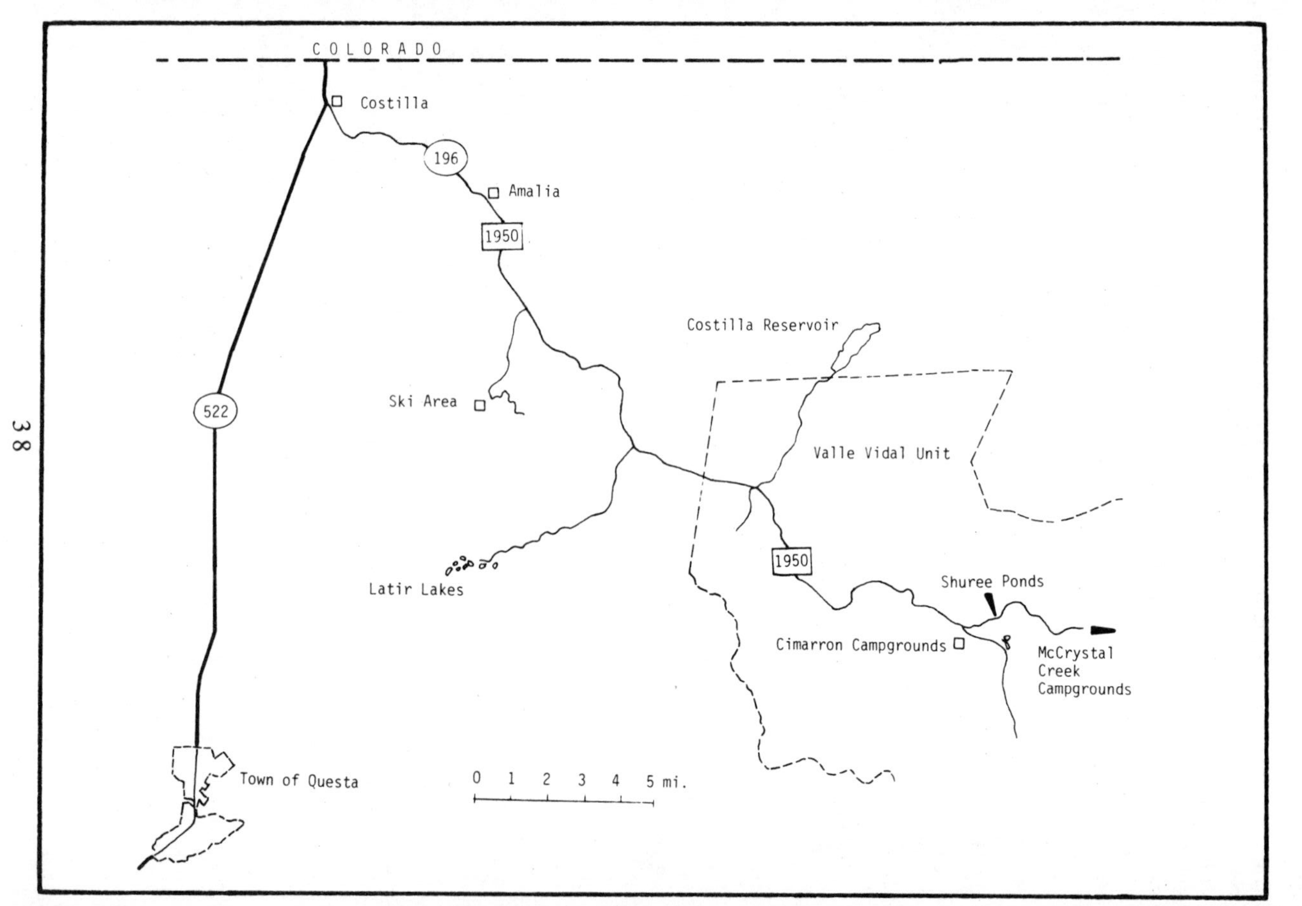

COLORADO
Costilla
196
Amalia
1950
Costilla Reservoir
Ski Area
522
Valle Vidal Unit
Latir Lakes
1950
Shuree Ponds
Cimarron Campgrounds
McCrystal
Creek
Campgrounds
Town of Questa
0 1 2 3 4 5 mi.

In the conifers and willow-alder growth along the way, look for Hammond's Flycatcher, Clark's Nutcracker, Red-breasted Nuthatch, Golden-crowned Kinglet, Pine Grosbeak, and Red Crossbill. There is also an opportunity here to find rare species, such as Black Swift, in migration. The mixed conifer stands and areas of dense Colorado blue and Engelmann spruce provide habitat for Northern Pygmy and Saw-whet owls and Three-toed Woodpecker.

Mountain Chickadee

NORTHEAST

Wesley Cook, Roland Goodman, John Hubbard, Sue Huntington,
Adolph Krehbiel, John Parmeter, Christopher Rustay

Varied habitats, together with the many transients which regularly follow the flyway crossing northeastern New Mexico, contribute to good birding in the region. Well over 250 species have been identified in sparsely populated Union County. This is big-ranch country. Most of the better birding spots are on large private holdings, and one must obtain permission to enter. DO NOT trespass on private lands, and above all else, if given permission to bird on a private holding, always immediately close all gates through which you pass -- an unwritten law in livestock country.

Bordered by Colorado and the Oklahoma and Texas panhandles, Union County has an average elevation of about one mile: Clayton is at 5,050 feet, and the land gradually rises to Sierra Grande Mountain, 8,720 feet. The terrain east and south of Clayton is relatively flat, but the northern part of the country contains numerous canyons.

A large ridgelike lava flow extends from Sierra Grande east to Rabbit Ear Mountain (5,940 feet), seven miles north of Clayton. This high point was a landmark for travelers on the southern branch of the historic Santa Fe Trail, which passed just north of the mountain.

Because of the elevation and summer precipitation, the warmer months are pleasant, with cool nights. Except for an occasional blizzard, winters tend to be fairly mild.

CLAYTON AND ENVIRONS

Clayton is the largest town in the the region, offering motels, food, and gasoline. Chimney Swift has become an urban summer resident in recent years, and Blue Jay an uncommon resident. Ungrazed native sod at the municipal airport affords habitat for Cassin's, Savannah, Lark, and Grasshopper sparrows as well as Lark Buntings during the breeding season. Another good site near Clayton is the municipal sewage disposal area. To reach it, go south on First Street from Main Street to Dorsey Road. Turn left (east) on Dorsey Road and go about 1.5 miles to Dellinger Ranch headquarters. Ask permission to drive through the pasture to the "lagoons," four immense, concrete-lined ponds with ultimate flow of clear water from the final one onto pastures beyond. The entire area is fenced and locked, but access is generally available to interested birders. Numerous ducks and some shorebirds, including Wilson's Phalarope, can be seen at the ponds during migration, and sparrows can be found in the nearby weedy areas.

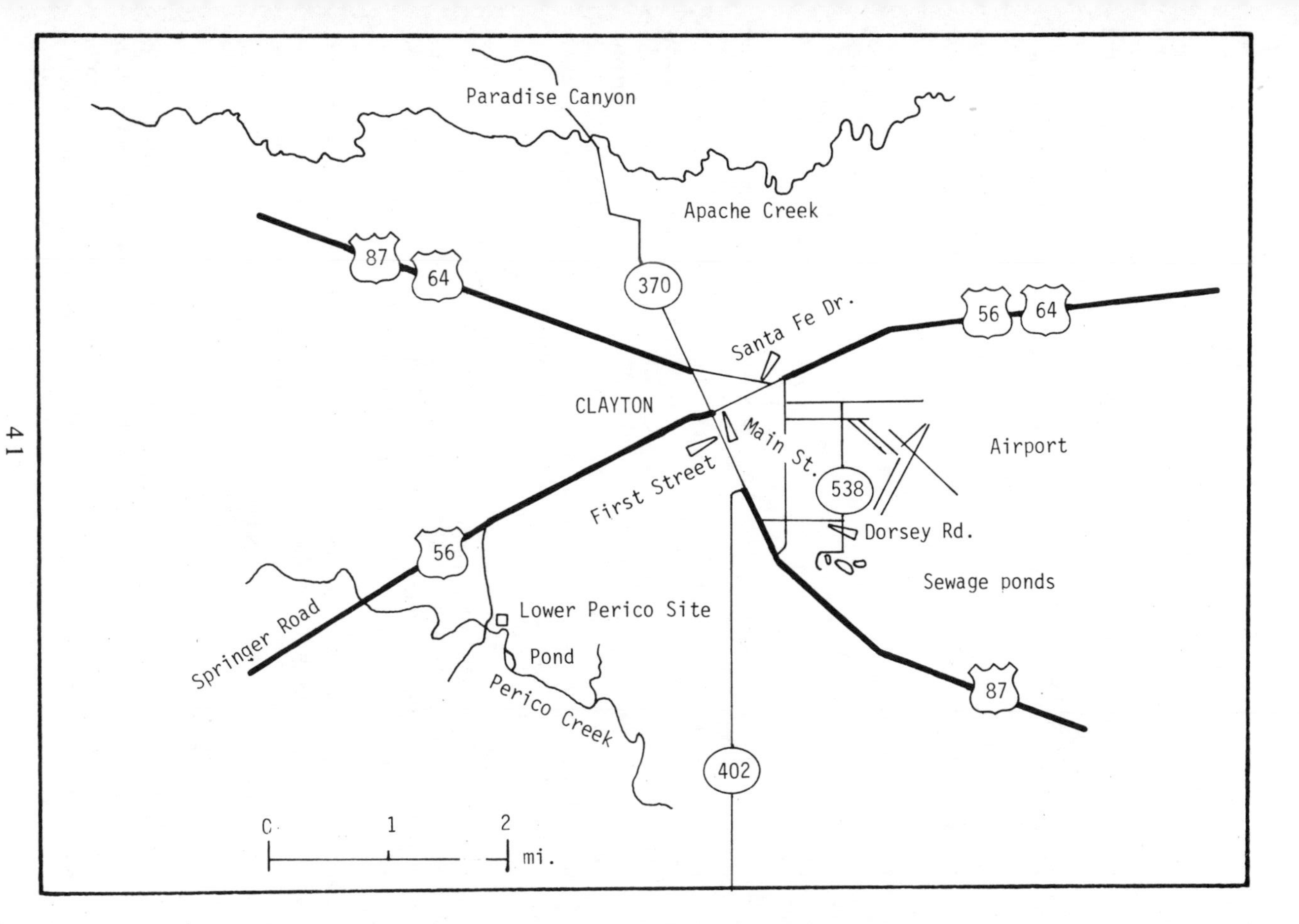

Paradise Canyon
Apache Creek
87
64
370
Santa Fe Dr.
56
64
CLAYTON
Main St.
Airport
First Street
538
Dorsey Rd.
56
Sewage ponds
Lower Perico Site
Springer Road
Pond
87
Perico Creek
402
C
1
2
mi.

THE FLATLAND STRIP

Most of Union County's farming is done in this strip of land, about 12 miles wide, east of NM 402 and bordering Oklahoma and Texas. There are no permanent streams, although following rains, temporary pools are formed by east-flowing creeks. Because the area has considerable land in grain crops, the resulting stubble furnishes plentiful food for birds, as do also the winter wheat fields where Canada Geese and some ducks feed. Scattered ponds and reservoirs attract waterfowl plus phalaropes and other shorebirds. Long-billed Curlews and American Avocets historically summered abundantly there, and they exist in lessened numbers today. Increased farming has decreased the habitat required by these species. However, the rodents always found in cultivated fields have tended to attract hawks to the area.

PARADISE CANYON

Locally known by the above name, the canyon of upper Apache Creek is a choice birding site. About three miles north of Clayton, it consists of a narrow gorge approximately 0.5 mile long between steep, 300-foot-high, lava-capped slopes. Perpetual springs emerge just above the principal gorge, but the flow disappears into the rocky floor shortly after leaving the canyon. Junipers, pinyon, and oak scrub, plus some cottonwoods, line the canyon floor and slopes. Noteworthy birds here in winter are Mountain Bluebird, Townsend's Solitaire, American Tree Sparrow, Song Sparrow, Dark-eyed Junco, and Pine Siskin. In summer, look for Rufous-sided Towhee and Lark Sparrow. Turkey Vultures ride the thermals, as does an occasional Golden Eagle, Red-tailed Hawk, or Prairie Falcon. Rufous-crowned Sparrows have been found here, especially on the high bench below the north rimrock.

To reach Paradise Canyon, leave downtown Clayton on north US 87 to NM 370 which veers off to the right, just before the overpass on US 87 toward Raton. Follow NM 370 about two miles until it goes down the hill into Apache Canyon and through a gap between two mesas; go left and upward to a locked gate (there also may be a haystack here) on the left.

Having previously secured permission and a key from the owner, W.R. "Bill" Watters in Clayton (505-374-9609), one can drive into the canyon and explore this lovely watered area. The road into the canyon is rocky and eroded, requiring a high-clearance vehicle.

PERICO CREEK

Perico Creek flows eastward through central Union County, crosses NM 18 three miles south of Clayton, and soon reaches the Texas Panhandle, there becoming part of the South Canadian River system. Each spring numerous migrants follow this watercourse. Some head for the mountains to the west, while others continue northwest along a branch of the Central Flyway, crossing the northeast corner of New Mexico.

The following breeding/summer species may be anticipated: Turkey Vulture, Northern Harrier, Swainson's, Red-tailed, and Ferruginous hawks, Golden Eagle, American Kestrel, Scaled Quail, Mountain Plover, Long-billed Curlew, Greater Roadrunner, Great-horned Owl, Belted Kingfisher, Lewis's Woodpecker, Say's Phoebe, Western Kingbird, Barn Swallow, Northern Mockingbird, Brown Thrasher (rare), Blue Grosbeak, Canyon (Brown) Towhee, Red-winged Blackbird, Northern (Bullock's) Oriole, and Song Sparrow. Migrants include: Spotted and Solitary sandpipers, Common Nighthawk, House Wren, Gray Catbird, Hermit, Swainson's and Gray-cheeked thrushes, Veery, Mountain Bluebird, Blue-gray Gnatcatcher, Ruby-crowned Kinglet, Virginia's, Yellow (rare), Yellow-rumped, and Wilson's warblers, Western Tanager, Green-tailed Towhee, and Chipping and Clay-colored sparrows. Species to be found in winter are Rough-legged Hawk, Ladder-backed Woodpecker (a few also in spring and fall), Northern Flicker, American Tree and White-crowned (also in early spring and fall) sparrows, and Dark-eyed Junco.

There are two principal birding areas along the stream: the lower Perico site three miles west of Clayton and the upper Perico site 6 to 8 miles west of Clayton.

The lower Perico site is adjacent to the south side of US 56/64 at historic Pitchfork Ranch headquarters, currently owned and operated by Mr. and Mrs. Toney Dowlen. To reach ranch headquarters, start in downtown Clayton at the intersection of US 87 and 56/64; go west on 56/64 about 2.5 miles to a cattleguard on the left at the entrance to a ranch road. (A pit for caliche road material is located near the cattleguard.) Follow the ranch road about 1 mile to the Dowlen home, marked by a grove of trees along Perico Creek. Mrs. Dowlen is interested in birds, and birders making inquiry will receive a friendly welcome. However, courtesy demands that one phone ahead: 505-374-9614. As at all private ranches, the owners want to know in advance who is entering their land, and why.

Permanently flowing springs provide a constant source of water to tree-lined Perico Creek. Start birding around the Dowlen residence and continue downstream through a large cottonwood grove to a small impoundment about 0.75 mile distant. The entire area is productive year-round but especially so during spring and fall migrations.

The upper Perico site is part of a 25,000-acre spread known locally as the Old Otto Ranch. The late John S. Otto was an ardent conservationist who did not overstock his range or permit hunting of either deer or birds. Upper Perico Creek is a tree-lined watercourse fed by permanent springs, and there are also

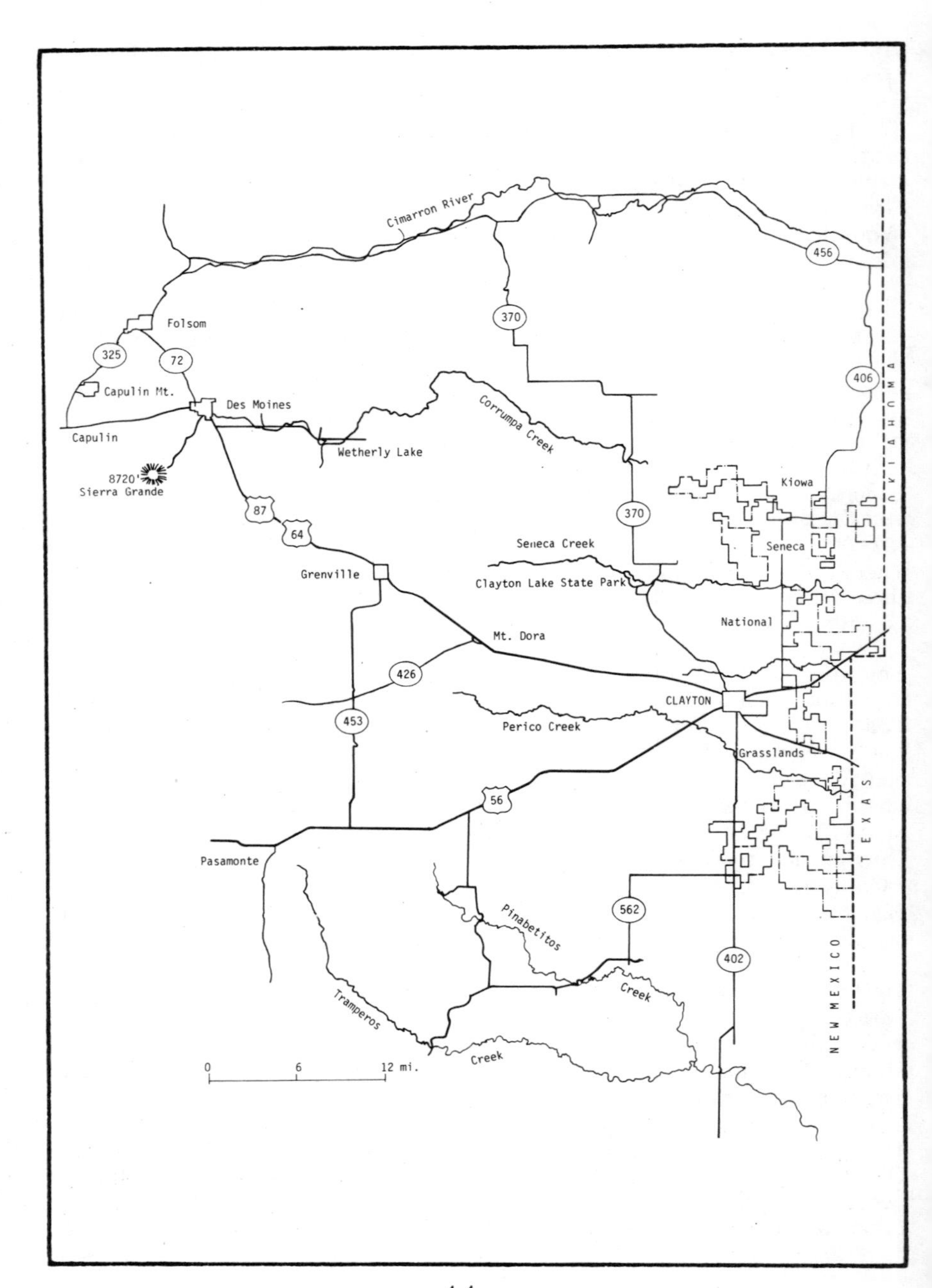
Cimarron River
456
370
Folsom
325
72
406
Capulin Mt.
Des Moines
Corrumpa Creek
Capulin
Wetherly Lake
8720'
Sierra Grande
Kiowa
87
370
64
Seneca Creek
Seneca
Grenville
Clayton Lake State Park
National
Mt. Dora
426
CLAYTON
453
Perico Creek
Grasslands
56
Pasamonte
Pinabetitos
562
402
Creek
Trampero
Creek
0
6
12 mi.
NEW MEXICO
TEXAS
OKLAHOMA

three reservoirs about 0.5 mile away. These stock-watering impoundments attract bird species not usually found on shallow creek waters. To reach the site, begin in Clayton at the intersection of US 87 and US 56. Go west on US 56 (Springer Road), over the top of a hill at the west edge of town (on the left is the Clayton Hotel), and about 100 yards farther to a dead end, then turn left onto an unmarked dirt road. It is about 6 miles to the ranch headquarters (marked by an abandoned concrete silo and various buildings), where one should ask for directions to the creek and reservoirs. Authorization for entry is required from Mr. or Mrs. Ron W. Jenkins, the present operators. Telephone 505-374-2815 or write in advance to the Jenkins at Clayton, NM 88415.

Be sure to reclose all gates immediately after driving through them. Remember, too, that all cattle encountered are range animals; though not necessarily dangerous, they are not to be trusted. Keep alert and use caution when afoot in their presence.

Birding can be good both upstream a mile or more along the meanders of Perico Creek and downstream past a small impoundment and marshy area. At several points upstream there are pools which are attractive to ducks, while various waders and shorebirds may be seen on the reservoirs. A likely place for Mountain Plover is on the prairie north of the creek and roughly two miles northwest of headquarters.

Another Perico Creek Site, with similar birdlife, is located upstream on the Heringa Ranch, which adjoins the Old Otto Ranch on the west. Access to these holdings must be secured from Mr. or Mrs. J. W. Heringa (505-374-9011); their mailing address is Clayton, NM 88415.

CLAYTON LAKE STATE PARK

This 440-acre State park and wildlife preserve straddles Seneca Creek and is reached by driving north from Clayton on US 87 until NM 370 veers to the right just before a railroad overpass. Go north on NM 370 for about 10 miles to a sign for Clayton Lake State Park on the left.

Grassland, pinyon-juniper, and riparian habitats are found within the park. An earthen, rock-filled dam has created an artificial lake bounded by lava and sandstone walls. Where Seneca Creek enters the upper end of the lake and near some permanent springs, there is a marshy zone where Great Blue Herons have nested. In season, Horned, Eared, Pied-billed and Western grebes are found here, along with an occasional Common Goldeneye and other waterfowl. Many Canada Geese and a Bald Eagle or two usually winter on this impoundment, and Sandhill Cranes may stop here during migration.

DRY CIMARRON RIVER VALLEY

This east-west valley near the Colorado-New Mexico boundary is reached from Clayton by driving east 2.5 miles on US 56/64 and turning left (north) on NM 402 for about 38 miles to the intersection with NM 325. There one turns west onto a paved road which becomes dirt and gravel and traverses the 50-mile-long Dry Cimarron Valley, a beautiful flood plain lying between high mesas and steep cliffs. Several intriguing formations arise from the valley floor itself, two of these appropriately called Battleship and Wedding Cake mesas. The road is flanked by private ranches and irrigated farmland, so birding is restricted to the right-of-way.

The Dry Cimarron River starts many miles to the west, along the south slope of 8,000-feet-high Johnson Mesa in Colfax County. Valley habitats include grassland, shrubland, pinyon-juniper woodland, and various types of riparian growth. CAUTION: The 100-mile drive from Clayton to Folsom, at the west end of the sparsely populated valley, lacks stores, potable water, gasoline, food and lodging.

Summer resident birds of the valley include: Turkey Vulture, American Kestrel, Mourning Dove, Red-headed, Ladder-backed, Downy, and Hairy woodpeckers, Northern (Red-shafted) Flicker, Ash-throated Flycatcher, Eastern, Western and Cassin's kingbirds, Cliff Swallow, Common and Chihuahuan (occasional) ravens, American Crow, Plain Titmouse, Mountain Bluebird, Gray Catbird, Northern Mockingbird, Sage, Brown and Curve-billed thrashers, Warbling Vireo, Yellow Warbler, Blue Grosbeak, Rufous-sided and Green-tailed towhees, Lark Sparrow, Lark Bunting, Northern (Bullock's) Oriole, House Finch, and Lesser Goldfinch.

SIERRA GRANDE

Union County's only true mountain is Sierra Grande, some 33 square miles of elevated land southwest of Des Moines, rising to 8,720 feet at the summit, roughly 2,000 feet above the surrounding plain. It is the highest point in the United States between longitude 104 and the Atlantic Ocean and supports New Mexico's easternmost stands of spruce along with woodlands of juniper, aspen, pinyon and ponderosa pine. Wooded areas, however, occupy only a small portion of the land area. Some 209 square miles of the massif is State-owned, but access is only by foot from the east. A rough road to the summit crosses private land on the north, and permission is required to enter.

Over 50 bird species have been recorded here during the breeding season. In the dominant open habitats, expect Ferruginous and Swainson's hawks, Golden Eagle, Horned Lark, Western Meadowlark, and Vesper Sparrow. Woodland and forest birds, several at their eastern breeding limits here, include Sharp-shinned and Cooper's hawks, American Kestrel, Wild Turkey,

Greater Roadrunner, Western Screech and Great Horned owls, Common Nighthawk, Broad-tailed Hummingbird, Northern (Red-shafted) Flicker, Lewis's and Hairy woodpeckers, Western Wood-Pewee, Dusky Flycatcher, Say's Phoebe, Cassin's Kingbird, Violet-green Swallow, Pinyon Jay, Black-billed Magpie, American Crow, Common Raven, Mountain Chickadee, Bushtit, Red-breasted and Pygmy nuthatches, Rock and House wrens, Ruby-crowned Kinglet, Mountain Bluebird, Hermit Thrush, American Robin, Northern Mockingbird, Warbling Vireo, Virginia's, Yellow-rumped (Audubon's), Black-throated Gray, and perhaps Grace's warblers, Hepatic Tanager, Black-headed and Evening grosbeaks (both apparently rare), Green-tailed and Rufous-sided towhees, Chipping and Lark sparrows, Brown-headed Cowbird, Red Crossbill, Pine Siskin, and Lesser Goldfinch.

Sierra Grande is of particular biological interest. Here, for example, Dusky Flycatchers inhabit blue spruce-aspen forest and juniper and juniper-pine woodland, habitats typically occupied elsewhere by Hammond's and Gray flycatchers respectively. The latter two are absent from Sierra Grande, as is the Dusky Flycatcher's normal habitat of fir-Gambel's oak forest. Other birds strangely missing from this mountain are such widespread breeders as Steller's and Scrub jays, White-breasted Nuthatch, Bewick's Wren, Solitary Vireo, and Dark-eyed Junco. Several other species, although recorded once or twice, are inexplicably scarce here. Sierra Grande is infrequently visited. There has been little field work during spring and fall when its isolated wooded areas surely attract numerous eastern migrants and vagrants.

CAPULIN MOUNTAIN NATIONAL MONUMENT

About 8 miles northwest of Sierra Grande, this area of about 775 acres embraces an extinct volcanic cinder cone. The monument is 3 miles north of the village of Capulin and about 6 miles south of Folsom, on NM 325. From the visitors' center, where a bird checklist is available, a well-maintained road circles the mountain, gradually ascending to the lip of the 450-foot-deep crater. An easy 0.25-mile footpath follows the rim, from which one can view portions of Colorado, Oklahoma, and Texas.

The monument's vegetation is predominantly pinyon-pine juniper woodland intermixed with various shrubby habitats and grasslands. Resident birds include Prairie Falcon, Wild Turkey, Scaled Quail, Great Horned Owl, Lewis's and Downy woodpeckers, Scrub and Pinyon jays, Common Raven, Bushtit, Mountain Bluebird, and Canyon and Rufous-sided towhees. During the breeding season there are also Ferruginous and Swainson's hawks, Common Nighthawk, Western Wood-Pewee, Say's Phoebe, Ash-throated Flycatcher, Cassin's Kingbird, Violet-green Swallow, Blue-gray Gnatcatcher, Solitary Vireo, Black-headed Grosbeak, Green-tailed Towhee, Vesper, Chipping, and Lark sparrows, Lark Bunting, and Lesser Goldfinch. Mountain Plover and Long-billed Curlew reportedly breed on grasslands near the monument. Many migrant species have been recorded here in spring and fall. Winter sometimes brings Rough-legged Hawk, Black-capped and Mountain chickadees, Townsend's Solitaire, and flocks of Chestnut-collared Longspurs, but little information is available on birdlife at that season.

WEATHERLY LAKE

This reservoir is on upper Corrumpa Creek, about 8 miles southeast of Des Moines. It is reached from Des Moines by going southeast on US 87 for 2 miles to a sign reading Weatherly Lake. Turn left and go east about 5 miles on a graded dirt road to the north side of the lake. Although the water level sometimes is lowered by irrigation, this impoundment seasonally attracts a substantial number of waterfowl and shorebirds. Permission to enter the Weatherly Ranch must be secured from the owner, A. D. Weatherly (phone 505-278-2871), whose ranch residence is 0.5 mile west of the lake.

TRAMPEROS CREEK VALLEY

Headwaters of beautiful Tramperos Creek rise just south of US 56, 3 miles east of Pasamonte Ranch headquarters, approximately 30 miles west of Clayton. This watercourse flows through a broad valley, often in the shadow of high mesas and buttes, providing good birding in a scenic setting at any season. During fall and winter, montane species wander down from the mountains (Clark's Nutcracker has been found here east of its usual range).

UPPER PINABETITOS CREEK

Upper Pinabetitos Creek, beginning in a rough setting of deep canyons, is one of the principal northern tributaries of Tramperos Creek. The best approach to the headwaters is from the north, not from the south on the Tramperos. From Clayton, drive 22 miles west on US 56, turn left (south) on an unnumbered road and go about 6.5 miles to a site on the creek locally known as Old Barney. Prospective birders must ask directions and secure permission from landowners. Max Sanchez (phone 505-374-9086) resides at the site of a former post office which gave the area its name. Another contact is (Thomas) George Gonzales (505-375-9002), and a third is Mrs. James (Fidelia) Taylor (505-374-9278), local head of the auto license office (374-9502).

This is rough woodland country (pine, juniper, and oak) contrasting with open grasslands. Birds rarely found breeding elsewhere in the county nest regularly here. Among these are Black-chinned Hummingbird, Ash-throated Flycatcher, Cassin's Kingbird, Brown Creeper, Curve-billed Thrasher, and Lesser Goldfinch. Other birds seen in the Upper Pinabetitos area during June include Red-tailed Hawk, American Kestrel, Lewis's and Red-headed woodpeckers, Willow Flycatcher, Rough-winged Swallow, Scrub and Steller's jays, Black-billed Magpie, Common Raven, Rock and Canyon wrens, Canyon Towhee, and Brown-headed Cowbird.

MAXWELL NATIONAL WILDLIFE REFUGE

This small refuge (about 3,300 acres) was established in 1966 for migrating waterfowl. It includes three lakes (numbered 12, 13, and 14), several small stands of trees, and fields where feed crops are planted. The refuge is open all year for birding and photography.

To reach the refuge, exit from I-25 at the town of Maxwell, 13 miles north of Springer and 26 miles south of Raton. After entering the village, turn right and go north for 1 mile on NM 445 (Third Avenue), then turn left (west) for 2.5 miles to the refuge entrance. Maps, a bird list and other information are available at headquarters. Phone is 505-375-2331.

The refuge is excellent for raptors. Up to four dozen Bald and Golden Eagles are present during the winter. Swainson's, Rough-legged and Red-tailed hawks, Northern Harrier and American Kestrel may be found at appropriate times of the year, and Prairie Falcons are occasionally seen year-round. American Avocet breeds in the refuge, and there are many migrating shorebirds including Sanderling and Marbled Godwit. Burrowing Owls are present in the prairie-dog town near NM 505 at the southeast corner of the refuge. Maxwell NWR is one of the best spots in the State to see Eastern Kingbird, which breeds commonly here. The trees often hold Tree Sparrows in winter and Red-headed Woodpeckers in summer. Grasshopper Sparrows and Dickcissels occasionally summer in the weedy areas. During migration the lakes attract numerous waterfowl, and Black Swifts have been seen with flocks of swallows.

South of the refuge there are three lakes between Maxwell and Wagon Mound on New Mexico Department of Game and Fish lands. Springer Lake is northwest of the town of Springer, Charette Lakes are southwest of Springer on NM 569, and there is a salt lake just northwest of Wagon Mound. Southeast of Maxwell, along the Canadian River, is the western section of the Kiowa National Grasslands. This area can be explored via NM 39. Chicosa Lake State Park, within the Kiowa grasslands, can be reached by taking NM 120 northeast from Roy.

LAS VEGAS NATIONAL WILDLIFE REFUGE

Situated at the base of the Sangre de Cristo Mountains and on the edge of the eastern plains, this wildlife refuge is a true gem. It encompasses grasslands, lakes, and ponderosa pine forest and provides particularly exciting birding from early August through late November. (Permission and a key are needed to visit the forested area, so Gallinas Canyon is not covered here.)

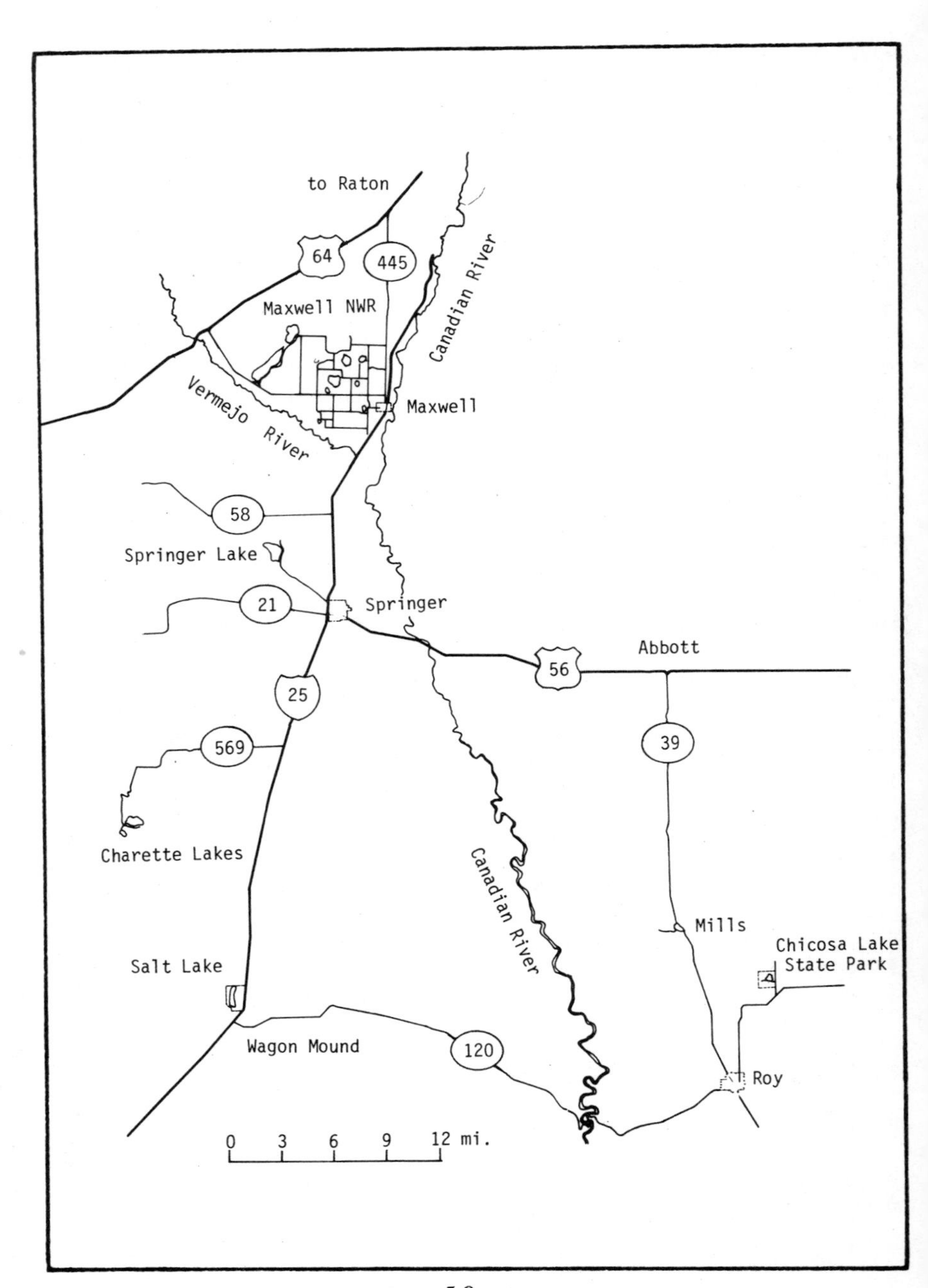

to Raton
64
445
Maxwell NWR
Canadian River
Vermejo River
Maxwell
58
Springer Lake
21
Springer
Abbott
56
25
39
569
Charette Lakes
Canadian River
Mills
Chicosa Lake
State Park
Salt Lake
Wagon Mound
120
Roy
0 3 6 9 12 mi.

To reach the refuge, follow I-25 to Las Vegas and take the University Avenue exit to NM 104. Turn east, away from the town; after 1.2 miles, a sign points south to the refuge. Take the first right turn after the frontage road. In spring, check the fields on the east (left) side of the road for Long-billed Curlews and Vesper Sparrows; in winter, expect Horned Larks. Watch the telephone wires for American Kestrels and the pole tops for Prairie Falcons and buteos. Weedy roadside growth hosts large numbers of sparrows in the fall, including the uncommon Clay-colored, and Lark Buntings may be abundant during late spring and early fall. Look for Ferruginous and Rough-legged hawks in winter.

At 3.5 miles the road crosses over a small creek and then turns sharply to the left. A frame house is on the right, followed by a row of trees attractive to migrants. Stop along the road just beyond the farmhouse and check for migrant warblers, especially in the fall. During migration, large flocks of Red-winged, Brewer's, or Yellow-headed blackbirds may be seen in the fields. In July and August, Rufous, Broad-tailed, and Calliope hummingbirds visit the roadside clover patches. In winter, look for the occasional Merlin in the trees; geese regularly feed in the fields. The refuge lies just beyond this row of trees, at 4.6 miles, after the road makes a sharp right turn. Listen here for Grasshopper Sparrows in the fields during spring and summer. Four of the refuge lakes are open for public viewing year-round. The first of these is Wigeon Pond, at 4.9 miles on the right. It provides waterfowl viewing at close range and, depending on water level, can be good for migrating shorebirds as well. Pronghorns sometimes are seen here also.

Refuge headquarters, on the left at 5.5 miles, are closed on weekends, but bird lists are available at the entrance. Park here and walk along the row of trees to the right. This area is reliable for American Tree Sparrows in winter and hosts an occasional owl. (Great-horned, Long-eared, Barn, and Western Screech are all possible.)

At 6.3 miles, beyond headquarters, Middle Marsh is visible on the right. Black-crowned Night-Heron, Great Blue Heron, Great-tailed Grackle, and Yellow-headed Blackbird have nested here. Check the adjacent fields for White-faced Ibis and Snowy Egret during migration.

Crane Lake, to the left, is not visible form the road; one must walk the short distance to the overlook. Bring a scope, as this is a large lake and too distant for binocular viewing. The near right shore is often good for shorebirds and Wilson's Phalarope in migration, while Sandhill Cranes and geese use the far right shore. Hooded Merganser is a good possibility here in winter. Franklin's Gulls may be found in the spring, Black Terns in late summer. The sun's angle makes viewing best late in the day. (This is another place to see pronghorns.) Beyond Crane Lake are more fields, with Vesper Sparrows nesting in summer and Western Kingbirds congregating during migration. Check for Bald Eagles and Rough-legged and Ferruginous hawks in winter.

As one continues, Lake McAlister becomes visible to the right. Descend a small hill and investigate the stand of Russian olives for Blue Grosbeaks and Yellow Warblers in summer. At the creek crossing, stop and check the reeds and surrounding vegetation for raptors, swallows, and sparrows. Past a small hill at 7.8 miles, the pavement ends, and a dirt road continues to Lake McAlister. Swainson's Hawks are here in summer and during migration. In the distant fields, Sandhill Cranes, Snow, Canada, Ross's and occasionally Greater White-fronted geese feed during migration and in winter.

After recent rains, this unsurfaced road can be muddy and passable only for four-wheel-drive vehicles. Just beyond a grove of trees on the right, at 8.2 miles, is a gate leading to Lake McAlister. It is closed after fishing season in the fall but opens again in the spring. Walk among the trees and brush at the south end of the lake, watching particularly for Lesser Goldfinches in summer, migrant warblers and sparrows in spring and fall, and American Tree Sparrows in winter. Water level permitting, the lake shore hosts a variety of shorebirds, including Semipalmated Plover, Killdeer, both yellowlegs, Solitary Sandpiper, Willet, Least and Baird's sandpipers, and Long-billed Dowitcher. The lake itself has a permanent population of American Coots. In summer look for Clark's and Pied-billed grebes and in late fall, Common Loons. Clark's, Western and Eared grebes, Osprey, and Black and Forster's terns are seen in migration, while Common Goldeneye, Common Merganser, and other bay ducks are easily found in winter, Fishing is permitted here, and during the season several boats may be on the lake. It is possible to drive along the western perimeter over a rough track.

The area beyond McAlister Lake is usually unproductive.

CONCHAS LAKE

Conchas Lake is a newly discovered birding "hot spot" located in the high plains of eastern San Miguel County. It can be reached by taking I-40 east from Santa Rosa for about 23 miles to Newkirk, then taking NM 129 north for 17 miles and turning east on NM 104. After about 6 miles, turn left (just beyond a golf course) at a turnoff marked for Conchas Dam and Conchas State Park. One soon reaches a flashing light at the south end of Conchas Dam; from here turn left to work the south shore of the lake or continue north (below the dam) to the Corps of Engineers residence area and north marina located along the lake's eastern edge beyond the dam. All of these areas are worthy of exploration, and indeed it is probably wise to stop and scope for birds at any point where the lake is visible. One can also drive south along the dam after reaching the Engineers residence area (most of the road atop the dam is one-way headed south), but this offers limited birding opportunities since parking on the dam is not permitted. For birding this large lake, a spotting scope is absolutely essential.

Conchas received very limited birding coverage prior to the winter of 1991-92, and it is hard to say what might be present during migration periods. In winter, water birds abound, especially diving ducks, and Common Goldeneye and Common Merganser can be as numerous as their names imply. Various other duck species, as well as Eared Grebe and Ring-billed Gull, are likely to be present in good numbers. Species that are probably regular in small to moderate mumbers include Common Loon, Horned Grebe, Greater Scaup, Red-breasted Merganser, and Herring Gull. From January to March of 1992 a number of outstanding rarities were found here, including the first photographically documented New Mexico records of Yellow-billed Loon and Mew Gull. A male Oldsquaw spent the winter here, and a Red-necked Grebe was reported and well described by several birders, though this last species remains unverified by photograph or specimen in New Mexico.

Land birding at this locality can also be quite good. The rocky areas around the dam and lakeshore have Canyon and Rock wrens and Rufous-crowned Sparrow. The trees and lawns around the Engineers residence are attractive to a variey of species, including wintering American Tree Sparrows, and a Field Sparrow was seen here during the winter of 1991-92. In the open countryside around the lake a variety of raptors may be seen, including Ferruginous Hawk and Prairie Falcon. A few Bald Eagles winter along the lake. If time permits, NM 129 between Conchas Lake and Newkirk can be checked for Mountain Bluebird and Cactus Wren.

WESTERN

Arch McCallum, Glen Hvennegaard

This region of mountains, plateaus, and mid-elevation grasslands begins about fifty miles west of Albuquerque and flanks I-40 for 80 miles to the vicinity of Gallup. It ranges in elevation from 6,500 feet at Grants to 11,301 feet at the summit of Mount Taylor, the highest peak in the western half of New Mexico. Vegetation zones, in ascending order, are grassland-shrubland, pinyon-juniper woodland, ponderosa pine forest, and subalpine grassland, the last two zones being found only on Mount Taylor. The Zuni Mountains, although being 2,000 feet lower, lack only a few of Mount Taylor's known summering species of birds.

The region's avifauna is distinctly northern in affinity. The notable "southern" forms are Whip-poor-will, Acorn Woodpecker, Black Phoebe, Scott's Oriole, Hepatic Tanager, and an intermediate population of the *dorsalis* and *caniceps* forms of the Dark-eyed (Gray-headed) Junco. The climate is delightfully mild in summer and early autumn but cold in winter. Birding is best from May 15 through October 15 but rewarding for the hardy throughout the year. The Bluewater Lake Christmas Count usually lists about 70 species in years when the lake does not freeze over, an impressive total for an area at this latitude ranging in elevation from 7,000 to 9,000 feet.

Accommodations and food are available in Grants and Gallup but scarce elsewhere; campgounds are available in the Cibola National Forest. All three loops detailed below require driving on fairly rough gravel or dirt roads, a fact of life here. All of these roads have been negotiated successfully (and without damage) in a very small car, but one should always drive slowly and be prepared to turn back during the mud season (late July and August). If one gets stuck, wait until someone comes by in a pickup truck with a chain, a fairly regular event. National Forest maps of the area are obtainable by mail or in person from the ranger station on Lobo Canyon Road in Grants or at Wingate, or from the U.S. Forest Service Office at 517 Gold Avenue SW, Albuquerque, NM 87102.

EASTERN ZUNI MOUNTAINS LOOP

This is the best trip in the region for birds, whereas Mount Taylor is the best for scenery. Begin at the junction of Santa Fe Avenue (the main road to Grants) and NM 53, just west of Grants, and set the odometer at 0.0 when passing McDonald's Restaurant. Proceed west on Santa Fe through Milan (or west on I-40 if in a hurry) and beyond on a divided highway that parallels the interstate. At 9.6 miles (Bowlin's Trading Post is visible) there is a turn-off for Bluewater, a Mormon farming village whose huge cottonwoods harbor, in summer, kingbirds, Yellow Warbler, Northern (Bullock's) Oriole, and other

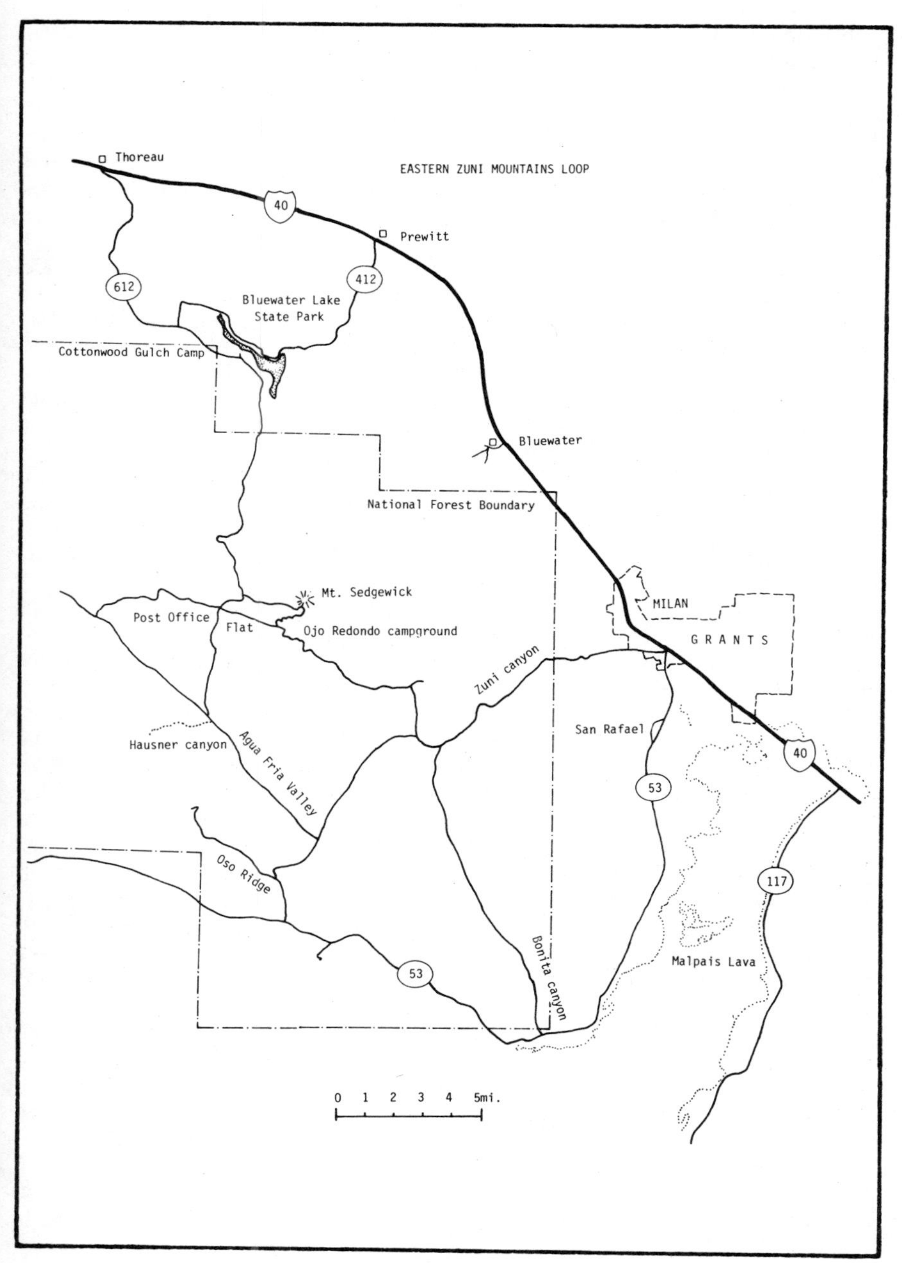
EASTERN ZUNI MOUNTAINS LOOP
Thoreau
40
Prewitt
612
412
Bluewater Lake
State Park
Cottonwood Gulch Camp
Bluewater
National Forest Boundary
Mt. Sedgewick
MILAN
Post Office
Flat
Ojo Redondo campground
GRANTS
Zuni canyon
San Rafael
Hausner canyon
Agua Fria Valley
40
53
Oso Ridge
117
Bonita canyon
53
Malpais Lava
0 1 2 3 4 5mi.

common species. This is NOT the exit for Bluewater Lake State Park. Continue on the access road to Prewitt and turn left onto NM 412 at 18.5 miles. Beyond, to the west, is Baca Boarding School, one of several low-elevation nesting sites of Brewer's Blackbird along I-40 from Grants to Gallup. Follow NM 412 about six miles to a settlement on the edge of Bluewater Lake. Continue to the end of the paved road in the State Park (camping available, but it is crowded). Go another 100 yards up the rough dirt road to an overlook of the dam and lake.

Scope the lake in migration and winter for diving ducks, loons, and Bald Eagles, but better views are available from the far side. Find a way down the cliff into the gorge that is commensurate with your surefootedness; the easier paths are 100 yards to the left. The object is to reach the base of the dam and work downstream. In summer, expect White-throated Swift, Black Phoebe (a disjunct northern population), Bewick's, Canyon, and Rock wrens, and other birds typical of pinyon-juniper-ponderosa pine country. In winter this is a good place for a variety of birds because it is warm and has open water. In addition to the species noted above, look for Belted Kingfisher, American Pipit, American Dipper, Winter Wren, Lesser and American goldfinches, and sparrows. One can climb out of the canyon on a road which crosses a wooden bridge about one mile below the dam. Black Phoebes nest under the bridge.

Return to the access road at Prewitt (odometer should be 18.5 as one turns left) and drive to Thoreau, watching the tree tops for Northern (rare) and Loggerhead shrikes and Sage Thrashers in winter and the railroad bank for Burrowing Owls in summer. (They nest on private land north of the tracks.) Large flocks of finches and sparrows also frequent these trees in winter. Turn left and go under the interstate on NM 612 (formerly Forest Road 178) at the Chevron station (odometer 28.5 miles). About two miles beyond, the road enters a small canyon where one should watch for the resident Northern Pygmy-Owl (especially on power lines) and Canyon (Brown) Towhee. About 6.5 miles from Thoreau (odometer 34.9 miles) a 25-mph speed limit begins. Just beyond the hill is Cottonwood Gulch, the most thoroughly explored birding spot on the north side of the Zuni Mountains. The 520-acre site contains shrub-grassland, pinyon-juniper woodland, ponderosa pine forest, and small riparian cottonwood groves. Habitat diversity is augmented by a spring-fed permanent stream which flows in the bed of Sawyer Creek. At least 56 species have nested here and several others breed nearby. The property is owned by the Cottonwood Gulch Foundation, which operates an educational summer camp here from June 15 to August 20. Birders and other naturalists are encouraged to visit throughout the year and take advantage of the variety of wildlife and the expertise of the staff, who will gladly show one around. However, advance notice of a visit will be appreciated. Call 505-862-7503 or write Cottonwood Gulch Foundation, P.O. Box 969, Thoreau, N.M. 87323. If this is impractical, visitors should stop at the caretaker's house (adobe building north of the paved road) and secure permission. If no one is home, park there and leave a note on the car windshield. The best birding is up the creek, from the bridge to the second fence. No collecting of any kind is allowed.

All three accipiters have nested at Cottonwood Gulch, as have Flammulated, Great Horned, Long-eared, and Northern Saw-whet owls. The Flammulated is common (but hard to find without assistance) from mid-June to mid-July. Nesting Dusky and Gray flycatchers can be compared. The State's first nests of Wilson's Phalarope and Savannah Sparrow were located nearby in 1980. Eastern Meadowlarks mingle with Westerns in the Bluewater Village area. Clark's Nutcrackers come down from the mountains in August, and the uncommon sparrows, such as American Tree, Lincoln's, Swamp and White-throated, may winter. Cottonwood Gulch has had its share of vagrant and rare visitors, including Broad-winged Hawk, Varied Thrush, Gray Catbird, Brown Thrasher, and Tennessee, Chestnut-sided, Black-throated Blue, Hooded, and Olive warblers, Northern Parula, and American Redstart.

From Cottonwood Gulch, drive up the road 1.2 miles and turn left (beware of mud) down a road to Bluewater Lake. Depending upon shoreline conditions, the lake is good in some years for shorebirds (August to October) and in most years, during migration, for ducks and grebes. Owing to the absence of marsh vegetation, few, if any waterbirds breed here. Check the mudflats along the lakeshore for shorebirds; Snowy Plover, Black-necked Stilt, American Avocet, Marbled Godwit, Red Knot, Sanderling, and Red-necked (Northern) Phalarope are unusual. The common gulls and terns are regular in season. Ducks, including Mallard, Gadwall, Pintail, Green-winged Teal, American Wigeon, Northern Shoveler, Redhead, Ring-necked Duck, Canvasback, Lesser Scaup, Common Goldeneye, Bufflehead, Ruddy Duck, and Common Merganser abound from September through December, with remnants remaining though the winter. A few Chestnut-collared Longspurs visit the grassland in September.

Return to the paved road (odometer 36.4 miles) and proceed southeastward to a sometimes muddy dirt track on the left (odometer 40.0 miles) to a point short of the dam. This overlook is less productive than that at the west end, but it does provide good views of deep water. Watch for Bald Eagles in winter and Osprey in migration.

Back on NM 612, turn left and continue southward into the high country. In Bluewater Canyon (odometer 43.1 miles) the road enters Williamson's Sapsucker habitat. This canyon offers fairly good birding and has nesting Belted Kingfishers and MacGillivray's Warblers, but otherwise no species not found more easily elsewhere. At odometer 49.4 miles, turn left on FR 504, along which is the most easily accessible mixed coniferous forest in the Zunis. There, in summer, one should find Red-naped and Williamson's sapsuckers,

Flammulated Owl

Cordilleran (Western) Flycatcher, Red-breasted Nuthatch, and Ruby-crowned Kinglet, in addition to the usual birds of ponderosa pine forest.

At the top of the canyon, a primitive road (504A) diverges on the left for the steep drive or hike to the summit of Mount Sedgwick, 9,256 feet, highest point in the Zunis. The view from the top is splendid. One may see Clark's Nutcracker here, and Hammond's Flycatcher nests in the Douglas-firs on the north slope. Continue on the main road to a T-intersection facing a meadow at odometer 53.6 miles. Ojo Redondo Campground to the left is pleasant, usually quiet on weekdays, and offers birds of ponderosa pine and mixed coniferous forests. Williamson's Sapsucker often nests in the aspens near the campground, and Hammond's Flycatcher nests near the summit of the ridge to the south. One can return to Grants via FRs 480 and 49 or continue west on this loop along FR 480 to Post Office Flat, where Brewer's Blackbird nests and Wild Turkeys are common in late summer. Turn left on FR 548 at Post Office Flat and proceed past Copperton (at 57.8 miles look for nesting Purple Martins in the aspens) to FR 50, at 60.5 miles, in the central valley of the Zunis. (A right turn leads to a rendezvous with the West Zuni Mountains Loop and to Ramah or Gallup.)

Straight ahead lies Oso Ridge and, along its 9,000-foot crest, the Continental Divide. Turn left on FR 50, and after 0.1 mile, a track leaves the road on the right. This is the access to Hausner Canyon, worth visiting for its magnificent blue spruces, Band-tailed Pigeon, Red-naped and Williamson's sapsuckers, Acorn Woodpecker, Whip-poor-will, Poorwill, Flammulated Owl, Dusky, Hammond's and Codilleran flycatchers, Clark's Nutcracker, all three nuthatches, and Orange-crowned, Virginia's, Grace's and Yellow-rumped (Audubon's) warblers. With a high-clearance vehicle one may drive the 1.8 miles to the first quaking aspens. It is a steep one-mile hike from there to the crest of the divide and another 0.5 mile beyond to Ojo Bonito Canyon, where a spring attracts many birds. From Ojo Bonito Canyon, one can hike cross-country to Little Water Canyon (about 2.5 miles) and to the deeper and wider Big Water Canyon, one mile to the west. The Hausner-Ojo Bonito-Water Canyon route is excellent for an overnight back-packing trip. (Take the USGS Valle Largo 7.5 minute quadrangle map, as well as adjoining sheets if visiting Big Water Canyon.) This area provides the finest example of the transitional quality that makes the biota of this mountain range so interesting. The other canyons have essentially the same birds (plus Olive-sided Flycatcher) as Hausner.

Back on FR 50 (odometer 60.6), continue southeast through the Agua Fria Valley until one meets the junction with FR 49, 66.3 miles, which leads to Grants. To continue the loop, bear right on FR 50 and ascend Oso Ridge. At the crest, 69.2 miles, one may take a 1.5-mile side trip to Oso Ridge Lookout, primarily for the view. From the 8,713-foot summit, on a clear day, one can see the Sandias 100 miles to the east, the San Agustin Plains 90 miles to the south, and Mount Baldy in Arizona 110 miles to the southwest. Dusky Flycatchers nest in the shrubs on the northeast slope of the peak. Continuing down the south slope of Oso Ridge, one reaches NM 53 (paved) at odometer 70.6 miles. El Morro National Monument, with its celebrated inscriptions, easily-seen Lewis's Woodpeckers and White-throated Swifts and uncommon Hepatic Tanagers, is 13 miles to the west. Ask for a checklist at the Visitors' Center where one may also obtain a key to the flora. To complete this loop, turn left at the FR 50/NM 53 junction, soon crossing the Continental Divide. Going down Cinder Hill, 72.7 miles, there is a panorama to the right across the 120,000-acre El Malpais lava flow, and at mile 76.6 the gray oak zone begins. Hepatic Tanagers are uncommon here, as they are throughout the Zunis. Look for them in the pinyons at the mouth of Bonita Canyon, odometer 81.6 miles, where Ladder-backed Woodpecker, rare in the area, is also present.

If a pull-off can be found, stop between mile posts 73 and 75 and listen for Eastern Meadowlark. Pass old San Rafael, site of Fort Wingate from 1862 to 1869, the road to Zuni Canyon (dry country birds), cross I-40, and return to the starting point.

MOUNT TAYLOR LOOP

This route begins in Grants at the junction of Santa Fe Avenue and First Street (NM 547). Go north on 547 for 0.9 mile, then turn right at the stop sign, watching for the Forest Service office where a Cibola National Forest map is available. At the first traffic light, 1.4 miles, turn left onto Lobo Canyon Road (NM 547 and FR 239), passing a large shopping center on the right. One now passes through several miles of greasewood-cholla cactus and then pinyon-juniper vegetation. Be careful not to trespass on private land.

At 10.9 miles is Coal Mine Campground, a pine-oak area surrounded by pinyon-juniper woodland. A good variety of birds can be found here, including Acorn Woodpecker and Virginia's Warbler. This is the last organized campground on the loop. Pockets of oaks, as in El Rito Canyon, 15.2 miles, support Dusky Flycatcher in summer.

Turn right on FR 453 (odometer 16.4 miles). After some 2 miles, one enters La Mosca Canyon and mixed conifer forest. Continue though the evergreens, aspen groves, and grasslands to a saddle (odometer 21.0 miles) between La Mosca Peak (which bristles with antennas) on the left and Mount Taylor to the right. Mount Taylor Trail 77, which begins here, ascends to a breath-taking panorama at the summit. One may walk the footpath or drive up the rough road which, after 1.2 miles, crosses the path. From here it is a steep 10-minute hike to the top, where at least one quarter of the State is visible -- from the Sangre de Cristos to the San Mateos, and southwest to the White Mountains of Arizona. On very clear days the La Platas in Colorado may be

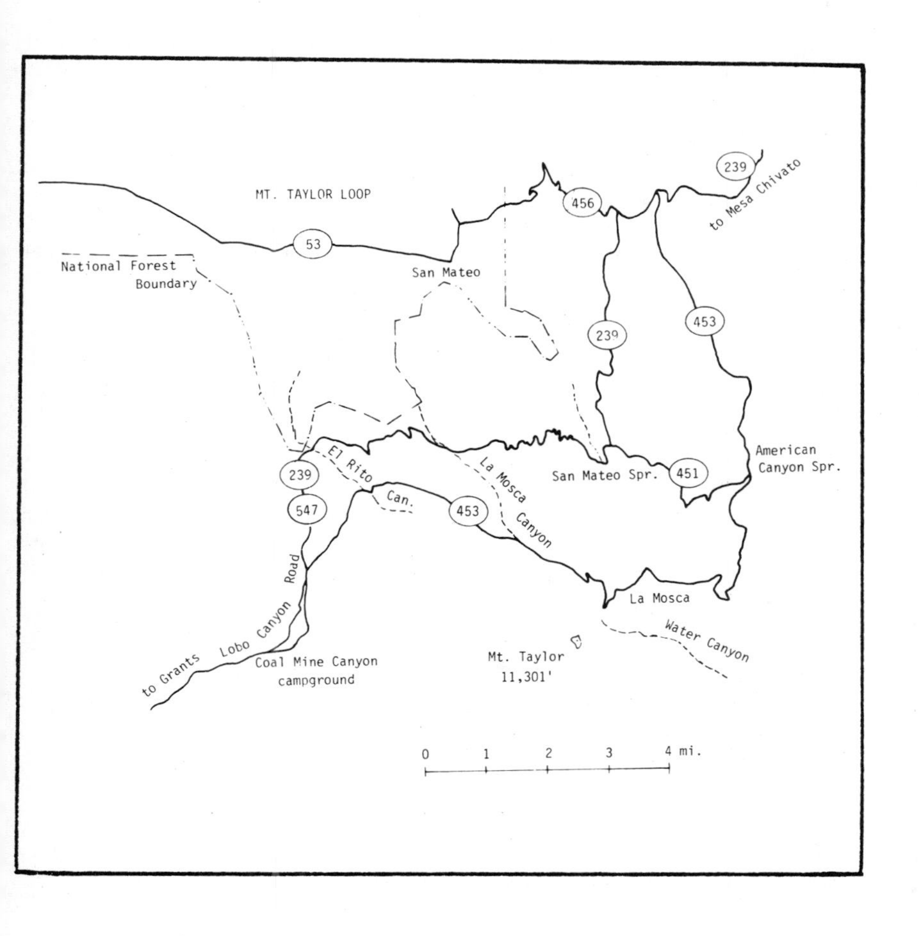
MT. TAYLOR LOOP
53
National Forest
Boundary
San Mateo
456
239
to Mesa Chivato
239
453
American
Canyon Spr.
San Mateo Spr.
451
239
547
El Rito
Can.
La Mosca
Canyon
453
Lobo Canyon Road
to Grants
Coal Mine Canyon
campground
Mt. Taylor
11,301'
La Mosca
Water Canyon
0
1
2
3
4 mi.

seen. Frequently encountered birds include Golden Eagle and Clark's Nutcracker. Common Nighthawks provide a spectacular aerial display at dusk.

Return to FR 453 at the saddle and drive up a steep stretch of road to La Mosca summit. This is the steepest section of the loop, but it is all downhill from here. American Pipits have been seen carrying food in the grassland below the summit and probably nest here. Although this is not true tundra, a few alpine plants are found on the windswept rocks below the fire lookout. From La Mosca one can see Water Canyon to the south and east. This lush canyon drains the former crater of a long-extinct volcano, the rim of which is readily apparent from this vantage point.

Continue on FR 453 through blocks of subalpine spruce-fir forest. Typical boreal birds inhabit these woods although, surprisingly, Hammond's Flycatcher appears to be absent. Below, on the steep, south-facing slope of Water Canyon, Orange-crowned and Virginia's warblers sing in the dense thickets of Gambel's oak.

One leaves the spruce-fir zone at mile 25.2 and enters an extensive grassland. Look for elk here as well as Poor-will, Black-headed Grosbeak, Vesper and Chipping sparrows. At American Canyon Spring, 26.8 miles, where the road re-enters the woods, Band-tailed Pigeons usually are common. (From here, it is possible to continue on FR 453 down American Canyon 5 miles to a junction with FR 239 leading northeast into the grasslands and oak copses of Mesa Civato.) To continue the loop, turn left on FR 451. This passes through dense, mixed coniferous forest, similar in physiognomy and birdlife to the spruce-fir stands. Golden-crowned Kinglets and Orange-crowned Warblers, as well as many of the more common mixed-conifer forest birds, summer here.

At the junction with FR 239, one returns to the pine zone. A right turn leads to the old Spanish town of San Mateo, where Charles Lummis lived and described Penitente practices around the turn of the century. Now it is surrounded by uranium-mining facilities.

To continue this loop, turn left on FR 239 which goes by San Mateo Spring, odometer 31.0 miles, a moist place with towering trees. Stay on FR 239 to return to Grants, passing the junction with FR 453 at odometer 35.8.

WESTERN ZUNI MOUNTAINS LOOP

This route places more emphasis on birds of lower elevations than the eastern loop, but it also penetrates country where most of the Zuni's montane species can be seen. Begin about 4 miles east of Gallup on 66 Avenue (old US 66) and set the odometer at 0.0 as one drives eastward under the I-40 overpass. At 2.4 miles, a side road passes under the interstate through a huge culvert.

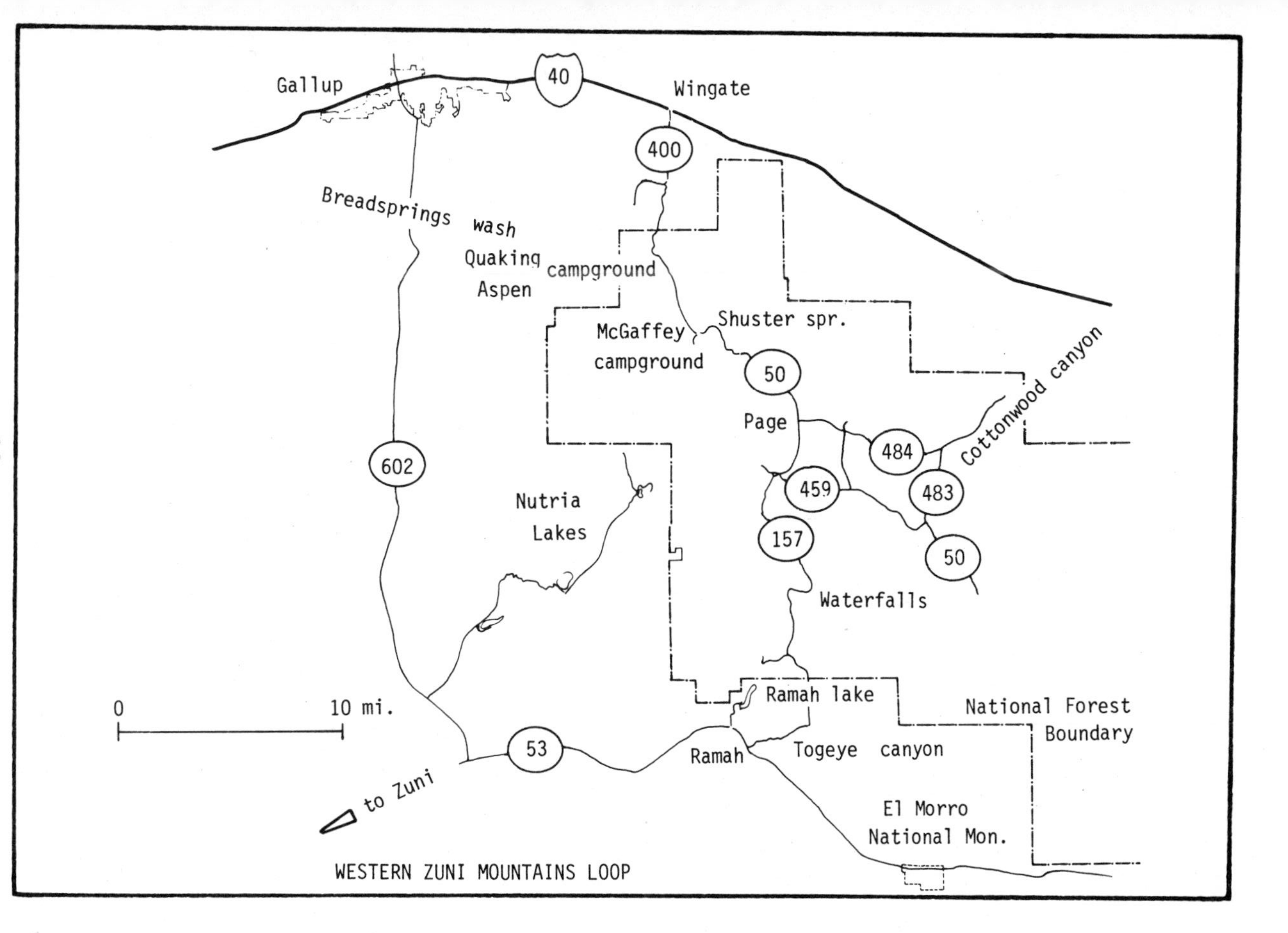

WESTERN ZUNI MOUNTAINS LOOP

About one mile along this road is an expanse of big sagebrush where Sage Thrasher and Sage and Brewer's sparrows are present during the breeding season. Watch out for coal trucks; there is a mine beyond.

Continue on this road past the turn to Red Rock State Park, where there is camping but poor birding. Brewer's Blackbirds nest in the roadside shrubs and Blue Grosbeaks along the washes. Cross the overpass just ahead to the right and proceed on NM 400 toward McGaffey. At Wingate High School, odometer 10.0 miles, there is a group of sewage ponds behind the rodeo grounds on the left, with nesting Great-tailed Grackles, Yellow-headed Blackbirds, and a few waterfowl. Above Wingate, the country changes gradually from pinyon-juniper woodland to ponderosa pine forest. Quaking Aspen and McGaffey campgrounds, at 18.4 miles, are in lovely settings and are good for birds of this forest type. (Flammulated Owls have been heard at McGaffey.)

At the campground entrance, NM 400 ends and becomes FR 50. Just ahead is McGaffey Lake, a favorite spot for local fishermen. However, birding is better around Shuster Spring, 19.4 miles, where American Coot, Sora, and a few teal rest. Continue east on FR 50 past the junction with FR 402, at 20.7 miles. At Page, 25.6 miles, now a mere crossroads, one may go straight ahead to Ramah on FR 157 or continue this loop by turning left on FR 50. At the junction with FR 484, at 27.9 miles, go straight toward Cottonwood Canyon on an ungraded track, being sure to close all gates securely, as one is passing though private land. At the junction with FR 483, five miles farther, one can see the big "V" of Cottonwood Canyon ahead. A large population of beavers is wreaking havoc in the dense stands of aspens in the canyon. Birds to look for in the vicinity include Golden Eagle, Northern Pygmy-Owl, Clark's Nutcracker (on the rim) year-round; both sapsuckers, Dusky, Cordilleran, and Olive-sided flycatchers, MacGillivray's Warbler in summer, and Winter Wren in winter.

Leave the Cottonwood Canyon area on FR 483, where Mallard, Belted Kingfisher, and Rough-winged Swallow nest along the creek and Brewer's and Vesper sparrows and Green-tailed Towhee abound in the shrubs. Rejoin FR 50 at 36.1 miles. A left (southeastward) turn leads to a rendezvous with the Eastern Zuni Mountains Loop. To continue, turn right into Monigan Canyon, at 36.8 miles. Meeting FR 459 at 40.6 miles, one may turn right and return to Gallup via McGaffey or continue on the loop to the left. Follow FR 459 to the junction with FR 157, at 44.1 miles; turn left (south) there and drive about 10 miles, mostly through private land, to the Cebolla Valley.

At 51.7 miles, a steep descent begins, and at 54.6 miles is a broad vista of towering variegated red and white cliffs and Ramah Lake. The lake is good for waterfowl and Bald Eagle except in summer, but this end of it is on Timberlake Ranch, a real estate development. To visit, cross the cattleguard to the right and follow the well-traveled road to the first ranch building where one should request permission for birdwatching.

After visiting the lake, return across the cattleguard and follow the main road, first over rolling hills, then through Togeye Canyon to NM 53, at 60.6 miles. Watch for Golden Eagle, Prairie Falcon, and among the pines, Hepatic Tanager. Ten miles farther, a left turn leads to El Morro National Monument (see above). To continue the loop, turn right toward Ramah and drive slowly under the towering poplars in this traditional Mormon town. At an orange picnic table on the left, at 61.8 miles, turn right again, heading north. Leave the poplars, pass some fields, and turn right in front of a large stone house to reach Ramah Lake State Park. In summer, the marshes below the dam are good for Sora, Virginia Rail, and Green-backed Heron (rare). Investigate the nearby willows for Indigo and Lazuli buntings and Blue Grosbeaks. Returning to NM 53, head west; for the next 12 miles one traverses a sagebrush-filled valley where Sage Thrasher, Sage Sparrow and Brewer's Sparrow are common during summer. At the junction with NM 602 (old 32), turn north toward Gallup. After 23 miles, the road descends into a valley choked with greasewood shrubs and dissected by deep arroyos. This is Broad Springs Wash, where Black-throated Sparrows are regular in summer and Bendire's Thrasher is also present. The sagebrush-clad hills nearer Gallup also support Sage Sparrows. The road enters Gallup from the south, but to avoid the town, take the by-pass to the left which leads to US 66 and I-40.

EL MALPAIS

El Malpais National Monument and National Conservation Area, administered by the National Park Service and the Bureau of Land Management, together protect over 376,000 acres of volcanic landscape, sandstone formations, pine forests, and wilderness areas. El Malpais (Spanish for "the badlands") contains diverse birdlife in various habitats, including grassland-shrubland, pinyon pine-juniper woodland, ponderosa pine forest, lava beds, and riparian zones.

A bird checklist (reporting over 190 species), area maps, road updates, and other information are available at the El Malpais Information Center in Grants (620 E. Santa Fe Ave., phone 285-5406) or at the new BLM Visitors' Center on NM 117. Groceries, restaurants, camping, and hotels are available in Grants.

The birding loop begins at exit 89 on I-40 (near a Stuckey's gas station), 5 miles east of Grants and 75 miles west of Albuquerque. Common birds to be encountered in most habitats include Turkey Vulture, Red-tailed Hawk, American Kestrel, Mourning Dove, Horned Lark, Violet-green Swallow, Common Raven, Mountain Bluebird, American Robin, Northern Mockingbird, Western Meadowlark, and Brown-headed Cowbird.

Proceed south on NM 117, a paved 2-lane highway, noticing Turkey Vultures soaring overhead and Scrub and Pinyon jays in the pines to the west. Northern Mockingbird, Townsend's Solitaire, and Lesser Goldfinch often perch on the fence wires and trees near the road. Flycatchers common along this route include Ash-throated, Cassin's and Western kingbirds, and Black and Say's phoebes.

Ten miles from I-40, turn into Sandstone Bluffs Overlook for a panoramic view of El Malpais (and its 5 different lava flows) to the west, Mount Taylor to the north, Cebollita Mesa to the east, and the Zuni Mountains to the west. Cliff Swallows and White-throated Swifts perform aerobatics over the precipice. Overhead, look for Turkey Vulture and Red-tailed Hawk. Both Rock and Canyon wrens inhabit the sandstone formations. Nearby are Band-tailed Pigeon, Greater Roadrunner, Mountain Chickadee, and Rufous-sided and Canyon (Brown) towhees.

After another 5 miles, one will see La Vieja ("the old woman"), a solitary sandstone block to the west. Watch for Prairie Falcons along the cliffs.

La Ventana ("the window"), the second largest natural arch in New Mexico, is 2.5 miles farther. A short walk from the parking area takes one to the base of this unique sandstone formation. Here also there are large numbers of Cliff Swallows and White-throated Swifts. In the pines and oaks at the base of the cliff, look for Acorn, Lewis's, and Downy woodpeckers, Red-naped Sapsucker, and Northern Flicker. Green-tailed Towhees have been seen near the road.

Driving south for 3.5 miles, stop at the Narrows, a picnic area in the pines on the east side of the road, to look for Lewis's Woodpecker, Mountain Chickadee, Hepatic Tanager, and Chipping Sparrow. Between the picnic site and the highway are unique pa-hoe-hoe lava flow formations which resemble coiled rope.

Continuing for another 13 miles, watch for Burrowing Owls that nest in the black-tailed prairie dog colonies to the east. As grass, rabbitbrush, and four-wing saltbush begin to dominate the landscape, typical prairie birds appear, such as Ferruginous Hawk and several sparrows, including Rufous-crowned, Vesper, Chipping and Lark. In spring and summer, Broad-tailed Hummingbirds are found feeding in the many wildflowers. Western and Mountain bluebirds inhabit the ponderosa pines farther up some of the canyons. American Kestrels perch on roadside fenceposts, and Golden Eagles soar overhead.

If the roads are dry, continue on county road 42 (a one-lane dirt road) for 33 miles to NM 53. In case of rain, however, return to I-40 via NM 117, as the road surface becomes extremely slick. At all times, drivers should proceed cautiously, watching for ruts and wet spots. After 11 miles, Cerro Brilliante (a cinder cone) is visible 0.5 mile to the south. The road turns north, passing by the western edge of El Malpais, bordered by the Chain of Craters, through older pine forests which support Wild Turkey, Western Wood-Pewee, Clark's Nutcracker, Plain Titmouse, all three nuthatches, Brown Creeper, and Western Tanager. This is the best area to hear or see Western Screech-Owl, Flammulated, or Great Horned Owl.

Approaching the junction with NM 53 (a 2-lane paved highway leading to Grants), one sees expanses of sharp "aa-aa" lava fields. On NM 53, one mile east of the junction, stop at Bandera Crater/Ice Caves, where Black-chinned and Broad-tailed hummingbirds frequent the feeders near the trading post, and Black-headed Grosbeaks and Dark-eyed Juncos (Gray-headed race) feed on grain nearby.

Near Grants, numerous potholes and wells along NM 53 attract waterbirds otherwise missing in this generally dry country. One of the best wetland sites is the San Rafael ponds (22.5 miles from Bandera), with Mallard, Blue-winged and Green-winged teal, American Coot, Sora, Killdeer, Spotted Sandpiper, Cliff and Violet-green swallows, Yellow Warbler, Common Yellowthroat, Red-winged Blackbird, and Great-tailed Grackle. Other breeding birds in similar wetland/shrub habitats in El Malpais are Black-crowned Night-Heron, Great Blue Heron, Gray Catbird, Blue Grosbeak, and House Finch. During migration, watch for waterfowl and shorebirds, Cattle and Snowy egrets, and White-faced Ibis. Winter residents include Bald Eagle, Northern Harrier, Merlin, Cedar Waxwing, Northern Shrike, White-throated and White-crowned sparrows, Cassin's Finch, and American Goldfinch.

Drive 2.5 miles back to I-40 (Grants-Milan turnoff) and the end of the birding loop. Be sure to report any unusual sightings to the staff at El Malpais Information Center.

CENTRAL

Pat Basham, Jim Black, David Cleary, Nancy and Steve Cox,
John Durrie, Robert Edens, Jr., J. Paul Fitzsimmons,
Larry Gorbet, Stephen Hoffman, William Howe,
Dustin Huntington, John Parmeter, Hart Schwarz,
Patricia Snider, Peter Stacey, Ross Teuber

ALBUQUERQUE

The largest city in New Mexico, like metropolitan areas elsewhere, has experienced extensive habitat alterations, but several good birding spots remain within the city limits. Habitats are diversified and range from riparian woods and brush along the Rio Grande to pinyon-juniper woodland in the Sandia foothills. The Sandia Mountains are just outside of town and easily accessible.

RIO GRANDE NATURE CENTER

The Rio Grande Nature Center is located within the Albuquerque city limits at the west end of Candelaria Road N.W. and is operated by the New Mexico State Parks and Recreation Division. There are approximately 270 acres within the Nature Center boundaries, which include large stands of old cottonwoods and associated willow, tamarisk, and Russian olive.

The Nature Center is open daily, except for a few holidays, from 10:00 a.m. to 5:00 p.m. During these hours, one may reach the cottonwood bosque near the river by walking west from the parking lot, following the main entrance path past the Visitor Center and across a small foot bridge spanning a drainage ditch. Before or after hours, one must park on the street and take the bicycle path that leads north/south along the ditch. (When using the parking lot, be sure to return to your vehicle by 5:00 p.m. or it might be locked inside the lot.)

In winter, White-crowned Sparrows and Dark-eyed Juncos are common around the Visitor Center, while House Finch and White-breasted Nuthatch are seen at any season. From inside the Center, (a small donation required) a large observation room overlooks a 3-acre artificial pond where resident Canada Geese and Mallards, as well as many other migrant and wintering waterfowl may be observed. The latter include Pied-billed Grebe, Gadwall, Northern Shoveler, Cinnamon Teal, Wood Duck, Redhead, Ring-necked Duck, and an occasional Mandarin Duck as well as Green-backed and Great Blue herons and Snowy Egret. Gambel's Quail frequent a feeder by the water's edge and Belted Kingfisher is commonly seen.

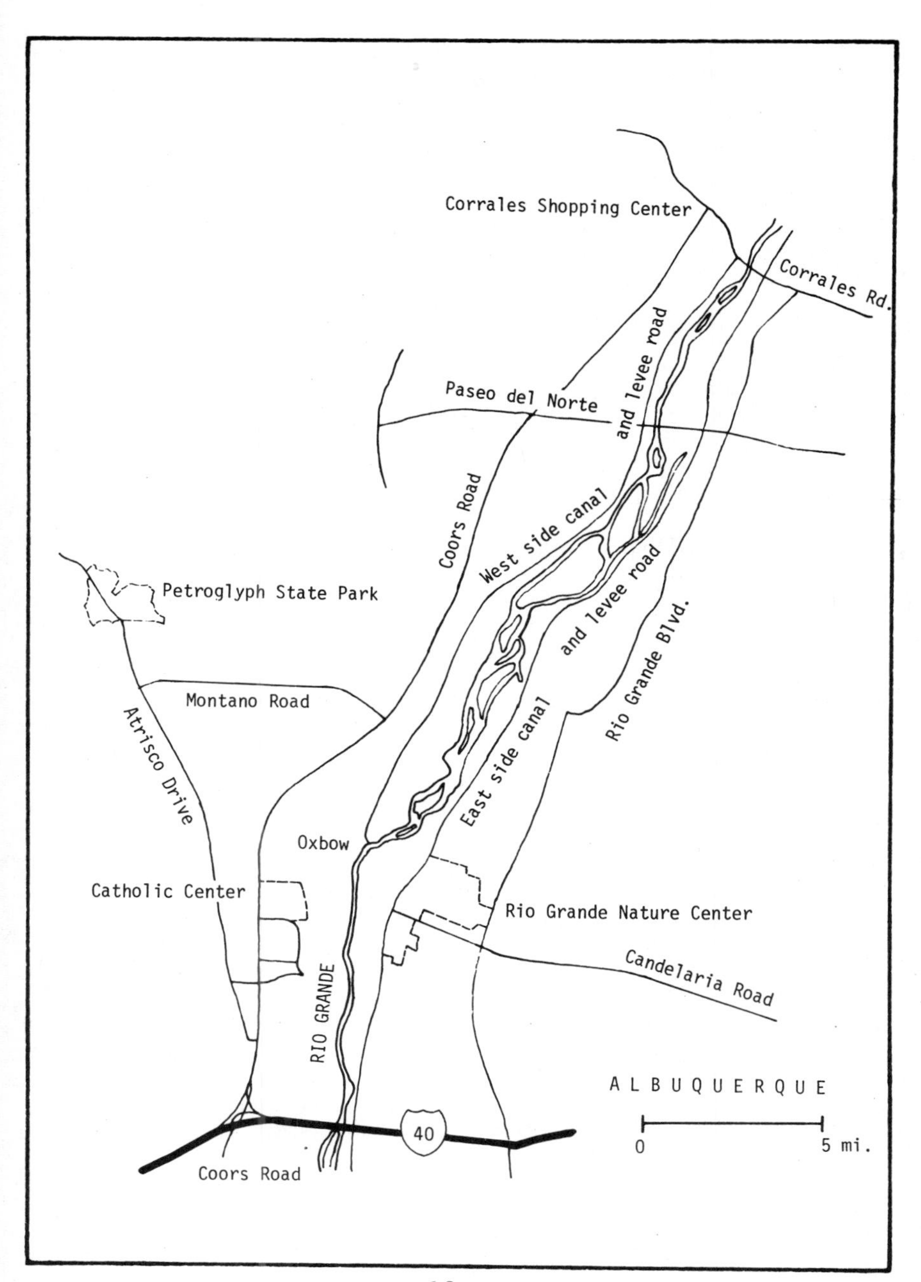
Corrales Shopping Center
Corrales Rd.
and levee road
Paseo del Norte
Coors Road
West side canal
Petroglyph State Park
and levee road
Rio Grande Blvd.
Montano Road
Atrisco Drive
East side canal
Oxbow
Catholic Center
Rio Grande Nature Center
Candelaria Road
RIO GRANDE
ALBUQUERQUE
0
5 mi.
40
Coors Road

Maps and checklists are available at the front desk. Inquire there also for a schedule of lectures, ecological exhibits and conducted bird-watching trips, as well as demonstrations of bird banding.

Of the three marked trails in the Nature Center, two, the River and the Bosque Loop, begin at the far end of the footbridge. To find the third one, the Ribbon of Green, turn south on the paved bicycle path instead of crossing the footbridge. Walk past the pump station on the east side, looking for the trail sign, which is partially hidden by shrubbery.

The River Trail leads through stands of cottonwood, Russian olive and tamarisk to the Rio Grande. The Bosque Loop meanders through the cottonwoods, but does not reach the river. The Ribbon of Green follows a perennial drainage ditch bordered by old fields, good for sparrows in migration. Please stay on the trails to reduce damage to the habitat. Northern (Red-shafted) Flicker and Black-capped Chickadee are usually present year-round as are Great Horned and Western Screech owls. Numerous wintering ducks may be seen on or near the river, and herons feed there in summer.

RIO GRANDE AND WEST MESA

Driving west on I-40, exit to the right onto North Coors Road, 0.5 mile after crossing the Rio Grande. Go north approximately 1.5 miles and turn right (east) at the St. Joseph-Ladera traffic light, where a sign indicates the Catholic Center. Drive straight back to the buildings and a parking area. Leave the car and walk east down the hill toward the river. Shrubbery on the hillsides sometimes attract wintering sparrows, and in summer one or two pairs of Burrowing Owls may nest in burrows along the dry river bank.

At a small cliff by the river, one has the option of walking along the top of the bank, which provides a good view of the canopy, or of going to the bottom to be nearer the trees. Water levels will influence how far one can go under the cottonwoods. If the water is low, one can sometimes find a way across the channel near the base of the cliff to a large dry area beyond, but birding can still be good from the cliff. Some trees are always accessible in the southern part of the area, although the birding to the north is generally better.

This area is called the "Oxbow." It is one of the most accessible nesting areas for the Gray Catbird in New Mexico and lures many migrants during spring and fall. The swampy sites attract ducks, including an occasional Wood Duck. Mosquitoes may justify use of repellents. One can walk north about one mile before fenced private land is encountered. Do not trespass.

If Burrowing Owls are not found here, return to Coors Road, turn left (south) and then left again at the Circle K. This will lead to roads which overlook the bluffs on the west side of the Rio Grande, where the species also may be found.

Returning north to the St. Joseph-Ladera traffic light, turn left (west) and proceed 0.3 mile to Atrisco Road. Proceed right (north) for 2.4 miles to Indian Petroglyph State Park, where Rock Wrens usually are calling among the prehistoric petroglyphs. Sage Sparrows often can be found in winter just off the road among the saltbush shrubs. (NOTE: The State Park has recently been made part of a more extensive National Monument, but at this writing there are no signs to indicate this.)

After leaving the park, go left (south) on Atrisco to Montaño Road (0.6 mile). Turn left (east) and proceed 3.8 miles to Coors Road. Turn left (north) and drive 2.3 miles to Corrales Shopping Center. Turn right (east) at the traffic light (an overhead sign indicates Alameda to the right and Rio Rancho to the left) and proceed 0.3 mile. Turn left (north) onto a broad dirt road/parking area just before the bridge over the river. Park here and walk past a closed gate for about 200 yards along an irrigation ditch on the right to a small wooden foot bridge which leads across the ditch to a dirt road on the east bank. The area between the ditch and the river contains some of the best accessible riparian habitat in the Albuquerque area.

The levee road, closed to vehicular traffic, parallels the ditch northward for eight miles. Several dirt roads and trails branch off to the river and all are worth exploring if time permits. This large area, termed the Corrales Bosque, can be good for transients and vagrants in migration and in winter one should check the bushes along the river for sparrows, and the sandbars for Horned Larks and longspurs. White-throated, Harris's and Golden-crowned sparrows have all been found in this general area, and a few pairs of Gray Catbirds nest along the river's edge. In and along the river, numerous ducks and shorebirds may be found.

Return to the intersection at Corrales Shopping Center and proceed right (north) for several miles, through Corrales to the far end of town. Look especially, except during summer, for Lewis's Woodpeckers which perch on the utility poles and dead trees along Corrales Road, particularly near orchards.

RIO GRANDE SOUTH OF ALBUQUERQUE

The Rio Grande from Isleta south to Bernardo is bounded on both sides by levee roads which provide access to 36 miles of excellent riparian habitat. These levees and secondary roads leading to the river serve as convenient paths from which one can observe a rich and diverse birdlife.

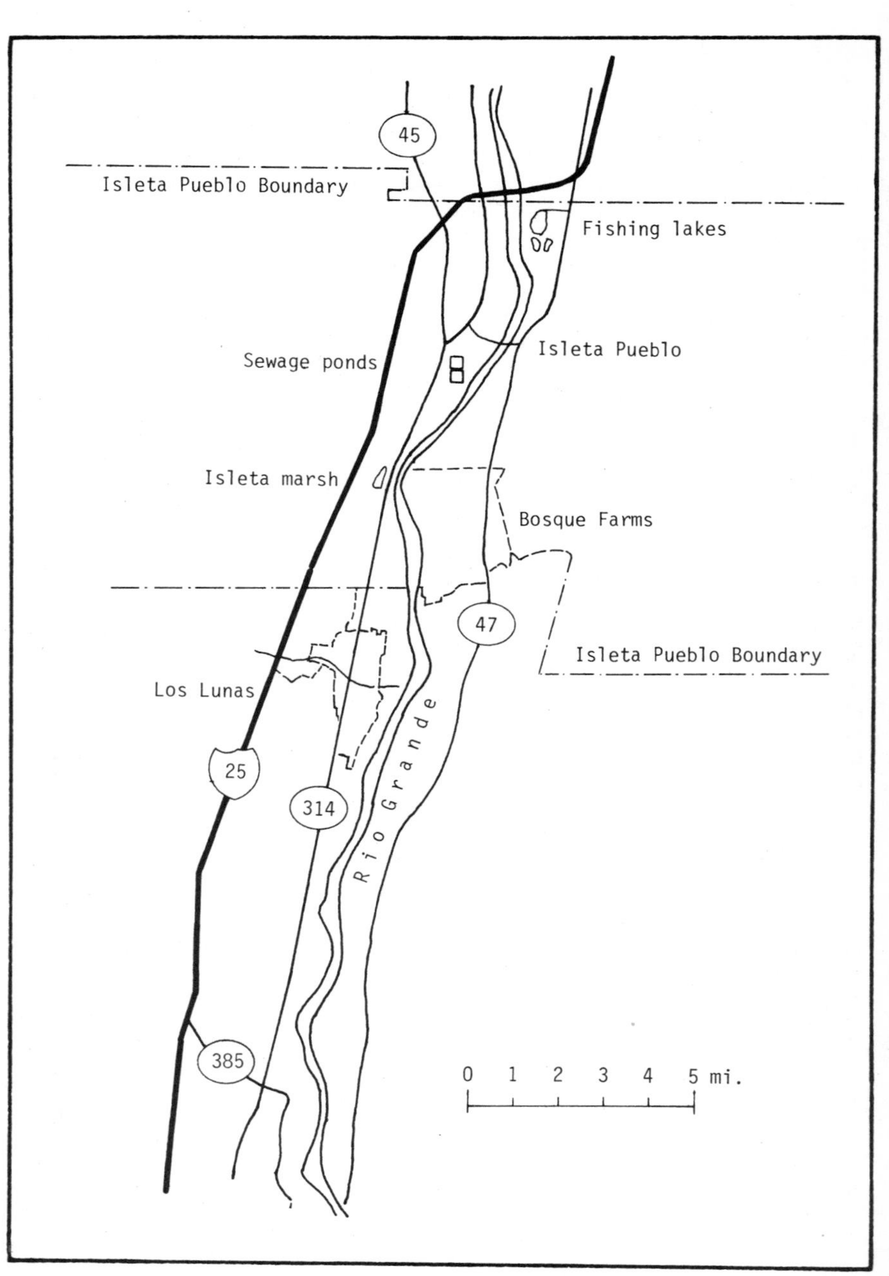
45
Isleta Pueblo Boundary
Fishing lakes
Sewage ponds
Isleta Pueblo
Isleta marsh
Bosque Farms
47
Isleta Pueblo Boundary
Los Lunas
25
314
Rio Grande
385
0 1 2 3 4 5 mi.

The Middle Rio Grande Conservancy District (MRGCD) owns most of the land between and including the levee roads. Its policy is to discourage widespread public use of the levees and the bosques (cottonwood groves) but there is no objection to birders entering at their own risk. The bosque is not the safest area, and cautions such as locking cars should be strictly observed; it is best not to bird alone here. Please remember to park off the levee. Pull off on the river side in order to make room for passage of maintenance vehicles, and be careful as the levee edges are soft and sandy in places. Large groups planning to visit the bosque should seek permission in advance from MRGCD (phone 505-247-0234).

Owing to the uniformity of vegetation throughout the middle Rio Grande Valley, all wooded/brushy areas along the river can be equally productive. Among the 80 breeding species are Cooper's Hawk, Yellow-billed Cuckoo, Greater Roadrunner, Great Horned Owl, Black-chinned Hummingbird, Western Wood-Pewee, Black-capped Chickadee, Gray Catbird, Yellow-breasted Chat, Summer Tanager, Blue Grosbeak, Black-headed Grosbeak and Indigo Bunting. Much less numerous are Mississippi Kite, Long-eared Owl, Red-headed and Lewis's woodpeckers, Willow Flycatcher, Eastern Kingbird, Mountain Chickadee, and Common Grackle.

Birding is most exciting along the Rio Grande during spring and fall when the cottonwoods attract migrant passerines, and when ducks, herons, and a few shorebirds utilize the river and its sandbars. During an extensive inventory in 1982, over 260 species of birds were observed in or near the bosque. These included such rarities as Red-throated Loon, Broad-winged Hawk, Peregrine Falcon, Whooping Crane, Sabine's Gull, Common Ground Dove, Sedge Wren, Northern Shrike, Red-eyed and Yellow-throated vireos, 26 species of warblers, Scarlet Tanager, and Harris's, Golden-crowned and White-throated sparrows.

ACCESS TO LEVEES: EAST SIDE OF RIO GRANDE

From Albuquerque, drive south on I-25 to the Broadway exit and continue south on NM 47 for 10 miles to Los Lunas. Bear right (west) on NM 6 and turn right (north) on the levee road just before crossing the river. One mile beyond, the road splits to follow both sides of the drain. Take the left fork, watching for Mississippi Kites which have been seen here regularly in summer. The levee continues north for 4.5 miles to the Isleta Pueblo Reservation Boundary, marked by a dirt bridge crossing the drain. Here one must turn around and return to NM 6.

Upon reaching NM 6, cross it to continue south on the levee road which follows the river and extensive cottonwood woodland for another 12 miles. The levee road is rough, though passable when dry, but it should be avoided during or after wet weather. Two miles south of NM 6, as one proceeds on the

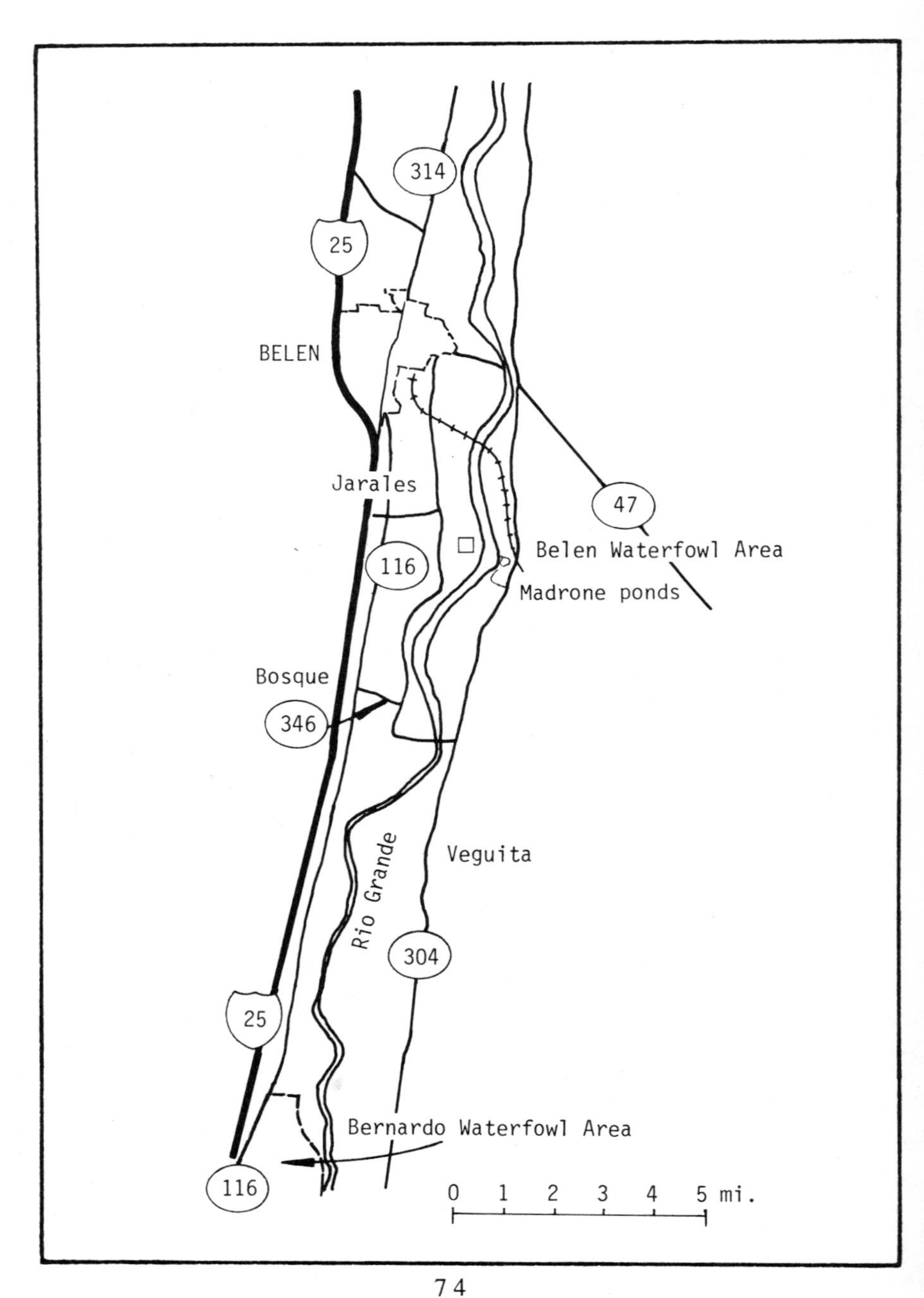
314
25
BELEN
Jarales
47
Belen Waterfowl Area
116
Madrone ponds
Bosque
346
Rio Grande
Veguita
304
25
Bernardo Waterfowl Area
116
0 1 2 3 4 5 mi.

levee road, the large agricultural fields visible to the east attract thousands of Sandhill Cranes and an occasional Whooping Crane in January and February. The road ends at NM 47, just north of the bridge at Belen. Upon reaching NM 47, turn right (south) for 0.4 mile and then right again on NM 304. From this junction, pass a railroad crossing, continue another 0.7 mile and turn right onto a dirt road following a line of utility poles toward the river. After crossing a small canal, park at an opening at the edge of the cottonwoods and walk north, following the drainage ditch. This soon leads to the Madrone Ponds, an area excellent for ducks, herons, and rails, as well as land birds. Exploring the entire vicinity of the ponds and along the river often yields interesting species. The brushy hillsides east of the cottonwoods attract Sage Sparrows in winter.

The levee continues south from Madrone Ponds for 4 miles to a bridge at the hamlet of Bosque (NM 346) and for another 10 miles to NM 60 and the Bernardo bridge. Lush riparian woodland extends throughout, but south of the Bosque bridge most of the cottonwoods have been cleared and replaced by tamarisk. The birdlife in these pure 'salt cedar' stands is much less diverse than that in the cottonwoods, but Northern Mockingbird, Blue Grosbeak, and Lark Sparrow are more common there.

ACCESS TO LEVEES: WEST SIDE OF RIO GRANDE

From Albuquerque, drive south on I-25 across the Rio Grande and exit at Isleta Boulevard (NM 314, old US 85). Continue south on NM 314 through the Isleta Pueblo to the extensive Isleta marshes, the largest remaining in the Middle Rio Grande Valley. This is reservation land and trespassing is forbidden, but one may view from the road. There is room to pull off at the south end of the marsh adjacent to a large pond which may have ducks, a few rails, and occasionally Least Bittern and Franklin's Gull. Eastern Kingbirds have bred at the north end of the marsh. The Isleta Indians consider it trespassing if one is more than 10 feet from the road, so please remain beside your vehicle when stopping here.

Continue south on NM 314, turning left (east) at the traffic light on Main Street in Los Lunas; this leads through town to the river. The levees can be reached by turning left or right immediately before crossing the river. The left turn follows the levee for 4 miles and exits on NM 85 just south of the marsh.

Another section of the west levee road goes south from Main Street and follows the Rio Grande for 12.5 miles before ending at the Belen bridge. Several side roads leading toward the river are worth exploring. A small pond 0.5 mile north of the bridge occasionally harbors Wood Ducks; there may be White-throated Sparrows in winter and Northern Waterthrushes during migration.

The Belen river crossing marks the boundary of Belen Valley State Park. The parking area between the levee and river contains many large cottonwoods, the site of the southernmost "colony" of Lewis's Woodpeckers known in the Rio Grande valley. From here, paths extend south through dense undergrowth with numerous dead cottonwoods. Red-headed Woodpeckers have been seen here at times. The levee can be followed south for 1.5 miles until the road divides at the railroad tracks. Make a sharp right turn to parallel the tracks, turn left to cross them, and take the first left turn which leads alongside a canal. This brings one back to the levee road which leads south.

The agricultural fields, soon visible on the right, are part of Belen State Game Refuge (Belen Waterfowl Area). This is a staging area for thousands of Sandhill Cranes in February, and one or two Whooping Cranes usually are present among them.

Not far beyond, at a bend in the levee, some narrow ponds on the left are good for Wood Ducks and other migrants. (The area also is one of the few places in the Middle Rio Grande Valley where leopard frogs can still be found in numbers.) Farther south, where one drives under two large gas pipelines, pull off the road and explore, especially near the southernmost pipeline. The area is productive in any season. Anywhere along the river edge in winter, the Russian olives attract fruit-eating species.

Three miles farther south is the bridge at Bosque. Before reaching it, one must turn west to NM 109 in order to cross a narrow canal, and then turn east again on the south side of the canal to return to the levee.

To reach the west side of the Belen State Game Refuge, turn right (west) at the Bosque bridge and right (north) on NM 109. The entrance to the Refuge is 3.5 miles beyond.

ISLETA LAKES AND RECREATION AREA

From Albuquerque, proceed south on I-25, about 5 miles past the Rio Bravo exit, to exit 215. When exiting, take the left fork marked "Isleta" and follow it as it crosses over I-25 and becomes NM 47. Take the first right turn (only a couple of hundred yards past the exit) onto a paved road, where a large sign indicates the Isleta Lakes and Recreation Area; then proceed for 0.9 mile, across the railroad track, to a building on the right where persons 14 years and older must pay an entrance fee of $1.00. (The fee for fishing is somewhat higher.) The area is owned and operated by the Isleta Indian Pueblo and provides facilities for camping and picnicking as well as fishing.

Three lakes flanked by extensive cottonwood groves and also brushy growth along an irrigation ditch along the west boundary provide habitat for a wide variety of birds during migration and breeding season. Species here are typical of those found elsewhere in the wooded/brushy areas along the Rio Grande, but some less frequently seen are Green-backed and Black-crowned Night herons, Swainson's Hawk, Black-necked Stilt, Belted Kingfisher, Black Phoebe, Ash-throated Flycatcher, Gray Catbird, Solitary Vireo, numerous warblers including Townsend's and Yellow-breasted Chat, Blue Grosbeak, Green-tailed, Rufous-sided and Canyon towhees, Brewer's Blackbird, Common Grackle, and Pine Siskin.

JEMEZ DAM

Sandhill Cranes (and occasionally Whooping Cranes) can be seen over Albuquerque as they migrate to or from their wintering grounds farther south in the Central Rio Grande Valley. The majority move north in February and south in November. For a special late afternoon treat in mid-November birders can head to the NM 44 exit on I-25. Drive 1.9 miles west on NM 44, then turn right and drive 6.2 miles to Jemez Canyon Dam. If a cold front is approaching from the northwest, and if there have been light southwest winds all day, it is likely that a large number of migrating cranes will pass near the dam heading for the sandbars on the Jemez River above the lake to roost. Starting about an hour before sundown, the cranes pour noisily across the sky.

SANDIA MOUNTAINS

Dominating Albuquerque on its eastern perimeter, the Sandia Mountains are an imposing sight, resembling a prehistoric leviathan that fossilized as solid granite. The west face, barren and forbidding, rises precipitously to a height of more than 10,000 feet, while the densely forested east side exhibits a gentler slope as it descends to meet the high plains. This "desert island" range is about 20 miles in length, extending northward from I-40 in Tijeras Canyon to the little community of Placitas.

The Sandias encompass a wide range of habitats, beginning with cholla-studded grasslands in the lower foothills and culminating in spruce-fir forest at the summit. This diversity in vegetative types has spawned a remarkable variety of birds; nesting species number well over 100, and more than twice as many have been recorded throughout the year. The best birding months are May and September, but even in winter one can find 50 or 60 species with a little effort.

Easy accessibility to all four life zones simplifies birding in the Sandias. From the center of Albuquerque it is about 10 miles to Embudito Canyon in the western foothills, 22 miles to Cienega Canyon on the east side, and 33 miles to the Crest itself, the latter trip taking less than an hour by car. An alternative way to the Crest is by means of the aerial tramway, reputedly the world's

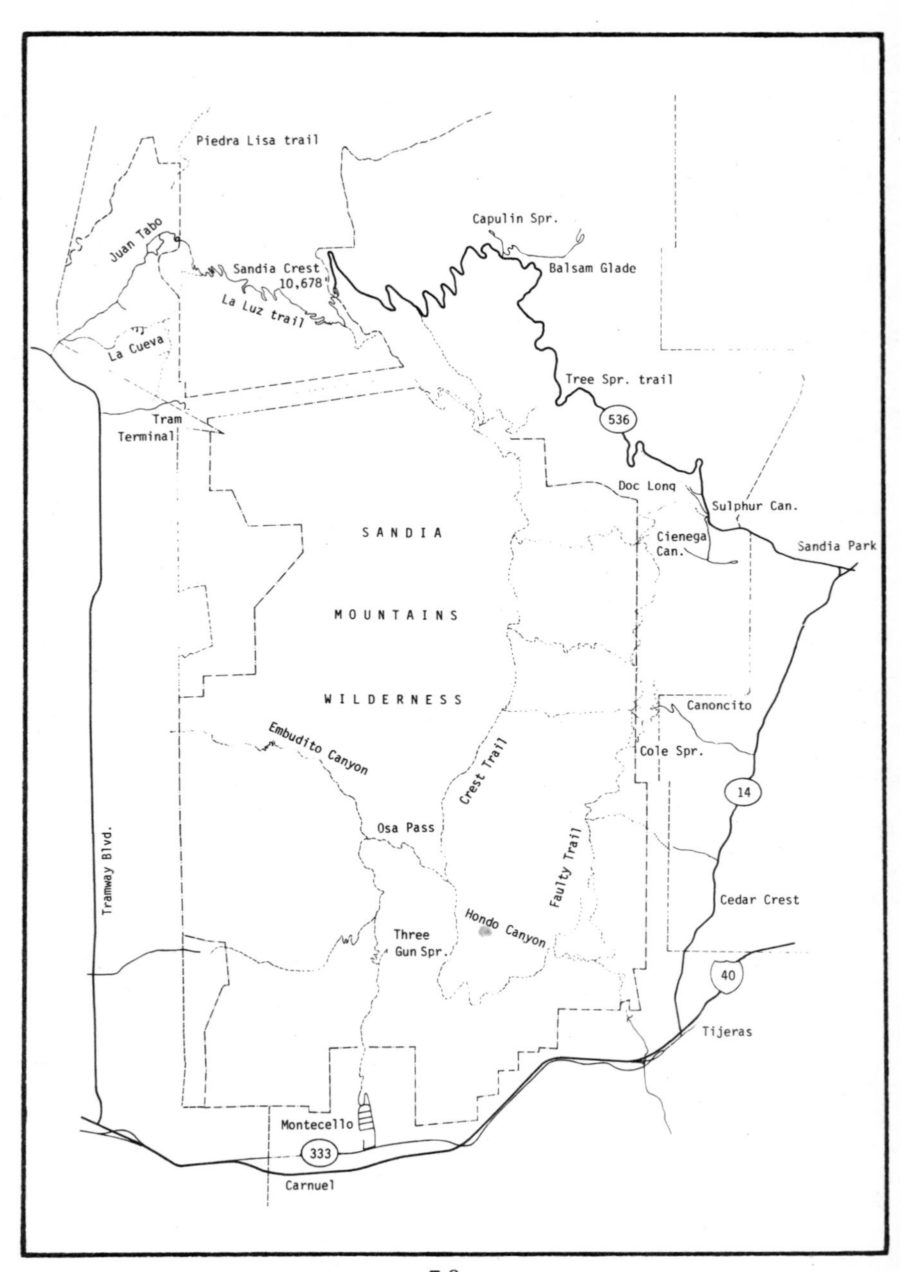
Piedra Lisa trail
Capulin Spr.
Juan Tabo
Sandia Crest
10,678
Balsam Glade
La Luz trail
La Cueva
Tree Spr. trail
Tram
Terminal
536
Doc Long
Sulphur Can.
S A N D I A
Cienega
Can.
Sandia Park
M O U N T A I N S
W I L D E R N E S S
Canoncito
Embudito Canyon
Crest Trail
Cole Spr.
14
Osa Pass
Faulty Trail
Tramway Blvd.
Cedar Crest
Hondo Canyon
Three
Gun Spr.
40
Tijeras
Montecello
333
Carnuel

longest, which whisks the visitor to the top in 15 very scenic and breath-taking minutes. The lower terminal is easily reached by going 4.3 miles north on Tramway Boulevard from the Montgomery intersection and then turning right (east) at the stop sign.

Birding is rewarding in the Sandias at all seasons. Spring begins early. By mid-February, resident Bewick's and Canyon wrens are in full song, and in early March the first White-throated Swifts are reconnoitering their favorite cliffs for prospective nesting niches. As Turkey Vultures begin to appear in mid-March, Crissal Thrashers may already be incubating their first clutch; by the end of the month, Red-tailed Hawks and Common Ravens are preparing to lay their eggs, while Black-throated Sparrows are returning in force, together with a few early Black-chins. This is just a prelude to the main migration in April and May.

When the heat of June and July suppresses bird activity in the foothills, the songs of Hermit Thrushes, MacGillivray's Warblers and Cassin's Finches enliven the highland scene. As early as the beginning of July and through August, Rufous and Calliope hummingbirds join the resident Broad-tails in the profuse wildflowers of mountain meadows near the Crest.

Autumn is pleasant, and winters are seldom austere in the Sandias, so that no hardships need be endured even when searching for Rosy Finches and Pine Grosbeaks on the Crest.

EMBUDITO CANYON

One of the most popular hiking and birding spots is this dry westside canyon. From the Montgomery-Tramway intersection, go 0.5 miles east on Montgomery; at the stop sign, turn left on Glenwood Hills Drive and continue for another half mile or so to a road going east to the Embudito trailhead parking area. The most productive birding is within the broad "wash" and the adjacent hillsides at the mouth of the canyon.

Wrens, thrashers and desert sparrows are some of the "specialties" of this brush-dominated landscape. Canyon and Bewick's wrens are resident and are joined by Rock Wrens in summer and House Wrens during migration, particularly in September. Crissal Thrashers, widespread residents in the foothills, are more often heard than seen; they become somewhat more conspicuous in February and early March, when courtship activities peak. Curve-billed Thrashers are more local in their distribution, often preferring the proximity of suburbia where it interfaces with undeveloped habitat. Look for Rufous-crowned Sparrow among the rocks on the south-facing slope of the canyon and, beginning in late March or early April, for Black-chinned and Black-throated sparrows.

Crissal Thrasher

Other species to be expected include resident Golden Eagle, Scaled Quail, Ladder-backed Woodpecker, Scrub and Pinyon jays, Bushtit, Canyon (Brown) and Rufous-sided towhees and House Finch. Additional breeding birds include Common Poorwill, Black-chinned Hummingbird, Say's Phoebe, Ash-throated Flycatcher, Cassin's and Western kingbirds, Blue-gray Gnatcatcher, Virginia's Warbler and Scott's Oriole.

Unusual species may appear during migration; during July of 1988 Cassin's Sparrows and Eastern Meadowlarks sang in the grasslands north of Embudito.

JUAN TABO

Compared to Embudito, Juan Tabo is more extensive and varied, comprising numerous small drainages in a depression extending from the semi-desert grasslands near Tramway to the pinyon-covered slopes of Juan Tabo Ridge. The higher elevations will be dealt with in the Piedra Lisa Trail section; the following pertains primarily to the lower foothills. To reach this area, go 4.3 miles north on Tramway from the Montgomery intersection to a stop sign; a marked road on the right goes to the lower tram terminal. Continue straight ahead, however, for another mile and turn right on FR 333; park at the pull-out immediately beyond the second cattleguard and examine the rather extensive cholla stands which are the best places to find numerous Black-throated Sparrows in summer and perhaps even a handful of hardy survivors in winter. Also look for Greater Roadrunner, Ladder-backed Woodpecker, Crissal Thrasher and Canyon Towhee year-round and summering Ash-throated Flycatcher and Northern Mockingbird. Although Brewer's Sparrows do not nest here, they often are present in substantial numbers from mid-April to mid-May.

For still greater variety, continue upward on FR 333 for another mile or so and turn right on the road to Tierra Monte subdivision; park just off the road at the bottom of the wash and hike either up or down the arroyo. Here it is easy to locate such year-round regulars as Scrub Jay, Common Raven, Plain Titmouse, Bushtit, Bewick's Wren, Crissal Thrasher, and Rufous-sided Towhee. In summer, listen for the melodious caroling of Scott's Oriole and the unique trilling of Black-chinned Sparrow. By August, a few montane species are already visiting the foothills, among them Band-tailed Pigeons in search of maturing acorns, and several flycatchers such as Olive-sided, Dusky, and Western Wood-Pewee. Later they are joined by a host of migrants including House Wren, Blue-gray Gnatcatcher, Orange-crowned, Virginia's and MacGillivray's warblers, Western Tanager and Green-tailed Towhee.

Lower Juan Tabo can be especially productive in the winter when a variety of birds are attracted to juniper berries and the seeds of mountain mahogany. At that season look for Ruby-crowned Kinglet, Western and Mountain bluebirds, Townsend's Solitaire, American Robin, Sage Thrasher, Cassin's Finch (in

Black-throated Gray Warbler

company with the abundant House Finch), Pine Siskin and Evening Grosbeak.

WATERFALL CANYON AND PIEDRA LISA TRAIL

This scenic trail traverses pinyon-juniper country above the Juan Tabo picnic compiex. From the Tramway intersection with FR 333, follow the latter about two miles until the pavement ends. Do not turn right toward the La Luz trailhead, but continue straight ahead for another 0.3 mile to the Piedra Lisa trailhead parking area. One must then walk another 0.3 mile along this dirt road before embarking on the trail proper, which diverges to the right. Along this first section of road in spring or summer, listen for Bewick's Wren and Black-chinned Sparrow, the latter being easily found amid rabbitbrush and Apache plume growing in the arroyos. From the road, the Piedra Lisa trail descends into a major drainage where Waterfall and Juan Tabo canyons meet; continue straight ahead, across the streambed. A sharp turn to the right leads up Waterfall Canyon, while the sandy wash between these two routes forms Juan Tabo Canyon.

A rewarding short hike from here is to go up the canyon to the first little cascade of water spilling over a large boulder; in dry years the water trickles to a stop here, but it usually runs year-round above this point. In summer look for Cooper's Hawk (nests upslope on south side of the canyon), Red-tailed Hawk, Broad-tailed Hummingbird, Olive-sided Flycatcher (uncommon, high on south side of canyon), Cordilleran Flycatcher, Violet-green Swallow (usually higher up the canyon near an old "burn"), Clark's Nutcracker, Solitary and Warbling vireos, Virginia's, Black-throated Gray, Grace's (in ponderosa pine), and MacGillivray's warblers, as well as Western Tanager and Black-headed Grosbeak. Rare migrants or vagrants have appeared here; for example, Red-faced Warbler in May 1977 and 1991, and a Carolina Wren for several months in 1991.

Although not providing the concentration of birds found in and around Waterfall, the Piedra Lisa Trail has a special charm owing to the many spectacular views along the way and especially the panoramic overlook from the Rincon, the high ridge (8,000 feet) which for the majority of hikers is the usual turnaround point. Here, from one of several granite outcrops, it is a thrill to watch the aerobatic White-throated Swifts or the Turkey Vultures and other raptors. On the return descent to Waterfall Canyon, listen and watch for Black-throated Gray Warbler, the primary denizen of the "pygmy forest." Other birds along this route include Band-tailed Pigeon (numbers vary greatly from year to year), Hairy Woodpecker, Plain Titmouse, Townsend's Solitaire, Chipping Sparrow and the highly unpredictable Red Crossbill. In winter, Cassin's Finch and Evening Grosbeak are sometimes common.

THREE GUN SPRING CANYON

A fine example of desert-like terrain is to be found at this broad box canyon bounded on three sides by high ridges, but open to the south facing Tijeras Canyon. To reach this area, take I-40 east from Albuquerque and exit at Carnuel (the first exit east of Albuquerque) shortly after entering Tijeras Canyon. Turn left at the stop sign and continue east on old US 66 for about 2 miles and make another left onto Monticello Street (FR 522), which very briefly parallels US 66. Continue north through the housing development, remaining on FR 522 as it jogs west and then north again. After a mile, a small parking area marks the beginning of Trail 194. It is about 2 miles to the spring at the base of the northern ridge and another 2 miles over the ridge to Oso Pass in the high country.

Several species of birds are more easily found here than elsewhere in the Sandias, among them Scott's Oriole, conspicuous from May to July in the area just north of Monticello residential area. A song suggestive of the Western Meadowlark reveals the presence of this handsome oriole (meadowlarks are absent from this section of the Sandias). In addition to the common Crissal Thrasher, Monticello supports an expanding colony of Curve-billed Thrasher, whose predilection for backyard chollas makes them particularly conspicuous. In early spring Pinyon Jays may nest here and Poorwill, though not often seen, calls its name incessantly from the hillside on almost any summer evening, shortly after sunset.

Other breeding birds at Three Gun Spring Canyon include Golden Eagle, Red-tailed Hawk, Black-chinned and Broad-tailed hummingbirds, Ash-throated Flycatcher, Scrub Jay, Plain Titmouse, Bushtit, Bewick's Wren, Blue-gray Gnatcatcher, Virginia's Warbler, Rufous-sided and Canyon towhees, and Black-chinned Sparrow. In winter, look for Western and Mountain bluebirds, Townsend's Solitaire, Hermit Thrush and Sage Thrasher. Rare species such as Anna's Hummingbird and Fox Sparrow have also been seen here.

HONDO CANYON TO THE WATERFALL

This area is unusual in the Sandias because limestone outcroppings, instead of the typical granite, predominate. Otherwise, the landscape is typical pinyon-juniper woodland. Follow Tijeras Canyon on I-40 for 5 miles beyond Carnuel and exit at the Cedar Crest-Tijeras sign. Bear to the right and take the Tijeras fork. At the stop sign, turn left, go under the overpass, angle off to the right, and continue along the road through Canyon Estates. After 0.75 mile, one arrives at a parking lot which is the southern end of Crest Trail 130. A half-mile walk along this trail brings one to the little travertine waterfall, a pleasant spot where birds come to drink and bathe.

Scott's Oriole

Birding can be good here at all seasons, but particularly in spring, fall and winter. The travertine and the streambed immediately above and below is the regular stopover for Winter Wren from mid-October to mid-November. As House Wrens may linger well into October, care must be taken to look for the Winter Wren's very short tail, strongly barred belly and warmer back tone, as well as its unique habit of bobbing to an upright position in two discrete stages. In November 1988, it was noted that a Winter Wren kept regular company with a male Hooded Warbler! Other rare warbler species recorded here include Worm-eating as well as Painted Redstart.

During winter, look for occasional Williamson's Sapsucker and more common Northern Flicker, Steller's and Scrub jays, Mountain Chickadee, Plain Titmouse, Bushtit, Golden-crowned Kinglet, Western Bluebird, Townsend's Solitaire, Hermit Thrush, Cassin's Finch, Pine Siskin and sometimes Evening Grosbeak. Should one want to explore beyond the travertine, either along the Crest Trail or the Faulty Trail, a Forest Service Wilderness map would prove useful. One can call the Sandia Range District at 505-281-3304 for directions.

SANDIA PARK

This general locale is one of the most rewarding in the Sandias because of its varied habitats, including pastures and cultivated areas. This diversity attracts many birds, some of which have only recently become established. Brewer's Blackbird, for example, is now a regular breeding species at or near Sandia Park Pond, arriving near the end of April and usually remaining through July. Say's Phoebes and Barn Swallows have also followed in man's footsteps and benefitted from the clearings and structures he provides.

To reach Sandia Park, drive east on I-40 through Tijeras Canyon and then north on NM 14 about 7 miles from the Cedar Crest exit. Just past the new Post Office on the left, turn left onto NM 536, which is the road to the Crest. After 0.75 mile, where the paved road goes right, bear left and park along the dirt road across from the first house on the left where the owners feed hummingbirds. From April through September, this is one of the best places to observe these dynamic Lilliputians of the bird world. In spring there are only Broad-tails, but at the beginning of July they are joined by the migrant Rufous and Calliope. At this time a few Black-chins may appear, although they are much more numerous in the foothills and in Albuquerque itself. July is the best time for enjoying the hummingbirds, not only because four species are usually present, but because many of the birds are colorful, pugnacious males. By August an influx of females and young adds considerable energy to the activity around the feeders and provides an identification challenge for the serious birder.

SANDIA PARK POND

This small, man-made oasis is 0.6 mile from NM 14 on NM 536, to the left of the road and partially hidden by shrubbery. Although the pond is private property and surrounded by a chainlink fence, it is possible to view it from the road without trespassing. Many interesting migrants and accidentals have been seen at or near the pond such as Arctic Loon (once), Pied-billed Grebe, Great Blue Heron, Black-crowned Night-Heron, several species of ducks, Common Snipe, Spotted Sandpiper, Solitary Sandpiper (late April and late July), Belted Kingfisher, Lewis's Woodpecker, Palm Warbler, Common Yellowthroat, Nashville Warbler, and Northern (Bullock's) Oriole. During summer, look for Turkey Vulture, Mourning Dove, Common Nighthawk, White-throated Swift, Ash-throated Flycatcher, Cassin's Kingbird (more common along NM 14), Violet-green Swallow, American Crow (small nesting colony), Virginia's Warbler, Black-headed and Blue grosbeaks, and Lesser Goldfinch. In winter, Cedar Waxwing and a variety of finches may be present.

CIENEGA CANYON

If this canyon were not so heavily used, it might well be the best birding area in the Sandias. Here a permanent stream meanders through a meadow, an aspen grove, and ponderosa pine forest. Two routes approach this canyon. The first is best followed on foot. From the "hummingbird house," 0.1 mile from Sandia Park Pond, follow the dirt road south, taking the fork that seems to go straight ahead, angling off slightly to the right. After 0.25 mile, the road dead-ends at two gates; the one on the right leads into Cienega Canyon. This first short segment, beginning at the gate, is private property. The owners, however, have no objection to hikers if the usual courtesies are observed. To take the other route, one must return to NM 536, go one mile up the mountain and turn left. Immediately, there is a fork, each road having a gate which is closed in winter. Straight ahead leads into Cienega Canyon; the right turn takes one up Sulphur Canyon. Half a mile or so along the latter, beyond the paved road and picnic sites, Whip-poor-will and Hammond's Flycatcher (late May) have been heard in spring. In April, Painted Redstarts have occasionally appeared near the Sulphur Canyon gate and immediately below it in Tejano Canyon near the Doc Long Picnic Area. The lower part of Tejano Canyon, between Sandia Park Pond and the Cienega turn-off, attracts a variety of birds, including occasional Lazuli Buntings in summer.

Cienega Canyon is less than a mile beyond the gate. At the stop sign, one can turn left and drive down the canyon a short distance to a picnic site at the end of the paved road, continuing on foot and emerging again at the "hummingbird house." Alternately, one can turn right at the stop sign and park at one of the many picnic sites. Some of the birds here include Hairy and Downy woodpeckers, Red-naped Sapsucker in the aspens, all three nuthatches, House Wren, Western Wood-Pewee, Cordilleran Flycatcher, Steller's Jay, Common Raven, Hermit Thrush, Solitary and Warbling vireos, Virginia's, Yellow-rumped and Grace's warblers, Western Tanager, Black-headed Grosbeak, Rufous-sided Towhee, Chipping Sparrow, and Pine Siskin.

The road up the canyon passes a meadow and terminates at a small parking area, beyond which begins the 2.25-mile Cienega Trail leading to the Crest. After dark on May and June evenings, one is likely to hear the soft hooting of a Flammulated Owl, especially above the spring where there is less background noise. It is a surprisingly common bird and will respond to even poor imitations of its call. Although it may sound fairly distant, the bird may be directly overhead. Watch for movement. With patience, one can usually see the owl clearly with a flashlight.

The Hepatic Tanager is relatively rare in the Sandias and is most likely to be found in September as a migrant. However, in summer, look for it near the sign at the bottom of the road leading into Cienega. In spite of the male's bright coloration, it can be most unobtrusive and inconspicuous. The only indication of its presence may be its call, which resembles that of the Hermit Thrush, a common nesting species in the Sandias. Another place where the tanager might be found is along NM 14, where any large ponderosa pine is worth examining.

TREE SPRING TRAIL AND CAPULIN SPRING

About 5 miles up the Crest road (NM 536) from the Sandia Park Pond is the beginning of Tree Spring Trail. A new parking area left of the road marks the trailhead from which point it is a 2-mile hike to the Crest. Many of the birds will be similar to those described later for Capulin. In June and July, Orange-crowned Warbler breeds here about a mile up the trail. This species' distribution is spotty in the Sandias at this season, although it is abundant during September at all elevations. Other warblers nesting here are Yellow-rumped, Virginia's and MacGillivray's. Townsend's and Wilson's warblers are fall migrants, starting in mid-August. If one has missed the Flammulated Owl in Cienega, try searching along this trail in May or June.

An ideal place for higher-altitude birds is Capulin Spring (8,800 feet). From the Sandia Park Pond, it is 7 miles to Las Huertas junction, where NM 165 veers to the right and continues as a dirt road to Placitas. Bear left here for about 0.5 miles to the Capulin turn-off and then turn right again onto a narrow road that passes a cattleguard and several picnic sites. Park at or near the northernmost, and the spring is just off to the left, marked by a small fenced enclosure protecting the pump and by a hollow log through which the water is directed. One can sit here for hours, watching the birds come and go to bathe and drink, among them Western Tanager, Black-headed Grosbeak, Pine Siskin, Cassin's Finch, Dark-eyed Junco, Broad-tailed Hummingbird, and

Red-breasted Nuthatch. Other breeding birds easy to find here are Band-tailed Pigeon, five kinds of woodpeckers, including Williamson's Sapsucker, Olive-sided Flycatcher, House Wren, Hermit Thrush, Brown Creeper, Warbling Vireo, Ruby-crowned and Golden-crowned kinglets, MacGillivray's Warbler, Green-tailed Towhee, Chipping Sparrow, and Evening Grosbeak; Red Crossbill is also possible.

Although several species of *Empidonax* flycatchers can be seen in the Sandias during migration, only two are known to breed there. The Cordilleran is common from 7,000 feet up to the Crest, while the Dusky is relatively uncommon between 8,500 and 10,000 feet. In the Capulin area listen for the Dusky's simple, three-part "song" near the spring in the New Mexico locust scrub and at the end of the Snow Play Area road where an unnamed hiking trail goes off to the northwest.

THE CREST

At 10,678 feet, Sandia Crest offers some of the best and most accessible high-altitude birding in the State, lacking only American (Water) Pipit, White-tailed Ptarmigan and Gray Jay, which are near and above timberline in the Sangre de Cristo range to the north.

From the Sandia Park Pond, it is approximately 13 miles to the parking lot on the Crest. A 30-mile trail spans the entire Crest from Canyon Estates in the South to Tunnel Spring in the north. The most readily accessible area is the 3-mile stretch from the Summit House (upper tram terminal at 10,378 feet) to North Peak. The parking lot lies about halfway between these two extremes, so it is a good starting point for an easy walk in either direction. For the most part, one can either hike close to the rocky edge of the Crest with splendid panoramic views toward the Rio Grande Valley or follow the trails that wind their way through Englemann spruce and corkbark (sub-alpine) fir forest. The Crest is a good vantage point for observing Turkey Vulture, Golden Eagle, Red-tailed Hawk, White-throated Swift, Violet-green Swallow and Common Raven. A fairly good place for watching migrating hawks is at a point about a mile north of the parking lot, directly opposite the Needle, a massive pyramid-shaped granite structure almost equal to the Crest in height. Here, in September or early October, a number of hawks pass through the gap between the Crest and the Needle. This does not compare with the more famous hawk observation sites, but on a good day one sees a fair number of raptors that might include an occasional Ferruginous Hawk or even a Peregrine Falcon.

Visitors to the Crest in July or August should visit Kiwanis Meadow, situated about 0.5 mile south of the parking lot. At this season the wild flowers are at their best and hummingbirds abound.

Almost any time of the year, but particularly in fall and early winter, one may see Clark's Nutcracker. They often allow a close approach, especially as they concentrate on extracting seeds from the cones of limber pines. Although Cassin's Finch, Red Crossbill, Pine Siskin and Evening Grosbeak are relatively common during much of the year, three other finches reach their southern limit in the Sandias during winter: Rosy Finch, Pine Grosbeak, and White-winged Crossbill. All three subspecies of Rosy Finch are present most years, sometimes in small groups but more often in large swirling flocks moving along the edge of the Crest. The rare White-winged Crossbill should be looked for in fall or early winter, feeding high in Englemann spruce, perhaps in the company of Red Crossbills. It has been observed here at least six times within the last decade, once as early as August 30.

No trip to the Crest would be complete without seeking Three-toed Woodpecker, the least common of the regularly occurring woodpeckers. The southern subspecies inhabiting the Sandias closely resembles Hairy Woodpecker in size and basic black-and-white pattern, thus making it easy to overlook, unless one notices the dusky, barred flanks. Contrary to most field guides, this race does not have significant barring on the back. Carefully check every woodpecker heard. Most sightings have been in the forested area just below the Crest and between the upper tram terminal and the TV/radio antennas immediately north of the parking lot. The Three-toed is often remarkably tame and can be closely approached once it is found.

HAWK COUNTS: SANDIA AND MANZANO MOUNTAINS

Since 1985, hawk migration counts have been conducted annually in the Sandia and Manzano mountains to measure trends in raptor populations which serve as an important indicator for measuring ecosystem health. Each day throughout the migration season, official observers count all migrant vultures, hawks, eagles, and falcons passing the lookouts. Visitors are welcome to assist with the counts at both sites, where the most common species are Turkey Vulture, Sharp-shinned, Cooper's and Red-tailed hawks, Golden Eagle and American Kestrel. Less common are Osprey, Northern Goshawk, Swainson's and Ferruginous hawks, Merlin, and Peregrine and Prairie falcons. On a good day, 150 or more raptors may be seen.

In the Sandias, rare and uncommon species have included Black-shouldered and Mississippi kites, Bald Eagle, and Broad-winged, Rough-legged and Zone-tailed hawks. In the Manzanos, the less common species are Bald Eagle and Broad-winged, Rough-legged, and Zone-tailed hawks.

The Sandia Lookout is manned from mid-March to mid-May. Peak numbers of birds occur during the first two weeks of April on days with no east winds. Late morning is the best time to watch. This station, in the Cibola National Forest, is reached by traveling east on I-40 from Albuquerque. Take the

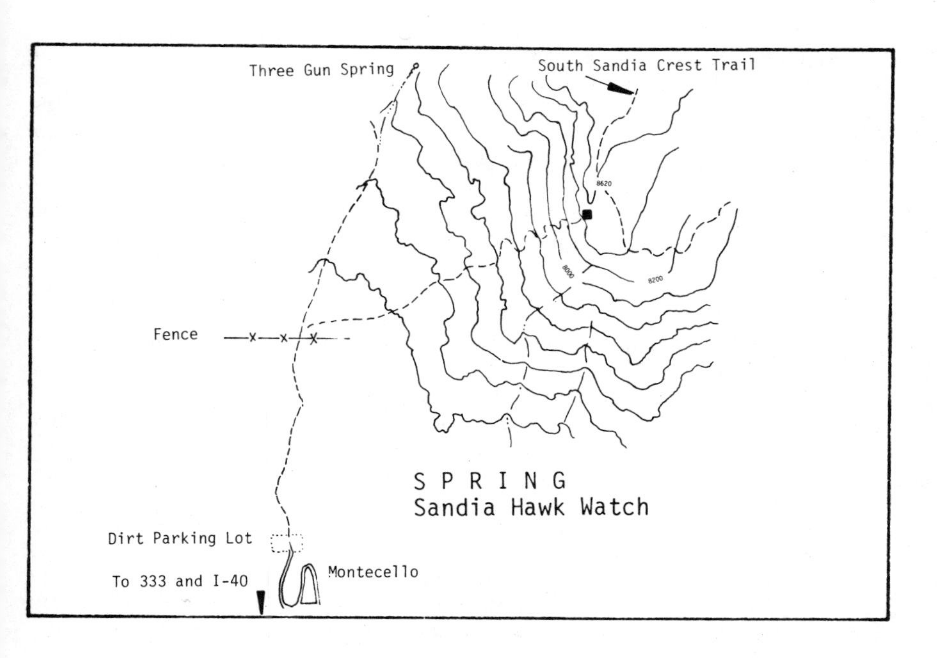
Three Gun Spring
South Sandia Crest Trail
8620
8000
8200
Fence
SPRING
Sandia Hawk Watch
Dirt Parking Lot
To 333 and I-40
Montecello

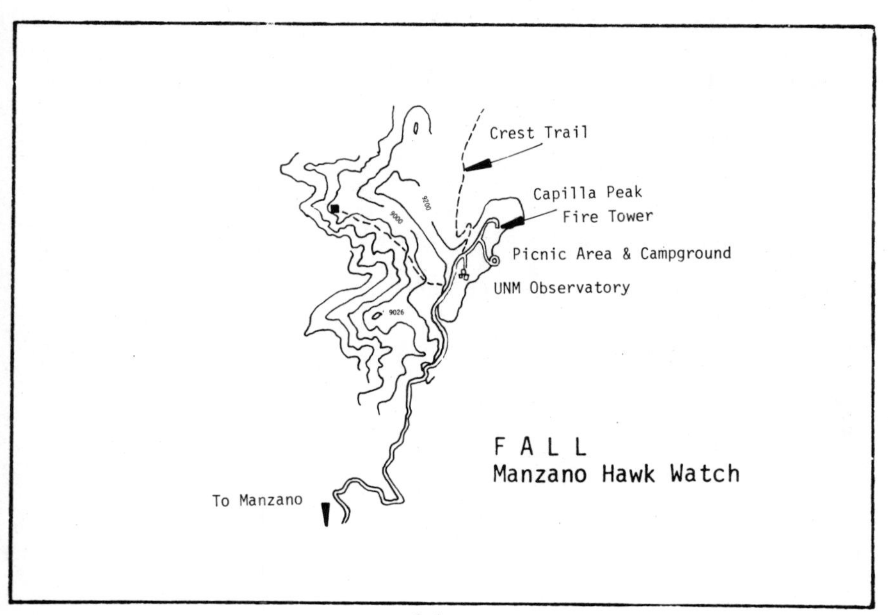
Crest Trail
9200
9000
Capilla Peak
Fire Tower
Picnic Area & Campground
UNM Observatory
9026
FALL
Manzano Hawk Watch
To Manzano

Carnuel exit, continue east on US 66 for 1.8 miles, and turn left into the Montecello subdivision. Follow Forest Road 522 to the Three Gun Spring Trailhead (Forest Service Trail #194). The Hawk Watch trail begins at the Forest Service boundary fence, from which a spur trail forks eastward across an arroyo and up the ridge to the observation point. This route is about two miles long and steep in places, with a total elevation gain of 900 feet. Wear sturdy hiking shoes, a hat, and sunscreen; bring food and plenty of water, and be prepared for cold conditions at higher elevations. Avoid stormy weather.

In fall, the count is conducted in the Manzano Mountains through September and October. The best flights are on early afternoons during the last two weeks of September and in early October, on fair, sunny days with moderate west or northwest winds. The Manzano station is a short distance west of the Capilla Peak Fire Tower and Campground. From downtown Albuquerque, take I-40 east, exiting at the Tijeras exit. Drive south from Tijeras on NM 337 (old NM 14) and NM 55 about 42 miles to the town of Manzano. NM 337 terminates as it joins NM 55, so turn right at this intersection. In Manzano, turn right (west) from the highway onto a dirt road (Forest Road 245) directly opposite a church. Drive a short distance and take the right fork; proceed 9 miles, past the New Canyon Campground, and proceed toward Capilla Peak Campground. As soon as the fire tower is visible ahead, park at the side of the road (about 200 yards south of the tower) and hike northwest across the meadow. A well-used recently constructed trail, rather steep in places, begins at a pile of stones in the meadow and follows the ridge crest westward for about 0.75 mile ending at the lookout, which is the site of the count operation. (NOTE: DO NOT take Crest Trail 170 which descends from the meadow into the canyon to the north.)

In addition to raptors, birds of the upper mountain slopes may be seen, including migrating White-throated Swifts.

For more information, write: HawkWatch International, Inc., 1420 Carlisle N.E., Suite 100, Albuquerque, NM 87110 or telephone 505-255-7622.

SEVILLETA NATIONAL WILDLIFE REFUGE

Sevilleta is located approximately 60 miles south of Albuquerque on both sides of I-25, between Bernardo and San Acacia, and comprises a total of 238,000 acres. It was acquired by the Nature Conservancy in 1975 with the stipulation that it be maintained primarily for wildlife use and open to the public only for approved research projects. In 1976 the property was turned over to the U. S. Fish and Wildlife Service.

Although public birding is not permitted, Christmas Counts were begun in 1986, and two breeding bird survey routes were also established. Indeed, surveys are conducted throughout the year, and thus far nearly 200 species have been identified on the refuge.

BOSQUE DEL APACHE NATIONAL WILDLIFE REFUGE

Bosque del Apache is probably the most popular birding spot in New Mexico, and it is one of the few places in the State where one is likely to encounter other birders. A visit to the refuge at about dusk on a winter day, when tens of thousands of cranes and geese are in the air, provides a most impressive sight.

Bosque del Apache is Spanish for "Woods of the Apache" and is derived from the formerly extensive groves of cottonwood trees along the Rio Grande, used as temporary camping areas by Indian bands before the arrival of white settlers nearly 300 years ago. The refuge was established in 1939 specifically as a wintering area for waterfowl and "Greater" Sandhill Cranes. At that time, only a few birds of this subspecies remained, and a mere handful visited the refuge. The construction of water channels and shallow marshes enhanced the recovery of these birds, and today they may be seen throughout the middle Rio Grande Valley, with 12, 000 or more at the refuge during the peak months of November-January. Small numbers of "Lesser" Sandhill Cranes mingle with the large flocks of Greater Sandhills.

The refuge is reached by going south from Socorro on I-25 for 9 miles to the San Antonio exit (US 380). Follow this road a mile east into the center of San Antonio, turning right (south) at the traffic light. San Antonio has gas stations, a small grocery store, the Owl Bar and Grill (famous for its excellent green chile hamburgers and cheeseburgers), and a Bed and Breakfast (Casa Blanca, 505-835-3027). In Socorro there are numerous motels, as well as a Bed and Breakfast (Eaton House, P.O. Box 536, Socorro, NM 87801, phone 505-835-1067); an RV campground, with hookups, is also available close to the refuge (see below).

Great-tailed Grackles are often seen in the vicinity of the large cottonwood trees near the main crossroad in San Antonio, and, except in winter, swallows of several species are numerous along the road through town. Driving south toward the refuge, watch for Crissal and Curve-billed thrashers and Pyrrhuloxias in the semi-desert vegetation, and in winter scan farm fields for Red-winged, Yellow-headed and Brewer's blackbirds and Sandhill and Whooping cranes. Cattle Egrets, Brown-headed Cowbirds, and Brewer's Blackbirds frequently accompany the grazing cattle, and ducks, Killdeer, American Pipits, and occasional shorebirds may be present in the fields when they are being irrigated or after a heavy rainfall.

White-crowned Sparrows are numerous in the roadside shrubs in fall, winter, and spring, and Savannah Sparrows may also be seen; Vesper, Lark,

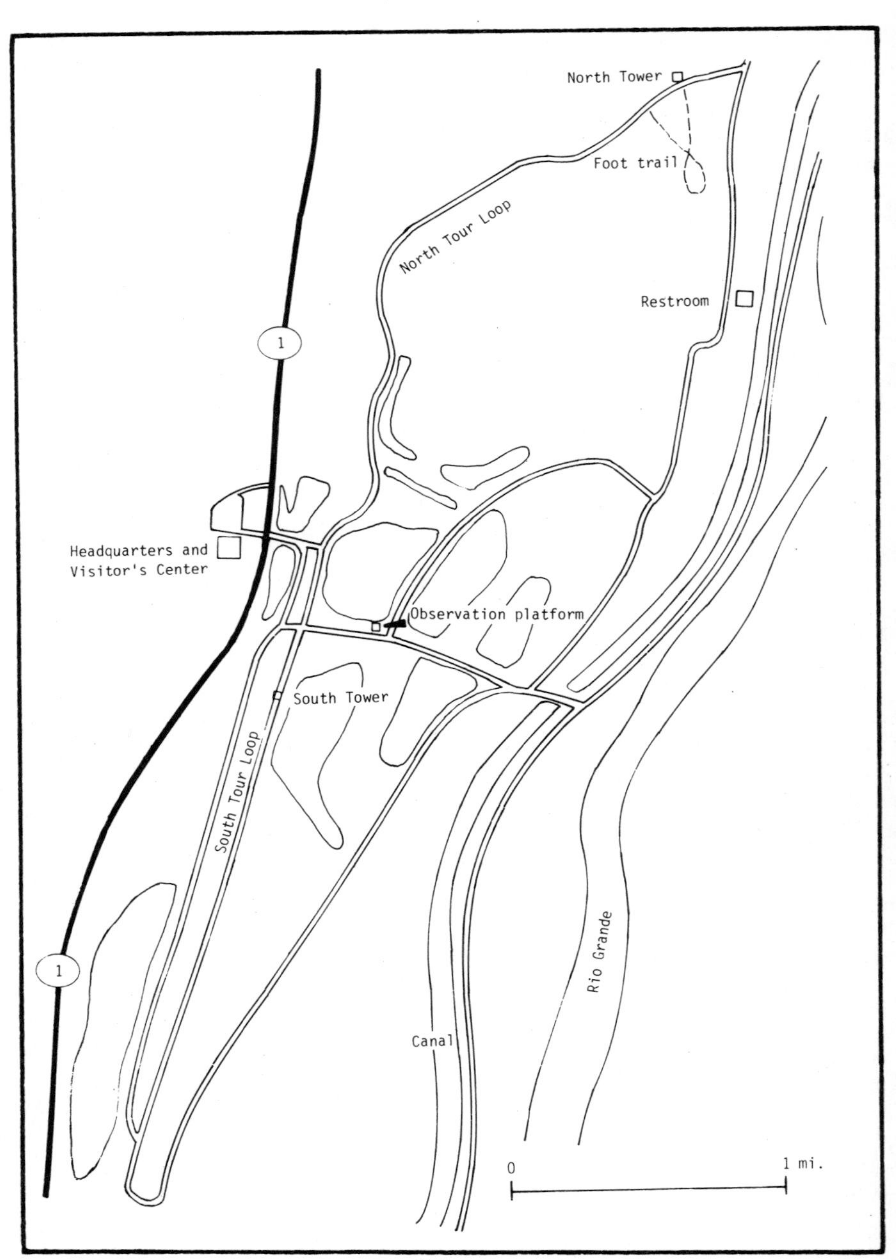

North Tower
Foot trail
North Tour Loop
Restroom
1
Headquarters and
Visitor's Center
Observation platform
South Tower
South Tour Loop
1
Rio Grande
Canal
0
1 mi.

and Song sparrows, as well as an occasional Cassin's, Black-throated, or Brewer's, are present during migration. On the power lines along the road watch for American Kestrel, Red-winged, Yellow-headed, and Brewer's blackbirds, Western Meadowlark, Loggerhead Shrike, and, in summer, Blue Grosbeak and Western Kingbird. The power poles are favored by Red-tailed and Cooper's hawks, especially in winter, and at dawn and dusk by an occasional Great Horned Owl.

Three miles south of San Antonio, on the right (west), just before the refuge boundary, is the Bosque Bird-watchers' RV and Trailer Campground, which was established by private interests to cater to visitors to the refuge. The usual hookups are available, and birders are welcomed. Feeders and shade trees attract various species, and in 1989 a Rufous-backed Robin made a rare appearance here. Just beyond the RV park, 3.2 miles from San Antonio, a small patch of scrub behind the refuge entrance sign shelters Pyrrhuloxias, Crissal and Curve-billed thrashers, and Black-throated Sparrows.

About 4.8 miles south of the refuge boundary, on the right, is the entrance to the visitor parking area. In winter, the feeding station at the visitors' center attracts various sparrows, including infrequent Golden-crowned, Harris's, and White-throated. Gambel's Quail, Rufous-sided, Canyon, and Green-tailed towhees, blackbirds, House Finches, and sometimes Pyrrhuloxias and Scrub Jays are regular visitors. The trees around the parking lot and visitors' center attract migrants in spring and fall, and for several years a pair of Vermilion Flycatchers nested there.

Except on weekends from April through September, when it is closed, visitors are encouraged to stop at the center to register, obtain bird checklists and self-guided tour brochures, and inquire at the information desk about species currently being seen. A few minutes can be well spent here viewing the interesting and well-conceived exhibits on the flora and fauna of the area. There is also an audio-visual room where slides and movies are presented.

Northwest of the visitors' center is the employee and temporary worker housing area with a large, well-kept lawn. Provided that visitors respect the privacy of the human residents, there is no objection to enjoying a picnic lunch on the grounds in company with the birds that are often present. There are convenient trash receptacles, a water fountain, and rest rooms outside the visitors' center.

The entrance to the 15-mile tour loop is directly across the main road from the parking lot exit. Bosque del Apache, along with other national wildlife refuges, charges an entrance fee of $2.00 per vehicle, but free access is accorded to those holding a valid duck stamp, Golden Eagle, or Golden Age pass. The fee program is important, as two-thirds of the proceeds are used for purchase of wetlands and the other third to administer the program.

A sign at the entrance gives refuge hours, which change seasonally, from one hour before sunrise to one hour after sunset. One must leave the refuge by closing time or risk being locked in. (Winter nights there can be cold!)

Bosque del Apache is an important resting and feeding area for migrating shorebirds in the middle Rio Grande Valley and has produced many rare shorebird records, including Buff-breasted Sandpiper, Ruff, Whimbrel, Upland Sandpiper, Dunlin, and Ruddy Turnstone. Common during migration in April-May and August-September are American Avocet, Black-necked Stilt, both yellowlegs, Western and Least sandpipers, Long-billed Dowitcher, Common Snipe, and Wilson Phalarope. Less common, but sometimes present, are Long-billed Curlew, Marbled Godwit,and Semipalmated, White-rumped, Baird's, Pectoral, and Stilt sandpipers. Waders such as Great Blue, Green-backed, and Black-crowned Night herons, Cattle and Snowy egrets, and White-faced Ibis are frequently seen in season, while less frequent are American and Least bitterns, Great Egret, and Little Blue Heron. Tricolored and Yellow-crowned Night herons and White Ibis are rare.

The wildlife drive covers four major areas; north farm fields, central marshes, south fields, and south pond. It is usually best to check the central marsh early in the day when activity is at its peak. Small, shallow ponds on either side as one enters the drive attract many dabbling ducks and/or shorebirds, depending on the season and water level. Shorebirds often feed around the edges of these ponds. Say's Phoebes are present year-round, and during migration many swallows, of all New Mexico species except Cave, fly over the ponds almost incessantly. It is always worthwhile to examine these ponds carefully, including the back areas and shorelines, by telescope.

Follow the road south, then east 0.3 mile to an intersection just beyond the bridge. Proceed straight ahead on the Middle Tour Route for 0.2 mile and, when it is open, turn left (north) on a narrow road with posts on either side. Closed October 1 to March 31 to prevent disturbance to the Whooping Cranes and Bald Eagles that roost in this area, the road is reopened after the Whoopers have migrated north, thus providing access to the center of the marsh. (During the winter months, one must continue east, then north on the Main Route.) Levels vary, but usually some water is present in the central marsh, and both Double-crested and Neotropic cormorants often perch on dead limbs on the right (east). When the water is low, Sora and Virginia rails may be heard, and if one waits quietly, they may come into view along the left side. In winter when water levels are higher, thousands of geese (Snow, with a few of the "blue" phase, Ross's, and Canada) rest on the ponds of the central marsh. One or two Tundra Swans are occasionally seen among the geese, and at least once a lone Trumpeter Swan remained for a few weeks.

Farther along the road, Swamp Sparrows and Black Phoebes are sometimes seen among the reeds near a pumphouse on the right, and Vermilion

Flycatchers may nest in the adjacent wooded area on the left. The marsh is frequently drained (to control botulism) after the cranes and waterfowl leave, but ducks, meadowlarks, and flycatchers tend to feed here. At dusk one can see Lesser and a few Common nighthawks. The road turns to the right along the north edge of the marsh (trees along the left side may harbor migrant warblers and flycatchers) before rejoining the main tour route which continues to the north (left).

The next section of the tour road passes fields on the left, a drainage ditch and cottonwood grove on the right, where porcupines may sometimes be seen in the trees. In late summer, Blue Grosbeaks are numerous in the fields, replaced by White-crowned and other sparrows in September and October. Later, from November through early February, thousands of geese (mostly Snow) and Sandhill Cranes feed here. About 10 per cent of the white geese are Ross's, and with careful scrutiny one should be able to distinguish them. Watch for Mallard-sized geese with shorter bills and more rounded heads. At close range note the lack of "grinning patch" as well as the blue-gray triangle at the end of the bill.

This is one of the best places to see Whooping Cranes. In winter one usually feeds in this section of fields, but it is often hidden among the corn stalks. At other seasons, in early mornings and late evening, watch at the far north end for introduced Wild Turkeys (Rio Grande race). In spring, the toms can be seen strutting along the levee.

Toward the end of the fields the tour road makes a sharp jog to the right across a culvert, followed by a sharp left turn. A broad strip of grass and a ditch backed by woodland parallel the road on the left, with a narrow strip of grass and cottonwood bosque along the right. In the breeding season, Summer Tanagers are often present in the bosque. Hawks, Mourning Doves, swallows, meadowlarks, flycatchers, and other passerines frequently perch on the power line and poles on the far side of the ditch. Later, sparrows, goldfinches (American and Lesser), juncos, and Pine Siskins feed in the grass and wild sunflowers. This is often a good place for Ladder-backed Woodpeckers.

Follow the road until it makes a sharp turn to the left (west) and passes under the power line, on which Brewer's and Red-winged blackbirds are often seen, while a Black Phoebe frequents the nearby culvert. Soon an observation tower, complete with permanent telescope, is obvious on the left. From this vantage point one may scan the fields to the north for wintering Whooping and Sandhill cranes, geese, ducks, and sometimes gulls as well as Bald Eagles in the distant trees. Western Meadowlarks and introduced pheasants (mostly hybrids between the Ring-necked and White-winged subspecies) often feed here, and look for Greater Roadrunner along the road or ditch. Mule deer and an occasional coyote may also be seen in these fields. Behind the tower (to the south), the Phainopepla has been seen in July in two separate years.

Whooping Crane

Farther along the road, on the left, is a small parking lot with the entrance to a foot trail. In spring and fall the adjacent large cottonwoods and willows may harbor several species of warblers, Northern (Bullock's) Orioles, and Black-headed Grosbeaks. Sometimes a Rose-breasted Grosbeak or Summer Tanager may be seen. Great Horned Owls nest in the large cottonwoods that top the remains of old dikes and sometimes are found when hiking the trail. In summer be prepared for mosquitoes, both here and around the marshes. Lark and Black-throated sparrows are present in the summer, replaced in fall and winter by White-crowned and Brewer's sparrows and Dark-eyed Juncos. A few Canyon and Rufous-sided towhees are resident.

The ditches that parallel this road are good for waders, ducks, and cormorants. Say's Phoebes, goldfinches, and Pine Siskins feed in the weeds along their edges. In winter the Red-shafted form of the Northern Flicker is a common sight. At times, Mexican-type Mallards or hybrids can be found in these ditches. Several years ago, "Mexican Ducks" were released to establish a breeding population here, but studies show that practically all have hybridized with the common Mallard. Occasionally, one with most of the characteristics of the Mexican form is seen.

This road eventually leads back south to the main middle tour route. To reach the south fields, drive across the east-west road toward another observation tower. The fields on the left are flooded in winter and are favored by waterfowl. One section of the south end, with deeper water, is particularly good for diving ducks and grebes. Well worth checking before reaching the end of this loop are some cottonwoods on the left, known as Rigby's Woods, named for a former manager of the refuge. These trees seem to be particularly attractive to passerines. In season they are good for Mourning Dove, Northern (Red-shafted) Flicker, Willow Flycatcher, Western Kingbird (an unusual Couch's Kingbird was seen in this area a few years ago), kinglets, warblers, including Yellow-breasted Chat, various sparrows, and blackbirds. Low-growing willows, especially good for warblers such as Yellow and Common Yellowthroat, line parts of the ditch on the right side, and pheasants may be expected in the grassy areas, often right on the roadsides. In season there are Song Sparrows, with an occasional Vesper or Savannah, while Marsh Wrens are present in the cattails.

The south pond is reached by taking the only available right turn shortly before reaching the southwestern end of the loop and just before crossing a culvert. The water is deeper toward the southern end and attracts diving ducks and coots. Both Neotropic and Double-crested cormorants are usually found ln the pond, and at times Pied-billed, Eared, Western, and Clark's grebes. In winter, Ring-necked Ducks and Common Mergansers are regular here, with an occasional Hooded or rare Red-breasted. Canada Geese nest on the platforms. The cattails around the edges of the pond harbor Black-crowned Night-Herons, American Bitterns, and a few Least Bitterns in

Black-throated Sparrow

season. Common Moorhens are sometimes seen near the cattails at the shallow upper (north) end of the marsh. During migration American White Pelicans are numerous; Black Terns and Ring-billed and Franklin's gulls are fairly common, with a few Bonaparte's Gulls joining them. In summer when the water level is lower, many shorebirds may be seen on the mud spits. These include Long-billed Dowitcher, Wilson Phalarope, both yellowlegs, and Least, Spotted, Western, and Solitary sandpipers.

This road comes out at the bridge at the beginning of the loop. Turn left to return to the main road and refuge headquarters. Another option, however, is to turn around at the upper end of the marsh and return to the cut-off where one exited from the tour road, continuing around the south loop. Where it turns to the left (east), the corner of the field on the left is often flooded and attracts several kinds of shorebirds. In autumn, goldfinches, siskins, and sparrows often feed in the ripened sunflowers, and sometimes Lazuli Buntings are seen here.

The return leg to the north has a variety of habitats, offering a good sample of birds recorded in the refuge and possibility for viewing the occasional wintering Swamp, White-throated, or Harris's sparrows in the weedy edges and cattails, as well as Greater White-fronted Geese on the pond among the commoner waterfowl. Merlin, Prairie, and Peregrine falcons are rare winter visitors, and uncommonly a Tricolored Heron has been found in the shallower portions of the marsh.

This road eventually returns to the east end of the two-way middle tour road, where one may bear right to rejoin the north tour loop or turn left to the visitor's center. It is also possible to turn left onto old route 85 from San Antonio and go south along the opposite (west) side of the south pond described above.

The left (east) side of this old highway is flanked by cottonwoods and dense thickets of tamarisk, often good for warblers and sparrows. An occasional break in the vegetation provides a vantage point for viewing waterfowl, waders, and shorebirds. CAUTION: This is a State highway, so it is dangerous and illegal to stop on the pavement; also, the dry and loose sand along the edge can be treacherous.

On the road's right (west) side, the cover is mostly low to moderately high brush, in season sheltering Crissal, Curve-billed, and rarely Bendire's thrashers, Pyrrhuloxia, Rufous-sided and Canyon towhees, and Black-throated, Sage, and White-crowned sparrows. Both Gambel's and Scaled quail are seen here, and sometimes a Verdin can be found in the low-growing mesquite.

Five to six miles south of the visitors' center this road passes under a railroad trestle. Birds in the vicinity are similar to those seen back toward San Antonio, but in the gullies and on dry slopes Rufous-crowned Sparrows and Rock Wrens may be found. In winter, a Golden Eagle often perches on the power line towers. From here it is about nine miles south to the junction with the San Marcial exit to I-25; a right (west) turn at the first gravel road takes one to the interstate. If returning to San Antonio and Socorro, turn around near the railroad trestle and retrace the route north past the visitors' center.

It should be noted that some of the refuge roads are closed to all entry by vehicle or on foot, a prohibition which should be carefully observed. Refuge personnel also appreciate having visitors come back to the visitors' center after their tour to report any interesting and/or unusual sightings. These reports are most helpful for other visitors to the refuge.

WATER CANYON

Water Canyon is one of the better birding spots in central New Mexico and is often combined with trips to the Bosque del Apache NWR. It is located in the Magdalena Mountains, an isolated volcanic mountain range west of Socorro, which is large enough to contain numerous motels and a KOA Campground. For those wishing to spend the night in the canyon, there is a pleasant but primitive campground (no water); for information write Magdalena Ranger District, Cibola National Forest, Box 45, Magdalena, NM 87825.

The highest point in the range, South Baldy Peak, rises to an elevation of 10,787 feet and can be reached by a primitive but quite passable dirt road. It is therefore possible to investigate in a single visit numerous habitats ranging from semi-desert grasslands at the base of the mountains to spruce-fir and aspen forests at the top. Although the Magdalena Range is geologically part of the mountain fringe that borders the Rio Grande valley, the vegetation and animal life show affinities with those of the Mogollon Plateau in the southwestern part of the State. Several birds reach or closely approach the northeastern limit ot their breeding ranges at or near Water Canyon, among them Elf Owl, Bridled Titmouse, and Red-faced Warbler.

The turnoff to Water Canyon is exactly 16 miles west of Socorro on US 60 which traverses grasslands with conspicuous yuccas and cacti and occasional groups of pronghorns. The paved entrance road goes left (west) just past a green 124-mile post and a mile beyond Water Canyon Lodge, passing through high desert grassland before it enters the canyon. Western Kingbird, Chihuahuan Raven and Loggerhead Shrike are often seen on the telephone wires. Watch also for Greater Roadrunner, Sage and Curve-billed thrashers. Lark Bunting, Cassin's and Lark sparrows, and Eastern and Western meadowlarks. During migration there can be large concentrations of Broad-billed and Black-chinned hummingbirds. Stop 2.3 miles up the road where occasional water in an earthen tank attracts Scaled and Gambel's quail, bluebirds, and other species. Nearer the canyon (beyond the Cibola National Forest Boundary sign), there are Curve-billed and occasionally Bendire's thrashers in cholla cactus stands, and watch for both Black-throated and Black-chinned sparrows.

As one enters the canyon, high red cliffs are obvious on the left (east). Drive to the windmill which is also on the left. The land here is not posted, but it is private and remains open only as long as visitors do not abuse the privilege. In the open pinyon-juniper habitat surrounding the windmill, look for Gambel's Quail, Ladder-backed Woodpecker, Say's Phoebe, Western and Mountain bluebirds, Canyon (Brown) Towhee, Brewer's, Chipping, and Black-chinned sparrows, and possibly Scott's and Northern (Bullock's) orioles. Near the cliffs, Band-tailed Pigeon, White-throated Swift, Canyon Wren, Blue Grosbeak, and Lazuli Bunting are likely. A pair of Great-horned Owls roosts and nests in the small caves in the face of the cliffs; they often are visible from the road.

Continue along the paved road to the Water Canyon Campground where a 14-day stay with no fee is permissible. The campground is situated within prime montane riparian habitat, with many narrow-leafed cottonwoods, gray and Gambel's oaks, Arizona walnut, and box-elder. Search the entire area both up and down stream from the campground. Nesting birds include Cooper's Hawk, American Kestrel, Western Screech, Great-horned, Flammulated, and occasionally Elf owls, Common Poorwill, Broad-tailed and Black-chinned hummingbirds, Northern Flicker, Acorn Woodpecker, Western Wood-Pewee, Ash-throated Flycatcher, Violet-green Swallow, White-breasted Nuthatch, House Wren, Solitary and Warbling vireos, Black-headed Grosbeak, Rufous-sided Towhee, Chipping Sparrow, Brown-headed Cowbird, Western and Hepatic tanagers, and Lesser Goldfinch. In the pinyon-juniper habitats (mainly on the west side of the canyon) look also for Gray Flycatcher, Scrub and Pinyon jays, Mountain Chickadee, Bridled Titmouse (irregular), Bushtit, Blue-gray Gnatcatcher, Black-throated Gray Warbler, and House Finch. During migration, the cottonwoods attract many warblers, including Townsend's, Wilson's, and MacGillivray's. Winter residents and visitors include Steller's Jay, Clark's Nutcracker, White-breasted and Pygmy nuthatches, Townsend's Solitaire, and Red Crossbill. It is also worth checking the cliffs above the canyon for Golden Eagle, Prairie Falcon, Red-tailed Hawk, and Common Raven.

A number of unexpected or irregular species have been documented near the campground and should be watched for; these include Violet-crowned and Magnificent hummingbirds, Painted Redstart, Rose-breasted Grosbeak, and Indigo Bunting.

A productive side-trip from the campground is in North Fork Canyon along Forest Road 39, which branches west froom the main road near the entrance to the campground. The road is passable in most years to four-wheel-drive vehicles, but it is usually best traveled by foot. The habitat is mostly montane riparian and ponderosa pine forest. Species found here include Montezuma Quail, Wild Turkey, Red-tailed Hawk, Flammulated, Western Screech, Northern Pygmy, and occasionally Northern Saw-whet owls, Whip-poor-will, Cassin's Kingbird, Gray and Cordilleran (Western) flycatchers, Bridled Titmouse, and Black-chinned Sparrow.

In the middle of the campground, a dirt road crosses the stream bottom and continues up the east side of the canyon to Langmuir Laboratory, operated by the New Mexico Institute of Mining and Technology and devoted primarily to the study of lightning (summer thunderstorms can be intense in these mountains). The lab, atop the mountain, is open to the public during most of the summer. The access road is narrow but easily passable by passenger car, and the view from the top alone can make the trip worthwhile. About two miles from the campground, the stream narrows and the road passes next to a steep slope underneath some cliffs. Here one should search for Red-faced Warblers which are often found along the stream and in the adjacent stands of Gambel's oak. By walking upstream along the road, a pair can usually be located. This area also supports Whip-poor-will, Dusky, Olive-sided, and Cordilleran flycatchers, Steller's Jay, Hermit Thrush, and Virginia's and Grace's warblers.

The next section of the Langmuir road traverses mixed areas of pinyon-juniper, ponderosa pine, and spruce-fir forests. The birding along this section is not particularly rewarding, but as the road nears the top, it goes through a stand of large Douglas-fir surrounded by sub-alpine grassland with some aspen. Birds here include Wild Turkey, Northern Goshawk, Band-tailed Pigeon, Red-naped and Williamson's sapsuckers, Hairy Woodpecker, Clark's Nutcracker, Red-breasted and Pygmy nuthatches, Mountain Bluebird, Townsend's Solitaire, Green-tailed Towhee, Dark-eyed Junco, Pine Siskin, and Red Crossbill. From here it is a short drive to the Laboratory.

GREEN CHAPARRAL TURF RANCH

At this ranch, six miles east of Moriarty, Mountain Plover and McCown's, Lapland, and Chestnut-collared longspurs may be seen at times within a stone's throw of I-40. The most convenient access is gained by leaving I-40 at exit 203 and proceeding to the stop sign on the north side of the interchange, across from an RV campground. Go left (west) on the north frontage road, which parallels the interstate, for 2.5 miles. The Turf Ranch will be apparent on the right.

The hospitable owners of Green Chaparral are Wayne and Barbara Webb whose home and offices are situated to the rear of the ranch property. It is important to check in with one of the family or staff before birding. They will direct visitors to favored areas for both plovers and longspurs and provide necessary information about where (and where not) to drive and walk on the sod farm.

The longspurs are wintering species, but some may be seen as early as October and as late as April. Sightings are most assured in mid-winter. By late February some of the birds have begun to acquire their attractive breeding plumage. Finding them is a matter of tracking down the large flocks of Horned Larks that dominate the ranch scene in winter. On a given winter's day, one might see 800 Horned Larks, 40 each of McCown's and Chestnut-collared longspurs, and five to ten Laplands. A Prairie Falcon or Merlin may sometimes be seen harassing these mixed flocks. Mountain Bluebirds and Sage Thrashers also are found on the ranch in winter.

The Mountain Plover is primarily a migrant through this area, although an occasional bird may remain into summer. Peak months are May and September. Like its relative, the Killdeer, which is also present at Green Chaparral, the Mountain Plover is quite approachable by car, and it is not unusual for a flock to settle next to one's vehicle.

Mountain Plover

GRASSLANDS TURF RANCH

The Grasslands Turf Ranch, located near Los Lunas in Valencia County, is the best locality for observing grassland bird species in the central Rio Grande Valley. The birding can be good at any time of the year, and this site is particularly well known for wintering longspurs and for Mountain Plover during the spring and fall migration periods. To reach the turf ranch, travel south from Albuquerque about 20 miles on I-25. The first exit -- Exit 203 -- one reaches after crossing the Valencia County line is marked for Los Lunas and NM 6. Leave the interstate here, turn west on NM 6, and go about 100 meters to the first dirt road on the right, which is marked for the Grasslands Turf Ranch. Take this road north for one mile (paralleling the interstate on its west side), where the entrance to the turf ranch is reached. The whole turf growing area is surrounded by dirt roads, and there is an additional east-west dirt road that bisects the property. This central road is often the best area from which to observe birds.

Longspurs are generally present here from late October to early April, with the largest numbers present from November to March. During the winters of 1990-1991 and 1991-92, McCown's was the commonest species, with a population sometimes exceeding 100 birds. Chestnut-collareds can also be numerous but appear to be more sporadic in occurrence. Lapland is decidedly rare but in at least some winters one or two are present and can be found by patiently working through the flocks of McCown's. The longspurs sometimes form mixed flocks with the Horned Larks that are also present, though segregated flocks are equally common. The birds can be hard to find and difficult to approach, so patience and a spotting scope are essential. By February, at least some of the longspurs are likely to be coming into breeding plumage. Learning the calls of these birds can be a real help in locating them, and it is best to look on a day that is not too windy.

Mountain Plovers are present here during both spring and fall. In spring, birds may be seen from early March through April, but numbers rarely exceed ten individuals, and finding them on a given day can be a hit-or-miss proposition. They are much more numerous in fall, appearing from late July until early October, with rare stragglers into November. During the peak months of August and September, dozens and sometimes hundreds of individuals may be present. The best viewing strategy is to scan with a spotting scope from the central dirt road.

Other shorebirds may be seen here in migration, especially during fall. In August and September up to 30 Baird's Sandpipers have been seen here in one day, and Pectoral and Upland sandpipers have both been noted on several occasions. In September of 1991, New Mexico's first photographically documented Buff-breasted Sandpiper was present there for about ten days.

Spring and fall migrations also bring many sparrows to Grasslands. These are best found around the edges of the turf ranch, especially along the south edge where there is a row of small trees. Regularly seen species include Savannah, Vesper, Lark, Black-throated, Chipping, Brewer's, and Lark Bunting. Clay-colored Sparrow has been seen here in fall and may be regular in small numbers during September. Other birds to look for at this location include Burrowing Owl in spring and summer, Ferruginous Hawk in winter, and Scaled Quail year-round.

The turf ranch is private property, and birders should act with due consideration when visiting. Stay on the dirt roads; do not jump fences or walk across the turf. In addition, the roads can be very slick and muddy after heavy rains, so take care not to get stuck. The owners, Mr. and Mrs. Charles Webb, have been very generous about granting access to birders, and it is the responsibility of visiting birders to see that these congenial relations are maintained.

In spring, the two or three miles of NM 6 just west of the turf ranch turnoff are probably the best location in the central Rio Grande Valley for finding Bendire's Thrasher and Eastern Meadowlark. Both species are best sought early in the morning and are difficult to find after mid-morning. Drive slowly and look for thrashers perched atop the junipers or pinyon pines or the larger bushes. A few pairs of Bendire's seem to be present here each year, beginning in late March or early April. The meadowlark is best located by stopping along the road every half mile or so and listening for its distinctive "see-you-see-yer" song. These birds may be found singing as early as the first week of March and appear to be most numerous about two miles west of I-25. Western Meadowlarks are also present and singing here, so one has a chance for direct comparison. Chihuahuan Ravens may also be found in the same area.

EASTERN

David Cleary

FORT SUMNER

Fort Sumner lies on US 60 about 84 miles northeast of Roswell and is reached by taking US 285 north from Roswell for 37 miles, then turning right (northeast) on NM 20 and going 47 miles. The extensive cottonwoods and tall grasses distinguish this area from the lower portions of the Pecos Valley. In and near the cottonwoods are numbers of breeding Bobwhites, Blue Jays, and Common Grackles and probably the highest density of Red-headed Woodpeckers in New Mexico. Large numbers of migrants also pass through Fort Sumner, and rarities such as Red-bellied Woodpecker have appeared here.

The best location for the jay and woodpecker is a grove of mature cottonwoods near the playing fields on the east side of Fort Sumner High School. The school is near downtown Fort Sumner, several blocks east of the intersection of US 60 and US 84. The grove is reached by following a dirt road parallel to the irrigation channel behind the school. Bobwhites are usually here as well as on the eastern bank of the Pecos River. To find them in the latter area, park just before the bridge on westbound US 60 at the edge of town. Walk upstream through a stand of cottonwoods and toward a railroad trestle about 1.5 miles away. If no quail are seen along the way, investigate the row of tamarisks beyond the trestle (which sometimes shelters a Great Horned Owl).

Two or three Dickcissels have been recorded yearly since 1987 on June Breeding Bird Surveys south of Fort Sumner National Monument, and Long-billed Curlews probably nest annually on the plains. The monument and surrounding agricultural areas are southeast of Fort Sumner and are reached by taking NM 212 south off US 60/84 for four miles. The male Dickcissels sing from shrubs bordering alfalfa fields. Swainson's Hawks are conspicuous on roadside poles in this area, and Barn Owls have been seen in summer in the primitive camping area (eastern side) below the dam at Sumner Lake State Park (Sumner Lake is also known as Alamogordo Reservoir). To reach the park, go north from Fort Sumner on US 84 for 10 miles, turning left (west) on NM 203, the access road. In migration and winter, Sumner Lake is good for ducks, gulls, and terns, while Mountain Bluebirds, Townsend's Solitaires and Canyon (Brown) Towhees are present in the nearby juniper groves. Large flocks of Sandhill Cranes frequent the agricultural fields southeast of the lake. Common Raven is to be expected in winter, whereas Chihuahuan Raven is more likely in summer.

SOUTHWEST

Marian Zimmerman, Dale Zimmerman, Ralph Fisher

Southwestern New Mexico harbors numerous species absent from the remainder of the State or not regularly present in other sections. The birds here are more representative of southeastern Arizona than of the rest of New Mexico -- species such as Common Black-Hawk, Montezuma Quail, Violet-crowned and Broad-billed hummingbirds, Gray-breasted (Mexican) Jay, Bridled Titmouse, Red-faced Warbler, Painted Redstart and Varied Bunting to name a few specialities. A central point for birding the area is Silver City (elevation 5,900 feet) with suitable motels, restaurants and other services. From there, most of the sites discussed may be conveniently visited on one-day trips. From the East, two major routes lead to Silver City: NM 152 through the Black Range from the Rio Grande Valley, and NM 26 and US 180 from Hatch and Deming as detailed below. The latter route is recommended during winter/early spring as snow and ice can make the tortuous Black Range road inconvenient or dangerous. Silver City also is served by NM 90 from Lordsburg and southeastern Arizona.

HATCH - DEMING - SILVER CITY

The vast open country between Hatch and Deming, traversed by NM 26, hosts large numbers of wintering raptors -- Golden Eagle, Northern Harrier, Prairie Falcon, and Red-tailed, Ferruginous, and Rough-legged hawks in particular. During summer, Swainson's Hawks are fairly common here, but they depart in autumn. If traveling this road between dusk and dawn, one should watch for Short-eared Owl (rare) during winter and Burrowing Owl in the warmer months. Great Horned and Barn owls are present throughout the year. On warm winter days, Crissal Thrashers sometimes are seen atop shrubs in brushy arroyos near Deming. Sage Thrasher, Lark Bunting and various sparrows are present in the same habitat, and Loggerhead Shrike and Western Meadowlark are regular at this time of year. Another winter attraction is the longspur flocks. Far-ranging, and sometimes difficult to find, they will congregate at water sources like the earthern stock tanks north of the crossroads known as Nutt (about 18 miles from Hatch). If one parks there and waits for the birds to appear, they can often be seen well, as opposed to fleeting glances of foraging flocks. Toward spring, they may be in nearly complete breeding plumage. Virtually all are Chestnut-collared, but be alert for an occasional McCown's -- formerly fairly common here but now rare. The Savannah Sparrow is the usual open-country sparrow, often visiting water tanks with longspurs and Horned Larks.

Spotted Owl

THE BLACK RANGE

The route to Silver City via the Black Range offers attractive and varied montane scenery and, from spring through autumn, numerous interesting birds. Take NM 152 (formerly 90) and follow signs for Hillsboro (17 miles from 1-25, 58 from Silver City). The first few miles through desert foothills are seldom productive, but birding anywhere along the road once it enters the Gila National Forest can be rewarding. Just beyond the summit of the road at Emory Pass, look for Olive Warbler, scarce here but possible. Also watch for Wild Turkeys along the road. One of the few convenient places to stop is Iron Creek Campground where there may be Red-faced Warblers as well as rather tame Golden-mantled Ground Squirrels and Tassel-eared Squirrels. Some of the side canyons hereabouts offer habitat for the Spotted Owl. Picturesque Gallinas Canyon, farther along the road and marked by a sign, is another good birding site (and excellent for wildflowers). The common Black Range birds include many species listed later under the Pinos Altos Mountains.

As NM 152 leaves the Black Range, it descends to the Mimbres River and skirts the Fort Bayard Military Reservation a few miles after passing the extensive open-pit copper mine near Santa Rita. The traversed area is mostly pinyon pine and juniper woodland, interspersed with yucca-studded grasslands supporting, in summer, Scott's Oriole and Eastern Meadowlark. At the intersection with US 180, turn right and drive 10 miles to Silver City.

FORT BAYARD

Easily reached from Silver City is the Fort Bayard Military Reservation. The associated hospital and surroundings are under State jurisdiction, and the reservation itself is managed by the US Forest Service. The New Mexico Department of Game and Fish also maintains it as a wildlife refuge. Take US 180 east 8 miles from Silver City and then turn left opposite the village of Central. Signs on the highway may indicate both the Fort Bayard hospital and a native plant nursery. At the entrance gate (0.5 mile from the highway), a security guard may ask the purpose of your visit. Just beyond this point, take the right fork which skirts the eastern edge of the hospital grounds. The grassy fields on the right and lawns on the left often attract ground-feeding birds. Montezuma Quail have been seen along this section of road on occasion. Not far ahead, keep right at another fork where a small sign indicates Forest Road 536. After two more intersections (with stop signs) a second FR 536 sign indicates the route, now on broken blacktop but soon changing to gravel as it enters the reservation. The road winds through brushy oak thickets and juniper savanna, crosses cottonwood-lined Cameron Creek (usually dry) and enters grasslands bounded by pine and juniper woodland.

Sometimes it is worthwhile to explore Cameron Creek briefly before driving on. Across a cattle guard there is a fork where one keeps left on 536. About 0.6 mile farther is a smaller creek bed where one may park at the small camp site on the right (before the bridge). Follow the creekbed to the west (downstream), looking in the large oaks for Bridled Titmouse and Gray-breasted Jay and on the brush-covered hills above for Black-chinned Sparrow. After 0.5 mile, this smaller drainage joins Cameron Creek. Walking up the latter for about 0.75 mile will bring one to a lovely glade with numerous trees and "Horseshoe Falls," which flow only after reasonable rain. However, some permanent water from numerous "seeps" attracts many of the area's birds and mammals. Wild Turkey, Elk and Mule Deer often are seen here. (White-tailed Deer are present in the area but are best seen on or near the hospital grounds, especially in the evening.)

Several other sections provide good birding, and one should sample the various habitats. Do not drive off the roads or on trails signed against vehicular use. In spring, Eastern Meadowlarks nest in the grasslands, replacing the Western Meadowlark which winters abundantly throughout the region. At intervals, Montezuma Quail wander through and they have nested in various parts of the reservation. Examine groups of tall yuccas for Scott's Oriole, an uncommon summer resident. The cottonwood groves support breeding Cooper's and Red-tailed hawks, Great Horned and Western Screech owls, Western Wood-Pewee, Cassin's and Western kingbirds, Solitary Vireo, Black-headed Grosbeak, and Northern (Bullock's) Oriole. In more open or brushy places, expect Common Nighthawk, Ash-throated Flycatcher, Western Bluebird, Curve-billed Thrasher, Canyon (Brown) and Rufous-sided towhees. Along rock outcrops watch for Rufous-crowned Sparrow, and in dense brushy streambed growth, for Crissal Thrasher (rare). Long-eared Owl winters in dense oak and juniper thickets, and has nested here on occasion; the Saw-whet Owl has been recorded in migration. Winter birding usually is good, in some years producing Pinyon Jay, Townsend's Solitaire, and Green-tailed Towhee. At this season a check of large trees on the hospital grounds may disclose American Robin, erratic winter finches such as Evening Grosbeak and Cassin's Finch, or perhaps a roosting owl.

LITTLE WALNUT PICNIC AREA and BEAR MOUNTAIN

About 4 miles north of US 180 west in Silver City, on Little Walnut Road, is a picnic area maintained by the US Forest Service. It is good for a short trip from town, especially on weekdays, which have fewer local visitors. Park in any of the designated lots and wander among the tall pines as well as east of the developed grounds to the shallow arroyo where low willows, scrub oaks, pinyon pines and junipers provide diversity.

An hour in summer typically reveals Northern Flicker, Hairy and Acorn woodpeckers, Ash-throated Flycatcher, Common Raven, Gray-breasted and

Black-chinned Sparrow

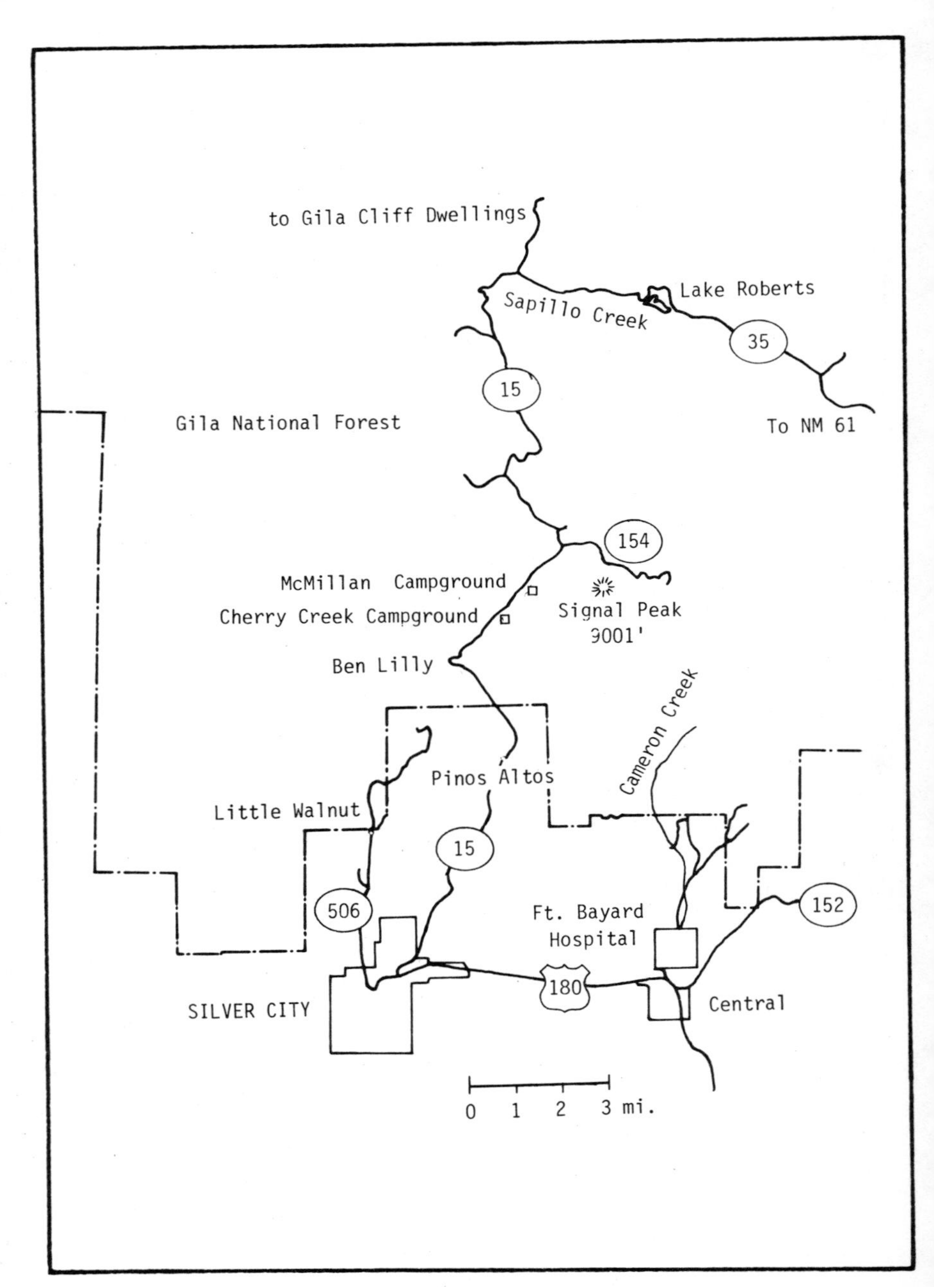
to Gila Cliff Dwellings
Lake Roberts
Sapillo Creek
35
15
Gila National Forest
To NM 61
154
McMillan Campground
Cherry Creek Campground
Signal Peak
9001'
Ben Lilly
Cameron Creek
Pinos Altos
Little Walnut
15
506
Ft. Bayard
Hospital
152
180
SILVER CITY
Central
0 1 2 3 mi.

Scrub jays, Bewick's Wren, White-breasted Nuthatch, Bushtit, Western Bluebird, Bridled and Plain titmice, Solitary Vireo, Hepatic and Western tanagers, Dark-eyed (Gray-headed) Junco, Rufous-sided Towhee, and Chipping Sparrow. Sometimes Violet-green Swallow and Purple Martin are seen overhead. The Gray Flycatcher frequently breeds here and the Red Crossbill nests sporadically. The latter often is present in winter along with Red-naped and Williamson's sapsuckers, Steller's Jay, Ruby-crowned and (rarely) Golden-crowned kinglets, Townsend's Solitaire, Pygmy and Red-breasted nuthatches, and several forms of Dark-eyed Junco. Among the many transient species possible are various warblers, Cassin's Finch, Pine Siskin and goldfinches.

Another profitable trip north of Silver City is to the the vicinity of Bear Mountain. From US 180 west, turn north on Alabama Street (0.3 mile west of Little Walnut Road) which becomes Cottage San Road and finally FR 853 (unpaved). At 5 miles from US 180, turn onto FR 858. The first mile of this trail, which combines a ponderosa pine-Gambel's oak community with pinyon-juniper-scrub oak, is often very birdy. Many of the species are the same as Little Walnut, including Gray Flycatcher (breeding). In addition, Hutton's Vireo has been seen here. There are several potential mud holes, so use care if visiting during the summer rainy season or after winter storms.

PINOS ALTOS MOUNTAINS

Some of the region's best birding is in the canyons of this low mountain range accessible via NM 15 branching north from US 180 in Silver City. This road passes through Pinos Altos (8 miles distant) and soon enters the Gila National Forest. Gray-breasted Jay, Cassin's Kingbird, Western Bluebird and other common species are seen from the roadway (as are, rarely, Montezuma Quail), but the best birding areas begin at Cherry Creek Campground, 13 miles from Silver City. The canyon here is a traditional site for Painted Redstart, although it is uncommon in some years. Look for it along the creek near the road. The Red-faced Warbler is sometimes with the redstarts, but more often is a short distance above the creek on the canyonsides. In scrubbier growth on the drier south-facing slopes breeds the Virginia's Warbler, while nesting among pinyon pines and junipers are a few Black-throated Gray Warblers. Grace's Warbler is widespread among the tall ponderosa pines.

Hutton's Vireo is fairly regular here, but scarce; the common vireos are Solitary and Warbling. Some years the Greater Pewee (Coues's Flycatcher) may be heard singing near McMillan Campground, a mile or so farther along the road. Northern Pygmy Owl, formerly regular, is now hard to find, but imitating its call to attract passerines sometimes stimulates the owl itself to call. Flammulated and Spotted owls are also a possibility, especially up McMillan Canyon. Both Whip-poor-will and Poorwill may be heard on warm summer evenings. Other regular breeding birds in the Cherry Creek-

Painted Redstart

McMillan Campground vicinity are: White-throated Swift, Broad-tailed Hummingbird, Northern Flicker, Acorn and Hairy woodpeckers, Ash-throated Flycatcher, Western Wood-Pewee, Violet-green Swallow, Common Raven, Steller's Jay, Canyon and House wrens, Bridled Titmouse (rare), White-breasted Nuthatch, Western Bluebird, Hermit Thrush, American Robin, Western and Hepatic tanagers, Black-headed Grosbeak, and Dark-eyed (Gray-headed) Junco.

Three miles beyond Cherry Creek Campground, Forest Road 154 branches to the right and ascends 9,000-foot Signal Peak. Parts of this 7-mile road are deeply rutted, rocky and steep, with sharp curves. It is not recommended for low sedans, although the first few miles present no problem. This area supports a population of the Olive Warbler, best located by its song, which may be heard as early as February. However, this scarce bird is here at the edge of its range, and perhaps not present every year. Sometimes a pair may be found near the junction with NM 15 or thereabouts, during nesting season or later in mixed post-breeding bird parties. Yellow-rumped (Audubon's) and Grace's warblers are common breeders throughout, and the Greater Pewee is occasional. Red-naped and Williamson's sapsuckers, Downy Woodpecker, Cordilleran (Western) Flycatcher, Pygmy and Red-breasted nuthatches, Golden-crowned Kinglet, Orange-crowned Warbler, and Red Crosssbill are additional breeding species present in the Signal Peak forests, although some of them are scarce and/or irregular. Certain of these, e.g. the nuthatches and kinglet, are more numerous in autumn or winter when other high-altitude birds such as Three-toed Woodpecker and Clark's Nutcracker can appear. The Saw-whet Owl is known here, but its status is uncertain. The Spotted Owl is heard on occasion, and the Flammulated nests locally. Signal Peak often is productive during fall migration, with large numbers of hummingbirds and, at times, wood warblers (including Nashville, Townsend's and Hermit).

An annotated checklist of the birds of the Gila National Forest, published in October 1991, is available at the Silver City Ranger District office, 2915 East US Highway 180, as well as at the Gila Cliff Dwellings visitor center.

GILA CLIFF DWELLINGS NATIONAL MONUMENT - LAKE ROBERTS

From Cherry Creek Canyon, one may continue on NM 15 to the Cliff Dwellings National Monument and Lake Roberts. About 7 miles from the Signal Peak road junction, the highway descends in a series of switchbacks to Sapillo Creek, and soon it turns left at an obvious fork. From here it is 15 miles to the National Monument headquarters in Cliff Dweller Canyon where White-throated Swift, Canyon Wren, Painted Redstart and other species similar to those in Cherry Creek Canyon are to be expected. The Spotted Owl has been recorded along the foot trail to the cliff dwellings and elsewhere in the area. Along the river below the canyon, Common Black-Hawks may be found in summer, Bald Eagles in winter. A Peregrine Falcon

Bridled Titmouse

or Goshawk is always possible and Montezuma Quail are occasionally present in the hills and side canyons; they are impossible to predict. The same is true of the Pinyon Jay flocks which roam the countryside at most seasons (least commonly during early summer when they are usually in pairs).

From the Monument, follow the road back to its junction with NM 35 (which later becomes NM 61). Turn left, proceeding eastward around Lake Roberts, watching for Wild Turkey, Pinyon Jay (a few have nested on the hills above the lake), and Purple Martin (nesting in tall dead pines). Near the east end of the lake, turn right and drive through a small campground to a parking area close to the lake. The cattails, adjacent shrubby growth and ponderosa pines on the hillsides should be examined, and a short boardwalk enables one to penetrate the marsh slightly for summering species such as: Ruddy Duck, American Coot, Sora, Virginia Rail, Common Yellowthroat, Marsh Wren and Red-winged Blackbird. Black Phoebe, Steller's Jay, Solitary Vireo, Grace's Warbler, Pygmy Nuthatch, Canyon Wren, Blue Grosbeak and Chipping Sparrow breed near the campground. During migration, various ducks, grebes, Double-crested Cormorant, Ring-billed Gull and a few shorebirds are not unlikely.

The trip south through the upper Mimbres Valley can be rewarding if one explores some of the side canyons. Many of the land birds found around Lake Roberts are widespread in the valley, along with Gambel's Quail, Western Bluebird, Acorn Woodpecker, Violet-green Swallow, Rock Wren, Rufous-sided Towhee, and Rufous-crowned Sparrow plus species typical of grasslands and pinyon pine-juniper woodland. Also of interest in autumn and winter is Bear Canyon Dam and its impoundment, about 10 miles south of Lake Roberts.

LOWER MIMBRES VALLEY

An interesting loop can be made by taking NM 61 south from its intersection with NM 152 near the village of San Lorenzo. It follows the Mimbres River, bordered by stately cottonwoods, as well as willows, shrubby seepwillows *(Baccharis glutinosa)*, and other riparian plants. This association is in sharp contrast to the adjacent xeric slopes with their cacti, mimosas, low mesquites and scrawny junipers. In addition, there are extensive orchards, large weedy patches, dense brushy thickets, grassland and rocky bluffs which increase the diversity of the valley's birdlife.

The Mimbres, however, lacks certain of the choice southwestern riparian birds characteristic of the Gila River Valley not far to the west. One looks in vain here for Gila Woodpecker, Northern Cardinal and Abert's Towhee. Furthermore, the valley's cottonwood groves are all privately owned and posted against trespassing. There is no easy legal access to these, and unless known to local landowners, birders are discouraged from entering the woods on foot. However, a number of the more widespread riparian and upland species may be seen on a leisurely drive with frequent stops, perhaps even including a Common Black-Hawk soaring above the trees.

The highway leaves the river valley after 19 miles, and turns generally westward through desert and desert-grassland. The road passes by the entrance to the City of Rocks State Park with interesting geological formations but few unusual birds (Great Horned Owl, Say's Phoebe and Rock Wren nest there), and soon joins US 180 from Deming to Silver City. One can return to the latter on the highway through Bayard or cut across the grasslands on the Silver City-Grant County Airport road which turns left from US 180 and heads west, then north, connecting to the graveled Ridge Road. This joins NM 90, which becomes Hudson Street, on the south edge of town.

RIDGE ROAD - NM 90 LOOP

The topography and vegetation south of Silver City contrast with those north of town and support largely different bird communities. The following route provides some typical samples: Leaving Silver City to the south via Hudson Street and NM 90, turn left 1.1 miles from the last traffic light (Hudson and Broadway) onto Ridge Road. Take this 1 mile to Golf Course Road which turns off to the left (east). This short road descends through oak and beargrass-covered hills past the landfill and along the golf course, passing various weed patches, brushy fencerows and desert grassland. At the base of the hill, where the blacktop ends, it crosses a shallow wash (usually dry) which often is birdy during migration and winter. One can also visit some small ponds on that part of the golf course by going through or around the fence near the wash. Remember to avoid walking on the maintained greens and be alert for golfers playing through.

The domestic ducks on the ponds attract a few migrant waterfowl, herons (including Snowy and Cattle egrets), grebes and coots. In all seasons except summer, the golf course greens are good for American Pipits, Brewer's and Red-winged blackbirds, and Western Meadowlarks. From October through spring the weedy thickets hold hundreds of White-crowned Sparrows, rarely with a White-throated, Golden-crowned, or Harris's sparrow among them. Usually there are numerous Song and Lincoln's sparrows, sometimes a wintering Swamp or Rufous-crowned sparrow or a Green-tailed Towhee as well. Judicious "pishing" lures these skulkers into view.

In the more open places, less often in dense weed beds, are roving flocks of Brewer's and Chipping sparrows and Lark Buntings. Lesser and American goldfinches and Pine Siskins are frequent visitors to the elm trees and sunflower patches. During autumn and winter, up to 200 Common Ravens roost nearby and breakfast at the landfill in company with a few Starlings. Great-tailed Grackles, Red-winged Blackbirds, and at times, Chihuahuan

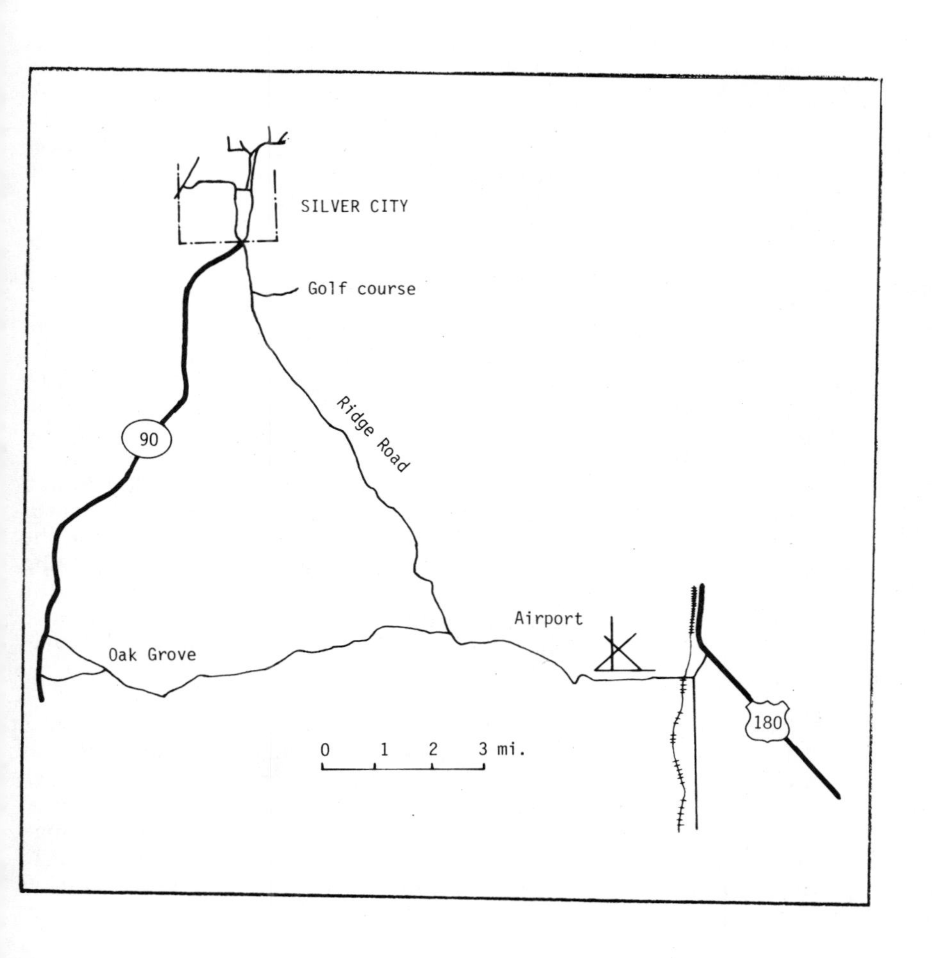
SILVER CITY
Golf course
Ridge Road
90
Airport
Oak Grove
180
0 1 2 3 mi.

(White-necked) Ravens. Between the landfill and golf course wherever mesquites and large cholla cacti remain, look for Curve-billed Thrasher, Cactus Wren, and Black-throated Sparrow. Red-tailed Hawks are resident, while a transient Prairie Falcon, wintering Ferruginous Hawk or Northern Harrier is also possible.

A half-mile walk across the flats to the vicinity of some conspicuous large cottonwood trees in the direction of town may disclose Northern Flicker, Bewick's Wren, Ruby-crowned Kinglet, Western or Mountain bluebird, Yellow-rumped Warbler, Savannah Sparrow and other wintering species. During the breeding season, Western Kingbird, Northern (Bullock's) and Scott's orioles, and Lark Sparrow are likely. American Kestrel, Scaled Quail, Killdeer, Mourning Dove, Greater Roadrunner, Ladder-backed Woodpecker, Say's Phoebe, Canyon (Brown) Towhee, and House Finch are present all year.

The road curves around the east end of the golf course, eventually joining a paved one (Taber Drive). Turn right to reach Lance Drive, which climbs back up to the Ridge Road. At the junction, turn left and continue away from town. The blacktop soon ends and the gravel road winds through hills studded with clumps of beargrass *(Nolina microcarpa)*. Birds are scarce in this typically windswept terrain but Horned Larks and Chestnut-collared Longspurs often are about in winter. Golden Eagle, Red-tailed Hawk, Northern Harrier and Loggerhead Shrike also are likely. Stop at intervals to investigate those areas of mixed beargrass and shrubs (mostly saltbush and low mesquite) for Sage Sparrow, which often winters here alone or in small loose groups with Vesper, Brewer's, and Black-throated sparrows or the occasional Sage Thrasher. Sage Sparrows are shy ground dwellers; stalking them is seldom productive, for they run off, thrasher-like, amongst the vegetation. However, they respond readily to "pishing," often ascending to the nearest bush-top where they look about briefly, pumping their longish black tails excitedly.

At 9.5 miles from Silver City there is a spur branching off to the west (right); keep left toward the Silver City-Grant County Airport. This open country has breeding Burrowing Owls in the large earthern kangaroo-rat mounds which are scattered in the flat overgrazed grassland; morning or evening is a good time to see them standing near their burrows. Also nesting where enough grass cover remains is the Eastern Meadowlark. Scaled Quail are widespread year round, while Vesper, Savannah, and rarely Grasshopper and Cassin's sparrows are present in winter.

Beyond the airport, a mile or so to the east, shortly past the railroad grade crossing, a gravel road turns southward. Along the first 2 miles, Burrowing Owls have nested regularly. In suitable grassy tracts farther on, Cassin's Sparrows sing on summer days, and Lesser Nighthawks trill in the very early morning and the evening. Swainson's Hawk, Lark Sparrow, and (among

Gila Woodpecker

scattered shrubs and yuccas) Bendire's Thrasher and Scott's Oriole also nest. Eventually a locked gate forces a return to the airport road. The entire area is privately owned, and birding should be confined to the roadsides.

Turn left and retrace the route back past the airport to the spur which branches west. It drops quickly to cross a bridge over a broad deep arroyo. A pair of Rock Wrens sometimes is found near the bridge, and flocks of sparrows feed in the weeds at the far end. Continue on this road, being wary of the few short stretches of sand, especially after a storm. (Always drive steadily through to firmer ground before slowing or stopping.) The shrub-covered hillsides, weedy grasslands, and dry washes with thickets of Apache-plume, oak, and hackberry are worth exploring in fall and winter for wrens, thrashers, towhees, and sparrows. Sometimes at that season a Phainopepla, Townsend's Solitaire, Mockingbird or Hermit Thrush may also be found, as well as wandering flocks of Western or Mountain bluebirds.

Several miles of hills, covered mostly with beargrass, usually yield few birds of interest except for Sage Sparrow, which sometimes winters here in numbers. Brushy thickets, cactus flats, and sandy washes with Emory's oak relieve the monotony after leaving the hills. Larger stands of oaks and some mine tailings on the right herald the approach to NM 90, 9 miles from the Ridge Road. From this junction, it is 10.4 miles north (right) to Silver City, and 35 miles southwest across the Burro Mountains to Lordsburg. The oak groves near this point are on Phelps-Dodge Corporation property, closed to the public, but from the roadway one may see Acorn Woodpecker, Gray-breasted Jay, Bewick's Wren, Bushtit, and possibly a Plain or Bridled titmouse. The roadside thickets and scattered oaks en route to Silver City harbor these resident species plus Ladder-backed Woodpecker, Gambel's Quail and, from spring through autumn, numerous other birds.

MANGAS SPRINGS

Along US 180, 18 miles northwest of Silver City, a line of cottonwoods and willows marks Mangas Creek, where permanent flowing water provides a small oasis in the mostly arid environment. For studying this area, look for an inconspicuous turnoff to the left at 4.5 miles from the Tyrone-Redrock road (between mileposts 96 and 95). This drops steeply to a small section of the old highway along the creek. Although the adjacent land is privately owned, the public right-of-way, below and parallel to the elevated new highway, provides good birding in all seasons. After descending from the main road there is a small marsh on the left, cut by a private gravel access road to several homes on the far side. Ample parking is available at this point, and the locals are used to birdwatchers on foot scanning the marsh. The cattails, shrubby willows and wet fields may contain such species as Canada Goose, White-faced Ibis, Common Snipe, yellowlegs, Solitary, Spotted and Pectoral sandpipers, Sora, American Pipit, and Yellow-headed Blackbird durlng migration seasons, and Song, Lincoln's and Swamp (the latter uncommon) sparrows in winter. Breeding birds include Killdeer, Sora, Virginia Rail, Common Yellowthroat, and Red-winged Blackbird. In the trees and thickets along the abandoned road one may find the following breeding species: American Kestrel, Red-tailed Hawk, Yellow-billed Cuckoo, Great Horned Owl and Western Screech-Owl, Northern (Red-shafted) Flicker, Ladder-backed Woodpecker, Cassin's and Western kingbirds, Bridled Titmouse, Bewick's Wren, Yellow and Lucy's warblers, Summer Tanager, Blue Grosbeak, Northern Cardinal, Canyon Towhee, Hooded, Scott's and Northern (Bullock's) orioles and Lesser Goldfinch. Zone-tailed Hawks and Common Black-Hawks, Elf Owl, Hairy and Acorn woodpeckers are only rare visitors from the Gila River 4 miles distant.

During spring and autumn, the Mangas area forms a "migrant trap" luring numbers of transients and vagrants; several rare species have appeared here. In winter, flocks of American Robins, bluebirds and Pinyon Jays frequently visit the creek for drinking and bathing as do Townsend's Solitaire, Ruby-crowned Kinglet, Yellow-rumped Warbler and numerous others.

GILA RIVER VALLEY

For most birders, southwestern New Mexico's prime sites lie in the Gila River Valley between Redrock and Mogollon Creek. If birding time is limited to one day in the vicinity of Silver City, it should be devoted to the Valley. Although much of the land is private, most owners readily grant birders permission to enter their property. A major portion of the Valley is owned by Pacific Western Land and Cattle Company and one should visit their office, about 1.5 miles north of Cliff on NM 293, and ask for a one-day permit if hiking away from the road is planned.

The several routes for Gila Valley birding involve driving northwest from Silver City on US 180. The first of these begins 25 miles from town where a black-top road, marked by a small sign to Bill Evans Lake, branches south (left). All the land adjacent to the road is privately owned to well beyond the lake, but many approaches to the river are unfenced, unposted, and widely used by picnickers and other visitors; the "off limits" areas are of limited importance for birds. The first few miles offer brushy thickets, cottonwood and willow bosques, dense riverine stands of seepwillow, and desert scrub with mesquite and cacti. Breeding birds include Red-tailed Hawk, American Kestrel, White-winged Dove (uncommon), Mourning Dove, Black-chinned Hummingbird, Acorn (now rare) and Ladder-backed woodpeckers, Cassin's and Western kingbirds, Black and Say's phoebes, Western Wood-Pewee, Vermilion (uncommon) and Ash-throated flycatchers, Rough-winged Swallow, Bridled Titmouse, White-breasted Nuthatch, Bewick's Wren, Lucy's and Yellow warblers, Yellow-breasted Chat, Summer Tanager, Northern Cardinal, Blue and Black-headed grosbeaks, Northern (Bullock's) and Hooded

Common Black-Hawk

orioles, House Finch and Lesser Goldfinch. Belted Kingfisher is a frequently seen transient. The Common Black-Hawk seldom nests here now due to reduced nesting sites and increased disturbance, but individuals breeding farther upstream still forage by the river or soar on rising thermals in late morning. Another visitor is the Zone-tailed Hawk, often flying along with the ubiquitous Turkey Vulture, Common Raven or Red-tailed Hawk. In side canyons and in nearby desert scrub are Plain Titmouse, Bushtit, Cactus, Rock and Canyon wrens, Phainopepla (local), Solitary Vireo, Black-throated Gray Warbler, Rufous-crowned Sparrow, and Scott's Oriole. (Gray Vireo is very rare.) The river often harbors Mallard (including "Mexican Duck" types) and Common Merganser with Killdeer and a few transient shorebirds as well as feeding herons -- Great Blue, with an occasional Green-backed (Green) Heron and Snowy Egret during migration.

At 3.5 miles from US 180 (pavement ends at 3.2), a short spur to the left leads to Bill Evans Lake, which usually has a variety of migrants and winter visitants. Pied-billed and Western grebes are regular, Eared Grebe now uncommon, while Horned Grebe is rare. Common Loons and most ducks on the New Mexico list have been seen here including the rare Surf Scoter. Neotropic (Olivaceous) and Double-crested cormorants and Ring-billed Gull are frequent visitors, while occasionally American White Pelican, Forster's Tern, and Wilson's Phalarope may appear. The Osprey is regular is spring and autumn; Bald Eagles, which winter along the river, sometimes fly over the lake, and Golden Eagle is possible at any season. A telescope is essential for optimal viewing here. The road to the boat-launching area on the back side of the lake gives access to typical upland birds.

Shortly south of the Bill Evans Lake turnoff, the river road (FR 809) enters a section of the Gila National Forest where scattered groves of sycamore, cottonwood, and other vegetation contain a high breeding bird density. Elf Owl and Western Screech-Owl, Brown-crested Flycatcher (rare, in sycamores), Bell's Vireo (in dense seepwillow stands), Bronzed Cowbird, plus most of the riverine woodland species mentioned above may be found here. Common Raven is the usual Corvus species of the Valley, but American Crows now reside here also and the Chihuahuan Raven is an uncommon visitor.

Another good route in the Gila Valley is along NM 211, which branches from US 180 to the right (northward) at 24 miles from Silver City. It crosses low rolling hills above the valley, then drops again to the village of Gila, 4 miles from US 180. Roadside birds in the breeding season include Gambel's Quail, Ladder-backed Woodpecker, Western and Cassin's kingbirds, Blue Grosbeak, Curve-billed Thrasher, Canyon Towhee, Black-throated Sparrow and Scott's Oriole. At Gila, turn left for 1 mile to the bridge across the river and park on the far side near a corral. One may follow a footpath upstream along the west bank for 0.3 mile to the end of the woods, then continue down from a channelization dike and along a fence bordering the west side of the trees.

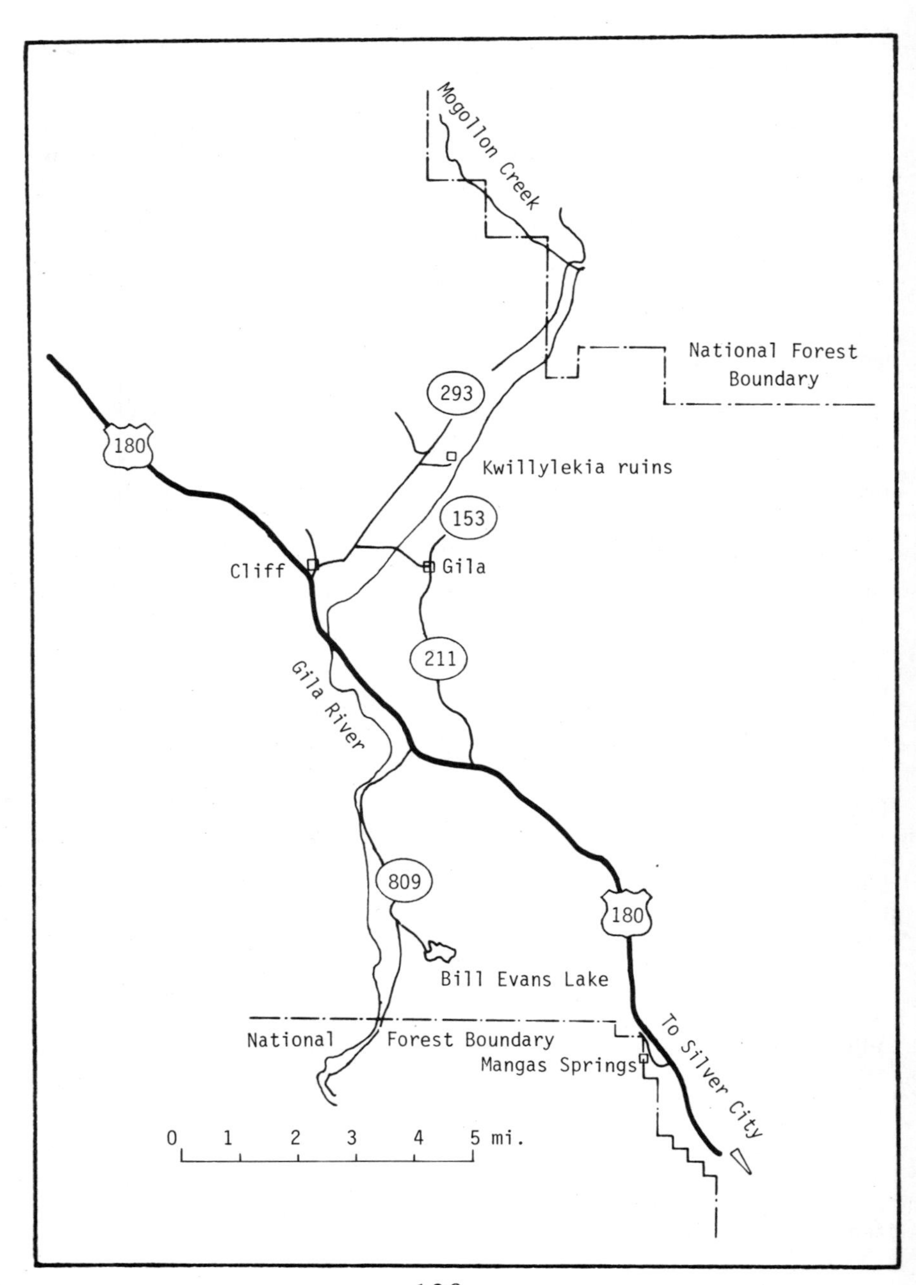
Mogollon Creek
National Forest
Boundary
293
180
Kwillylekia ruins
153
Cliff
Gila
211
Gila River
809
180
Bill Evans Lake
National
Forest Boundary
Mangas Springs
To Silver City
0 1 2 3 4 5 mi.

This will lead one back to the bridge. Many of the cottonwood bosque birds may be found here, and there are numerous vantage points overlooking the water.

From the bridge, continue on NM 211 toward Cliff, but at the junction with NM 293, turn right (north) away from the village and proceed up the valley. About 1.5 miles farther, a locked gate marks the entrance to Kwillylekia Ruins on the right. The ruins are closed, but one may park along the road and walk the lane to a stand of large cottonwoods and sycamores. If it is dry, one can cross an irrigation ditch and reach a dike, which follows the river for nearly 0.5 mile. This elevated path is ideal for seeing both the river bed and the trees on both sides. Be alert for Common Black-Hawks, which often nest in this section. They sometimes perch on stubs or low branches at the water's edge searching for prey.

Continuing north on NM 293, the blacktop turns to gravel, becoming Forest Road 755, and climbs gradually through dry hills, with Curve-billed Thrasher, Black-throated Sparrow, Scott's Oriole and other desert birds. After a bend to the right and another to the left, one drops steeply to normally dry Mogollon Creek. Here, under the magnificent sycamores, one may park and explore on foot the junction of the creek and the river. Although there is some posted private porperty to the left, beyond the creek bed, most of the land here is part of the Gila National Forest. Adjoining it to the south is the northern boundary of the Nature Conservancy's Riparian Habitat Preserve, which extends downstream for 2 miles.

While walking downstream along the river, watch for Common Merganser in the shallows and for Golden Eagle and Common Black-Hawk overhead. During migration, there may be unusual shorebirds, Green-backed Heron, White-faced Ibis, Merlin, or Peregrine Falcon. The sycamore-oak woodland is prime habitat for Elf Owl, Western Screech-Owl, Brown-crested Flycatcher, Bridled Titmouse, Gray-breasted Jay, Bewick's Wren, and Lucy's Warbler. Many of the riverine woodland birds listed earlier breed hereabouts, as well as Common Raven, a few American Crows, Yellow-billed Cuckoo and possibly Indigo Bunting. Watch for Willow Flycatcher, which formerly nested here, but has not been found in recent years. Also in summer, groups of Chihuahuan Ravens occasionally fly in to drink at the river. Rarely, the Gila Woodpecker is seen in the woods near Mogollon Creek, but it is disappearing from this part of the Gila Valley. A scarce New Mexico mammal, the Arizona Gray Squirrel, may be seen in the trees. (Rock Squirrels usually are atop scrubby oaks and among the boulders.)

FOREST ROAD 851 - BURRO MOUNTAINS

Forest Road 851, the "back road" to Redrock, passes through three distinct life zones. To reach it, take US 180 about 13 miles from Silver City where a left

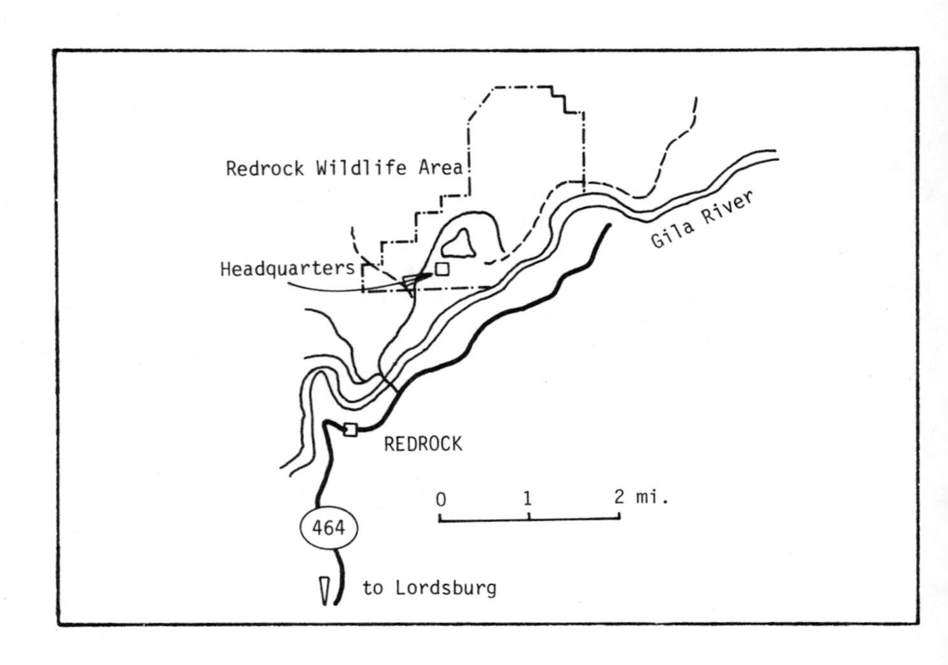
Redrock Wildlife Area
Headquarters
Gila River
REDROCK
0
1
2 mi.
464
to Lordsburg

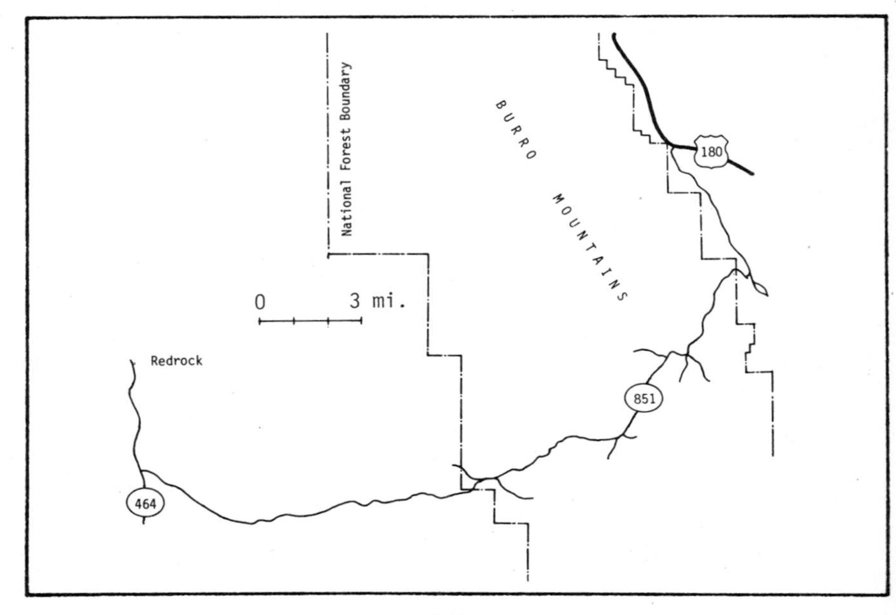
National Forest Boundary
BURRO
MOUNTAINS
180
0
3 mi.
Redrock
851
464

turn on Mangas Valley Road leads east toward the Phelps-Dodge Tyrone mine. After 4.8 miles, turn right on FR 851. From the junction it is 24 miles to NM 464 and 5 miles farther to Redrock. If traveling in a period of storms, check on surface conditions before leaving Silver City. This gravel road is regularly maintained, but portions may be difficult or impassable after heavy rain or snow. It crosses the Burro Mountains and follows sandy creek beds and canyon bottoms in places.

The first few miles of desert grassland support Ladder-backed Woodpecker, Cactus Wren, Curve-billed Thrasher, Black-throated and Lark sparrows, House Finch and, in winter, large flocks of Brewer's Sparrows. The road winds upward through chaparral and pinyon-juniper woodland where Scrub Jay is the most noticeable bird. Ash-throated Flycatcher and Black-throated Gray Warbler are present in summer while Plain Titmouse, Bewick's Wren and Rufous-sided Towhee are resident. The brushy canyonsides and dry streambeds are home to the shy Crissal Thrasher, most vocal and best seen in late winter and early spring. In oak stands, the Gray-breasted Jay and Bridled Titmouse may be found, and tall ponderosa pines have harbored breeding birds such as Northern Goshawk (rare), Zone-tailed Hawk, Wild Turkey, Acorn Woodpecker, Pygmy Nuthatch, Steller's Jay, Grace's Warbler, Solitary Vireo, and Hepatic Tanager.

Nine miles from the Mangas Valley, FR 851 joins a streambed and then climbs briefly up the side of a small canyon which falls away on the left. Where a cattleguard (the 3rd one) marks a narrow pull-off, there is a good vantage point for the terrain on both sides. Water often is found in this shaded spot long after other sources are gone, attracting wildlife from the surrounding area. In addition to species already listed, one may find Canyon and Rock wrens, Blue-gray Gnatcatcher and Rufous-crowned Sparrow, which nest nearby.

Brushy woodland and chaparral along the next few miles may produce Crissal Thrasher, Gray Vireo, and Black-chinned Sparrow, all difficult to find unless singing. Farther on, the lower slopes and foothills with clumps of beargrass, yuccas and scattered shrubs may produce Swainson's Hawk, Scott's Oriole, and Bendire's Thrasher. In autumn and winter, this area is good for Sage Thrasher and Brewer's and Sage sparrows. Golden Eagle, Prairie Falcon and Ferruginous Hawk all are more likely at this season, although the eagle and falcon are resident, as are the Red-tailed Hawk, Great Horned Owl, and Western Screech-Owl. Remember that this is rattlesnake country and the reptiles may be out even on sunny winter days.

At the Junction with NM 464 from Lordsburg, turn right toward Redrock. The mesquite- and acacia-lined streambeds along this paved road are the haunts of Greater Roadrunner, Crissal Thrasher, Cactus Wren, Verdin, Pyrrhuloxia, and other desert birds. Watch closely for Black-tailed

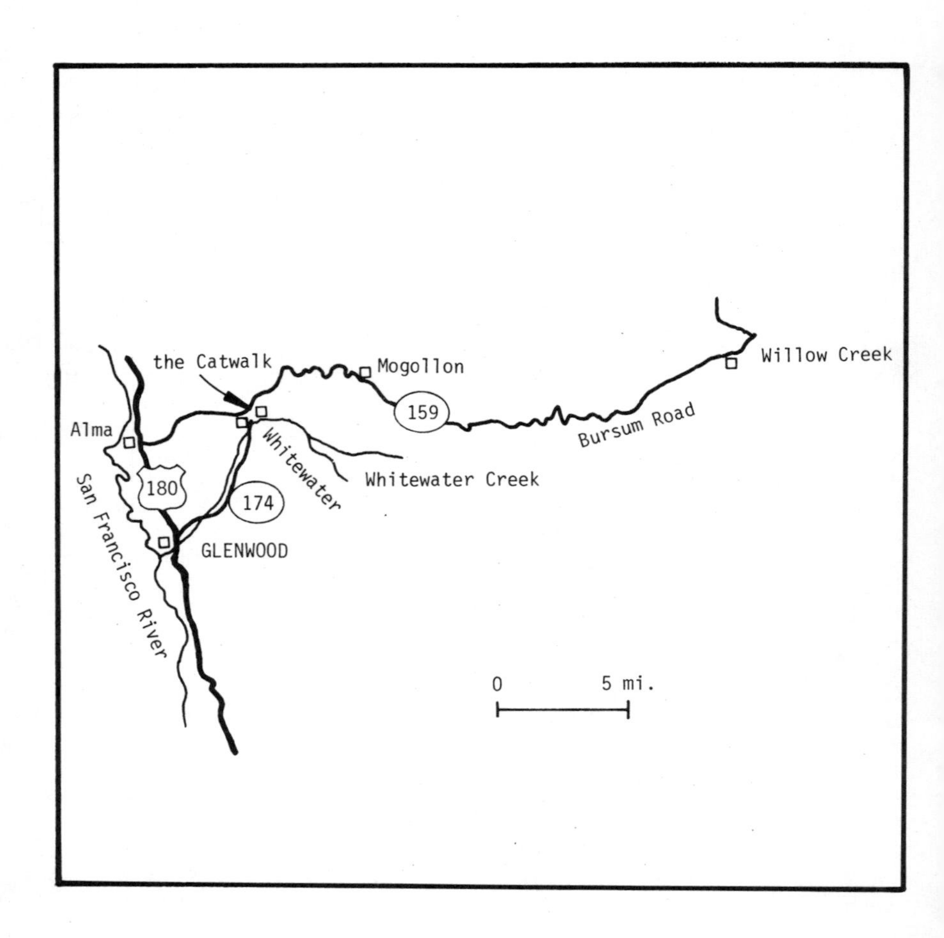
the Catwalk
Mogollon
Willow Creek
159
Bursum Road
Alma
Whitewater
Whitewater Creek
180
174
San Francisco River
GLENWOOD
0
5 mi.

Gnatcatcher, irregular here. (Blue-grays may be present during the non-breeding season.) Patches of desert-willow (*Chilopsis*), Fremont's cottonwood and Gooding's willow nearer the settlement of Redrock shelter additional species. Access to the river is limited, but one may find a few special species such as Bell's Vireo by going a mile or two up the road which turns off to the right on the east side, just above the main Gila River bridge. In late spring or summer the following are likely: White-winged Dove, Yellow-billed Cuckoo, Gila Woodpecker, Vermilion and Brown-crested flycatchers, Bewick's Wren, Lucy's and Yellow warblers, Abert's Towhee, Northern Cardinal, Blue Grosbeak, Hooded and Scott's orioles, and Lesser Goldfinch. Although rare, Common Black-Hawk and Zone-tailed Hawk sometimes are seen here. Also watch and listen for another rarity -- the Common Ground Dove. Great Horned Owl, Elf Owl and Western Screech-Owl all breed in the cottonwoods. In winter, flocks of American Robins and bluebirds are likely, and Yellow-rumped Warbler, Green-tailed Towhee, White-crowned, Chipping, Brewer's, Song and Lincoln's sparrows, and (rarely) Dusky Flycatcher are present.

Crossing the bridge, turn right, taking the dirt road 1.5 miles through desert shrubland to the New Mexico Game and Fish Department's "Wildlife Area." Drive in to the headquarters for permission to visit the marsh, in most years the best remaining place in the Gila Valley for ducks, shorebirds, herons and rails, and transient White-faced Ibis. If no one is home at the headquarters, one may still bird outside the fenced area. Dense thickets along the road are likely places for Crissal Thrasher and, sometimes, Pyrrhuloxia. In summer watch overhead for Common Black-Hawk, Cooper's, Swainson's, Zone-tailed, and Red-tailed hawks, Golden Eagle, and Prairie Falcon. A migrating Peregrine or Merlin is also possible. The road dead-ends in about two miles at a locked gate, forcing a return to Redrock, thence to Silver City or Lordsburg.

GLENWOOD

Another site for riparian birding is north of Cliff on US 180 near Glenwood, which serves as a base for hiking or horseback riding in the San Francisco River Valley. Like the Gila Valley, it contains excellent examples of the southwestern riparian ecosystem. In and near Glenwood itself, remnant cottonwood and sycamore trees attract a number of riverine woodland birds, including nesting Elf Owls. Access to the San Francisco River is gained by parking at the 2-story motel on the left (west) side of the highway and following Whitewater Creek about 0.5 mile to its confluence with the river. Common Black-Hawks are sometimes seen over the town, coming from their nest sites a few miles away, while Common Ravens and American Crows often feed together in nearby fields.

The best single place here is Whitewater Canyon, 5 miles from Glenwood. At the north edge of town, turn right (east) off US 180 where a sign indicates the "Catwalk," passing Los Olmos Lodge. Parking and day-use picnic facilities are

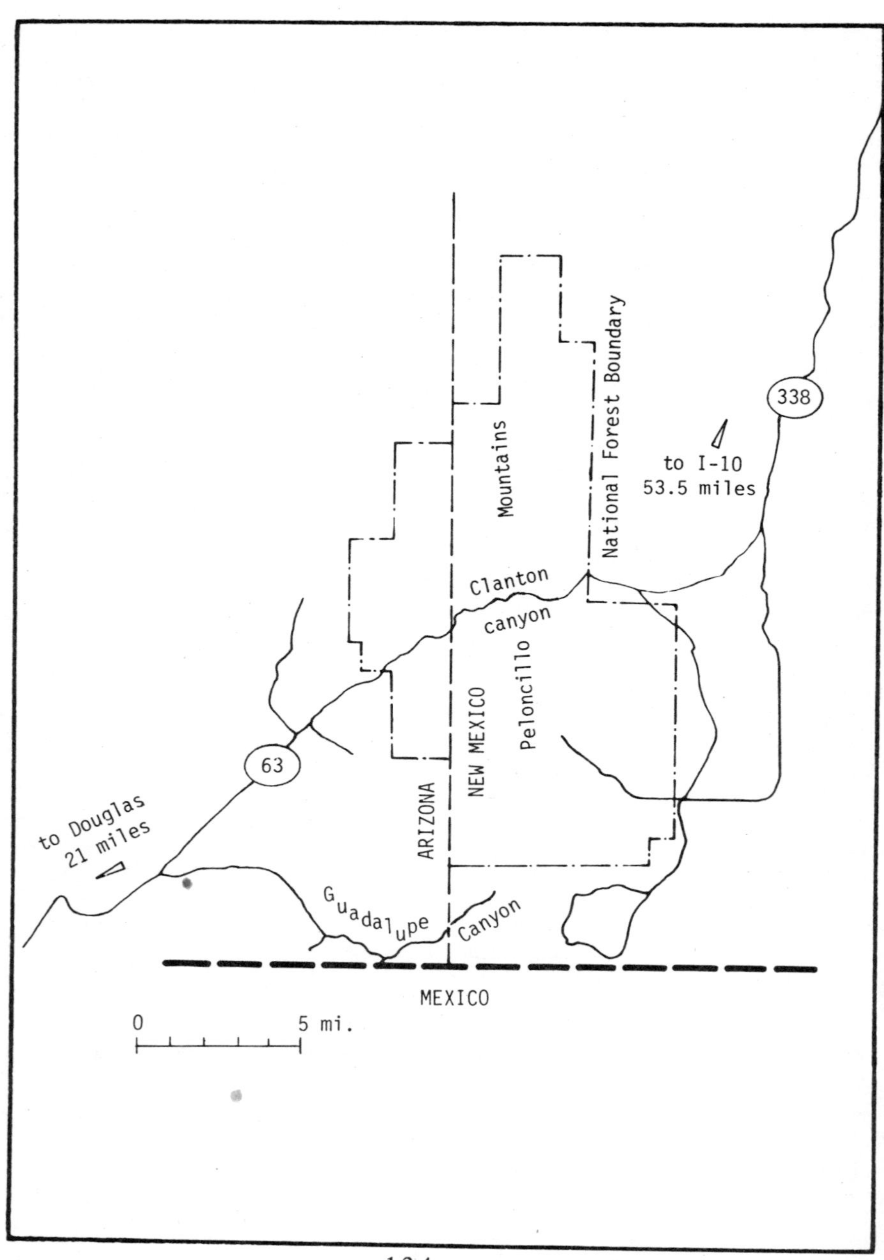
338
to I-10
53.5 miles
National Forest Boundary
Mountains
Clanton
canyon
Peloncillo
NEW MEXICO
ARIZONA
63
to Douglas
21 miles
Guadalupe
Canyon
MEXICO
0
5 mi.

available at the end of the road. The rushing stream along and under the catwalk is one of the few places in the region where one may expect to see the American Dipper. Other breeding species include White-throated Swift, Cordilleran Flycatcher, Violet-green Swallow, Black Phoebe, Canyon Wren, Solitary and Warbling vireos, Painted Redstart, Scott's, Hooded and Northern (Bullock's) orioles and Summer Tanagers. Bighorn Sheep are frequently seen here, as are Black-tailed Rattlesnakes.

Closer to Glenwood is a state fish hatchery, owned and operated by the New Mexico Department of Game and Fish. This is located on the Catwalk road, 0.25 mile from the highway. A pleasant picnic site in a grove of sycamores contains a table and rest rooms, and the nearby half-acre pond attracts various water birds year-round. In recent years, a small rookery of Great Blue Herons has become established, as well as a colony of Great-tailed Grackles. Also nesting here have been Common Black-Hawk, Ring-necked Pheasant, Common Yellowthroat, Yellow-breasted Chat, Blue and Black-headed grosbeaks, Northern Cardinal, and other riparian species.

MOGOLLON MOUNTAINS

Entering the Mogollons, 3.5 miles north of Glenwood, is NM 159, a steep, winding, often narrow mountain road requiring careful driving, especially in rain or snow. Near the erstwhile ghost town of Mogollon (9 miles from US 180), montane birding is decidedly worthwhile during summer. Noteworthy sites include Bursum Camp and Willow Creek Camp (10 and 17 miles, respectively, from Mogollon). Birding is often good along the highway itself as well as on the numerous hiking trails leading from it. In summer these offer a chance for Blue Grouse, Band-tailed Pigeon, Three-toed Woodpecker, Williamson's Sapsucker, Violet-green Swallow, Greater Pewee, Cordilleran and Olive-sided flycatchers, Ruby-crowned Kinglet, Red-breasted Nuthatch, Clark's Nutcracker, Olive, Red-faced, MacGillivray's, and Orange-crowned warblers, Green-tailed Towhee, Dark-eyed (Gray-headed) Junco, Red Crossbill, and other high-elevation species.

LUNA

The town of Luna, on US 180 about 40 miles north of Glenwood, is one of the few places in the Southwest Region where Lewis's Woodpecker is regularly seen. Near the south edge of town, in the vicinity of a prairie-dog colony on both sides of the road, they are likely to be noticed first on the adjacent power poles and fence posts, but they feed on the ground as well as in the pines. (Also breeding nearby are Vesper Sparrow and Mountain Bluebird, sometimes Yellow-headed Blackbird.) If the woodpecker cannot be located at Luna, look for it along NM 12 through Reserve. They are quite reliable along the road east of Apache Creek, about 12 miles beyond Reserve.

ANIMAS VALLEY-PELONCILLO MOUNTAINS-GUADALUPE CANYON

An overnight trip, perhaps better based from Lordsburg than from Silver City, takes one southward through the Animas Valley, across the Peloncillo Mountains to Guadalupe Canyon on the Arizona-New Mexico border. Ten miles west of Lordsburg, take NM 338 south from I-10. At the junction, just after exiting, there is a large playa which contains water briefly after rains. Cattle Egrets and several unusual shorebird species, including phalaropes and American Avocet, have appeared here. Along the road, Cassin's Sparrows may be heard singing locally in summer. Harris's Hawk (rare), Swainson's and Red-tailed hawks, Mourning Dove, Lesser Nighthawk, Greater Roadrunner, Western Kingbird, Northern Mockingbird, Bendire's Thrasher, Loggerhead Shrike, Pyrrhuloxia, Blue Grosbeak, Black-throated Sparrow and Scott's Oriole, are among the regular summer residents of the mesquite shrubland along this route. In winter, Ferruginous Hawk and Golden Eagle may be expected, and in some years, Rough-legged Hawk also. Sage Thrasher, and Brewer's and Sage sparrows likewise are present in winter, and Loggerhead Shrike may be fairly common then.

Most of the land along NM 338 is private, although little is fenced or posted. Aplomado Falcon, which used to inhabit this area, now is considered extirpated. The Animas Mountains to the east are home to White-eared Hummingbird (rare), Mexican Chickadee, and Yellow-eyed Junco. The Elegant Trogon also is known from the Animas, but its status is uncertain. The entire range is now owned by the Nature Conservancy, and future management and access is uncertain at this writing. A few of the Animas Mountain specialties may be seen in the Peloncillos but others must be sought in the more accessible ranges across the state line in Arizona.

Approximately 54 miles from I-10, turn right (west) on Forest Road 63 where a sign (not always intact) may indicate the way to Douglas and Clanton Canyon. This road crosses the Peloncillo Mountains and enters Arizona. Be sure to have adequate supplies of gasoline and water before leaving the village of Animas and check there on the condition of the road in the event of recent storm activity. Shortly after entering the National Forest, one may encounter Gray-breasted Jays in the open oak groves. Watch carefully for Strickland's (Arizona) Woodpecker, Hutton's Vireo, and, at night, Whiskered Screech-Owl. (Western Screech-Owl also inhabits the area.)

About 4 miles into the National Forest, a small picnic ground is evident immediately before the descent on the west side of the mountain. This is another place to seek Strickland's Woodpecker, and, in winter, Mexican Chickadee and Yellow-eyed Junco. From the picnic site it is 23.5 miles to Guadalupe Canyon. Only the upper end of the canyon is in New Mexico, thus within the scope of this publication, but habitat and birds are much the same on both sides of the state line. This boundary is about 3 miles from the entrance and is marked by a cattleguard and a small sign. Some 2 miles into the New Mexico portion of the canyon, topography and vegetation changes render it of little interest to birders. The road ends at a ranch house and to reach the upper section, one must proceed on foot or horseback.

The main part of Guadalupe Canyon, adjacent to the road, offers excellent birding with several Mexican specialties. The Buff-collared Nightjar sometimes is found here but is difficult to see. Western Screech-Owl, Common Nighthawk and Poorwill are the usual nocturnal birds. (Northern Mockingbirds, upon arrival from their winter quarters in Mexico, have been heard mimicking calls of the nightjar, so be wary of identifications based on voice only.) The rare Lucifer Hummingbird has nested in the Arizona portion of the canyon and should be looked for in New Mexico. Thick-billed Kingbird is uncommon but readily found among the many Cassin's and Westerns, and in mid-summer, the scarce Violet-crowned Hummingbird is present. Black-chinned and Broad-billed hummingbirds are common, while Costa's is rare and best sought in early spring. Other characteristic breeding birds are Brown-crested, Ash-throated, Dusky-capped and Vermilion flycatchers, Bridled Titmouse, Verdin, Crissal and Curve-billed thrashers, Bell's Vireo, Lucy's Warbler, Northern Cardinal, Blue Grosbeak, Hooded, Northern (Bullock's), and Scott's orioles. All are fairly easy to find. Northern Beardless Tyrannulet, Gray Vireo and Varied Bunting usually require more effort; these species often are found in the vicinity of the state line. The Common Black-Hawk has erroneously been attributed to Guadalupe Canyon in some bird-finding guides, but there are no records of the species there, where the habitat is entirely unsuitable. All reports pertain to Zone-tailed Hawk, a regular breeding species in the canyon.

Montezuma Quail

SOUTH CENTRAL

Warren Bloys, Nancy Dobbins, Bill Felten, Nancy Hutto
Bob and Kay Jenness, Catherine Sandell, Jerri Smith,
Jackie Talley, Kevin and Barry Zimmer

TRUTH OR CONSEQUENCES TO LAS CRUCES

Truth or Consequences, reached from nearby I-25, supports an abundance of motels, cafes, and gas stations, mostly along the business loop of I-25. Where this intersects NM 51, go east toward Elephant Butte Reservoir for 2.5 miles, turning left at the sign for the Hot Springs landing. When the road ends at a T-intersection at 2.0 miles, turn left and go 0.3 mile to Elephant Butte State Park. There, turn right and take the picnic grounds loop which provides several vantage points for viewing the lake.

Ring-billed Gull and Double-crested Cormorant are the most common birds, but depending on the season, there may be Western, Clark's, and Eared grebes, American White Pelican, Neotropic (Olivaceous) Cormorant, and various herons, egrets, and ducks. Fall and winter may bring rarities such as loons, and even an occasional scoter, Oldsquaw, or jaeger. A spotting scope is essential because the lake is large and viewing distances are great.

Return to NM 51, turn left, and drive 0.5 mile to another section of the state park. After 0.9 mile, turn left and go uphill to an overlook of the park. Rock Wrens abound, and Neotropic Cormorants are often seen below the dam. Follow a short loop back to the main park road, turn left at 0.7 mile at the end, and proceed 0.1 mile to the recreation area. Here there are more views of the lake, and the many junipers and cottonwoods attract numerous migrants in spring and fall.

Another large reservoir farther south may also prove productive. Take US 85 south from Truth or Consequences for about 16 miles, turning left at the sign for Caballo Dam. This road traverses the top of the dam and ends at 1.1 miles. The water below can best be checked with a telescope for Western and Clark's grebes, American White Pelican, Neotropic and Double-crested cormorants, herons, deep-water ducks, and gulls. Bald Eagles often are present in winter, and from October through February, Sandhill Cranes and flocks of geese (Canada, Snow, and Ross's, with an occasional Greater White-fronted) frequently pass overhead.

Below the dam is Caballo State Park, reached by a small road leading south from the top of the dam (0.3 mile from US 85 and just past the homes of the park managers). This small park lies along the Rio Grande and is heavily vegetated with tamarisk which may be swarming with migrant warblers in spring. Breeding birds include White-winged Dove, Yellow-billed Cuckoo,

Crissal Thrasher, Summer Tanager, Blue Grosbeak, Great-tailed Grackle, and Northern (Bullock's) Oriole. Coveys of Gambel's Quail are present throughout the year. In winter the river here is good for Hooded Mergansers and other ducks.

Return to US 85 and turn south (left); cross over the I-25 bridge, and turn left again after 1.1 miles at the sign to Percha Dam State Park. Go 0.4 mile and turn right, proceeding 0.8 mile to the park ($3.00 entry fee, self-paid; camping fee required).

This is a great spot in any season. If there is time for only one stop between Truth or Consequences and Las Cruces, make it here. The park contains a large remnant stand of cottonwoods, tamarisk, mesquite, and other woody species. It is one of the few samples of original habitat remaining along this section of the highly agricultural Rio Grande Valley. The river flows through the park, and there is a small dam at the north end of the camping area.

Neotropic Cormorants are occasional here but are more likely at Caballo and Elephant Butte dams where they are nearly as numerous as Double-cresteds. (Locating the cormorants is only half the battle; identifying them as to species can be a challenge, unless both species are together and readily compared. The Neotropic is a much smaller and slimmer bird than the Double-crested, but size is relative and at great distances is not reliable. During the breeding season, the Neotropic usually has a narrow white margin to the throat pouch, but the white border is inconspicuous for much of the year. One of the best marks is the shape of the posterior edge of the throat pouch. In the Double-crested, this presents in profile a semi-circular or rounded line extending from the eye to the throat. In the Neotropic, the pouch extends sharply back from the eye toward the rear of the face, then abruptly angles forward toward the throat. In flight, look for tail ratio differences; the Neotropic is very long-tailed, with almost half its length appearing to fall behind the trailing edge of the wing; the Double-crested's short tail appears to account for only a third of the bird's length, posterior to the wings.)

The long list of resident birds in the park includes Gambel's Quail, White-winged Dove (absent some winters), Barn Owl (in cottonwoods), Ladder-backed Woodpecker, Black Phoebe (near the dam), Verdin (in mesquite), Bewick's Wren, Crissal Thrasher, Phainopepla (sporadic), House Finch, and Lesser Goldfinch. These are joined in summer by Yellow-billed Cuckoo, Lesser Nighthawk, Black-chinned Hummingbird, Ash-throated Flycatcher, Western Kingbird, Lucy's Warbler (in mesquite), Summer Tanager, Black-headed and Blue grosbeaks, Great-tailed Grackle, and Northern Oriole.

Winter is an exciting time, especially in years when numbers of montane species move down to the valley. Hairy Woodpecker, Red-naped Sapsucker, Scrub Jay, Mountain Chickadee, Bridled Titmouse (sporadic), Brown Creeper,

Western Bluebird, Hermit Thrush, Ruby-crowned Kinglet, Yellow-rumped (Audubon's) Warbler, Fox (rare), Song, Lincoln's, White-throated and White-crowned sparrows, and Dark-eyed (Oregon and Gray-headed) Juncos are usually present. Steller's Jay has rarely wintered here.

Fall migration often brings rare vagrants to Percha. Eastern Phoebe, Eastern Bluebird, Winter Wren, Brown Thrasher, Black-and-White Warbler, and American Redstart usually put in annual appearances. Vermilion Flycatcher is casual, and such rarities as Northern Goshawk, Northern Parula, Pine Warbler, and Purple Finch have been recorded.

One may backtrack to the Caballo exit and take I-25 south toward Las Cruces. However, a more rewarding though longer route to the same destination is via US 85. This road crosses agricultural areas with plowed fields, pecan groves, salt-cedar (tamarisk) stands, and scattered cottonwoods. Raptors are common in winter, mostly Red-tailed Hawks and Northern Harriers, with a few Prairie Falcons and Ferruginous Hawks. The irrigated fields usually host shorebirds during spring and fall, while Greater Roadrunner, both ravens, and Great-tailed Grackle are here in any season. The Mexican race of the Mallard also is possible.

LAS CRUCES AREA

The city of Las Cruces (population 70,000) lies in the Rio Grande Valley some ten miles west of the imposing Organ Mountains. Local habitats include desert-grassland, pinyon pine-juniper slopes, oak-covered slopes and draws, pecan groves, brushy irrigation ditches, and tamarisk-cottonwood bosques (Spanish for "woods"). Motels, stores, service stations, and restaurants are abundant and diverse.

Perhaps the best nearby birding location is the "Old Refuge." In Las Cruces, take I-10 west to the Mesilla/NM 28 exit. Go south on NM 28 toward Mesilla for 1.0 mile and turn west (right) just beyond the Oñate Plaza on County Road 359. Drive 2.0 miles and pull off to the left immediately after crossing the Rio Grande (just before the road makes a big bend to the north). Park near the locked gate that blocks the levee road and walk south on the levee toward the salt-cedar bosque in the distance, scanning the river and its sandbars for ducks and waders. Cinnamon Teal are occasional from October through May, and Snowy Egrets are frequent visitors from spring to autumn. The Mexican race of the Mallard often is seen in the early morning hours. (Obvious hybrids are a common sight, but phenotypically characteristic diazi with pure green or yellow bills and dark brown body coloring also are frequently seen.) In winter, American (Water) Pipits and Savannah Sparrows are abundant along the river.

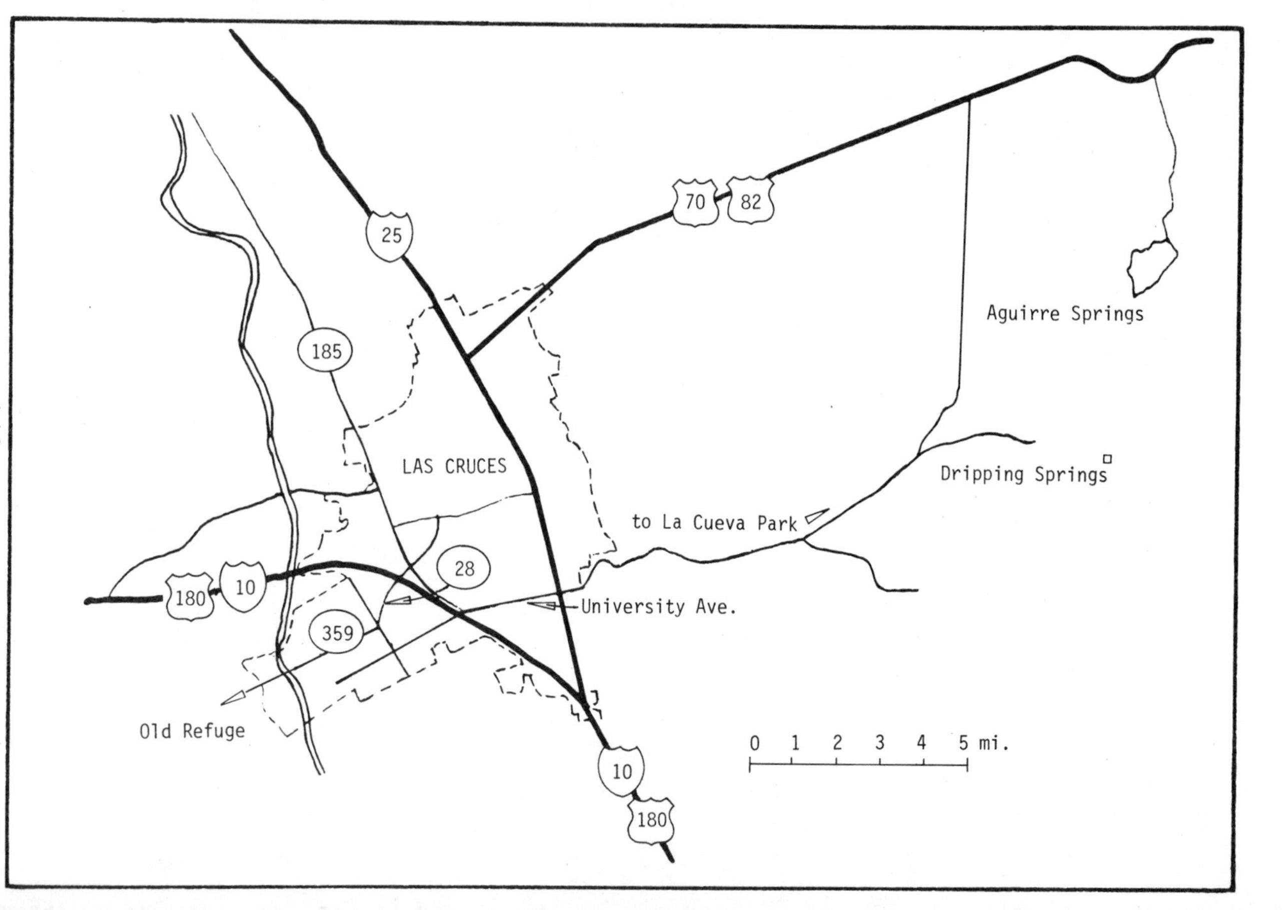
70
82
25
Aguirre Springs
185
LAS CRUCES
Dripping Springs
to La Cueva Park
28
180
10
University Ave.
359
Old Refuge
0 1 2 3 4 5 mi.
10
180

At one time a large cottonwood grove existed on the right, but most of these trees have died, the snags serving as perches for wintering raptors: Red-tailed and Ferruginous hawks, Prairie Falcon, and Merlin. In living trees, check for resident Phainopeplas which are often found near clusters of mistletoe which parasitizes the cottonwoods. The mistletoe berries also attract Western, and occasionally Eastern, bluebirds in winter.

Farther along, the levee bends to the right and intersects an old drainage ditch that runs north and south, paralleling the river. The dirt trail leading south along the right side of the ditch is especially productive in winter but may be good in any season. The ditch itself is choked with cattails where one may expect Marsh Wren in winter and Common Yellowthroat in summer. On open patches of water look for Common Moorhen (Common Gallinule) and Sora.

To the right of the trail is a large, mostly dry, cattail marsh with grassy swales and patches of tamarisk. This is a great place for wintering sparrows, including Lincoln's and Swamp (uncommon). Where patches of shrubby willows persist, listen and watch in summer for Willow Flycatcher. The vegetation at the south end of the refuge is mostly tamarisk with numerous cottonwoods and willows. Roosting Long-eared Owls (fall and winter) and resident Barn Owls often can be flushed from the thickets.

Other resident species likely anywhere along the trail include Gambel's Quail, White-winged Dove, Greater Roadrunner, Ladder-backed Woodpecker, Verdin, and Crissal Thrasher. These are joined in summer by Yellow-billed Cuckoo, Black-chinned Hummingbird, Western Kingbird, Yellow-breasted Chat, Summer Tanager, Blue Grosbeak, and Northern Oriole. Additional wintering species are Black Phoebe, Scrub Jay (some years), Hermit Thrush, Ruby-crowned Kinglet, Yellow-rumped Warbler, Pyrrhuloxia, and Dark-eyed Junco.

Upon leaving the Old Refuge, one may wish to recross the river and drive north on the east-side levee. The road is closed by a gate after 1.0 mile, but one may park and walk north for another 0.5 mile to the University bosque. This large stand of tamarisk and cottonwood is densely vegetated with a few trails running through it. Birding is usually less productive than at the Old Refuge, but summering cuckoos and tanagers may be easier to find.

A largely different set of birds inhabits Dripping Springs Natural Area (a fee area) and the west mesa below the Organ Mountains. Proceed east on University Avenue (marked by exits reading "New Mexico State University" on both I-10 and I-25). East of I-25, University Avenue becomes gravel-surfaced and winds up toward the mountains through creosote-bush desert. Numerous arroyos (gullies) filled with mesquite, Apache plume, little-leaf sumac, and acacias harbor many more birds than do the "flats." Resident species include Scaled Quail, Greater Roadrunner, Ladder-backed Woodpecker, Verdin, Cactus Wren, Crissal Thrasher, Black-tailed Gnatcatcher, Canyon (Brown) Towhee, and Black-throated Sparrow. In summer, also expect Poorwill, Lesser Nighthawk, Black-chinned Hummingbird, Ash-throated Flycatcher, Western Kingbird, and Scott's Oriole. Winter brings Pyrrhuloxias and large mixed flocks of sparrows, mostly Brewer's, Chipping, and White-crowned.

Follow the BLM signs to the A. B. Cox Visitors' Center and La Cueva Picnic Area. The road is paved for a short distance before again becoming gravel. Note a junction on the left where Baylor Pass Road turns north to US 70. Intersecting it are numerous arroyos suitable for any of the birds mentioned above. The windmill and water tanks a mile from the turnoff are especially attractive to birds.

To reach Dripping Springs Natural Area and La Cueva Picnic Area 2 miles beyond, continue on the main dirt road to the base of the mountains. The first half of this 6-mile trip from Las Cruces traverses desert-grasslands ornamented with an abundance of soap tree yucca, where Black-throated Sparrows are common throughout the year and Scott's Orioles are likely in spring and summer. As one climbs, Scaled Quail often can be seen in the early mornings calling from the tops of rocky outcrops which they share with Greater Roadrunner, Canyon Towhee, Rock Squirrel, Antelope Ground Squirrel, and Collared Lizard. Pyrrhuloxias and numerous sparrows also are present in winter.

The Cox Ranch Visitors' Center is at the very end on the road, where one can park and register after paying a fee of $3.00 per vehicle at the station. The naturalist on duty can answer questions about the trails and bird sightings. This is a Bureau of Land Management area, managed with the Nature Conservancy. The hours are: from 8 a.m. to 6 p.m., Friday through Monday, October through March; and from 8 a.m. to 8 p.m., April through September. The Visitors' Center is open Friday to Monday, from 9 to 5 year-round.

The best area for birds is the wooded ravine between La Cueva Picnic Area and La Cueva (a formation of red cliffs dominated by a cave). To reach this area, take the hiking trail to La Cueva which starts from the Visitors' Center or drive back down the entrance road to the first exit on the right; turn there, drive straight ahead, and park in the large lot on the right.

The best birding usually is along the lower reaches of Pine Tree Trail, marked by a sign at the lower end of the upper parking lot. This makes a 4.5-mile loop and requires about 4 to 5 hours to cover; it ends in the middle of the picnic area. An early start is important, especially in summer when temperatures may be over 80 degrees F. by 8 a.m., and a canteen is essential. Warm clothes that can be shed in layers are desirable in winter.

NEW MEXICO BIRD FINDING GUIDE, Revised Edition: Corrigenda

P. 103 Paragraph 1, first word: for "billed" substitute "tailed"
P. 144 Paragraph 4: for "Friday through Monday" substitute "daily"
Paragraph 6: disregard
P. 145 Paragraphs 2-5: disregard
P. 146 Paragraph 1: disregard
Following the first full paragraph, insert:

On the east side of the Organ Mountains is another great birding spot with a decided contrast in habitats from Dripping Springs Natural Area. Aguirre Springs and the Pine Tree National Recreational Trail are reached by traveling northeast on highway 70 from Las Cruces for 17 miles to the Aguirre Springs National Recreation Area turnoff. (Hours: from 8 a.m. to 6 p.m., daily, October through March; and from 8 a.m. to 8 p.m., April through September. There is a fee of $3 per vehicle.) Proceed right (south) on this access road, following BLM signs, 5.5 miles to the Aguirre Springs picnic area and campground. Just beyond the latter is a parking area for Pine Tree Trail, and hikers should allow a minimum of 4 hours to walk the 4.5-mile loop. The elevation rises from 5,700 feet at the trailhead to about 6,880 feet at the highest point. The route, which crosses several seasonal creeks, provides spectacular views of the granitic spires aptly named "Organ Needles" and "Rabbit Ears." An early start is advised in summer, when temperatures may be over 80 degrees F. by 8 a.m.; carrying a canteen is essential. In winter, warm clothes that can be shed in layers are useful.

The best birding usually is along the lower reaches of the Pine Tree Trail. The vegetation here is chaparral with mountain mahogany, Apache plume and scrub oak predominating, and junipers and Gambel's oaks scattered across the landscape.

Bird life along the lower part of the trail is similar to that in the campground except for increased numbers of Black-chinned Sparrows in the first half mile. (The species is most numerous from early April through the summer; many move to lower elevations for the winter.) Rock and Bewick's wrens, Canyon Towhee and Rufous-crowned Sparrow are common along most of the route, with Rufous-sided Towhees replacing Canyons as one climbs.

With heightened elevation, oaks and junipers increase and ponderosa pines appear, while cholla cactus, sotol and agave continue to give a desert flavor to this interesting montane community. In the pine belt, Broad-tailed Hummingbird, Western Wood-Pewee, Hepatic Tanager and Black-headed Grosbeak are common summer residents. In winter, Scrub Jay, Ruby-crowned Kinglet, Western Bluebird, and White-breasted Nuthatch are often seen. At any season, Acorn Woodpecker and Plain Titmouse may be encountered, sometimes with a Mountain Chickadee or two, and Canyon

Wrens are possible in the rock outcroppings along the trail. Golden Eagles are likely (some nest there) as are White-throated Swifts, Violet-green Swallows and Indigo Buntings in summer.

At the summit, the trail skirts pine forest with resident Hairy Woodpeckers. In summer a good place for Cordilleran (Western) Flycatcher, Solitary Vireo, and Grace's Warbler (uncommon) is in the vicinity of a primitive camp where a sign marks the half-way point on the trail. Most of the year, there are several small water-crossings along the upper reaches; near these streambeds -- especially the first one after the mid-point -- one should look for Virginia's Warbler, an uncommon summer resident. Steller's Jays, Cassin's Finches and other montane species visit the higher areas in some winters. Migration brings various warblers, including Townsend's and Black-throated Gray.

Resident birds include Gambel's Quail, Greater Roadrunner, Say's Phoebe, Verdin, Cactus, Bewick's and Canyon wrens, Crissal Thrasher, Phainopepla, Canyon Towhee, Black-throated and Rufous-crowned sparrows, and House Finch. These are supplemented in summer by White-winged Dove, Poorwill, White-throated Swift, Black-chinned Hummingbird, Ash-throated Flycatcher, Western Kingbird, Violet-green Swallow, Northern Mockingbird, and Scott's Oriole. (Gray Vireos sometimes have nested opposite La Cueva.) Winter brings Cooper's Hawk, Plain Titmouse, Ruby-crowned Kinglet, Western Bluebird, Hermit Thrush, Curve-billed Thrasher, Cedar Waxwing, Loggerhead Shrike, Yellow-rumped Warbler, Pyrrhuloxia, Rufous-sided and Green-tailed towhees, Dark-eyed Junco, Lark Bunting, numerous sparrows, and Lesser Goldfinch. In some winters the area is inundated with montane invaders including Steller's and Scrub jays, Mountain Chickadee, White-breasted and Red-breasted nuthatches, Western Bluebird, and Cassin's Finch.

The vegetation here is chaparral with mountain mahogany, Apache plume, and scrub oak predominating, and many junipers and Gambel's oaks are scattered across the landscape.

Bird life along the lower part of the trail is similar to that in the picnic area, except for the increased presence of Black-chinned Sparrow in the first half mile. The species is commonest from early April through the summer. (Many move to lower elevations during winter.) Bewick's Wrens, Canyon Towhees, and Rufous-crowned Sparrows are common along most of the trail.

With heightened elevation, oaks and junipers increase, and the first ponderosa pines appear. Meanwhile, cholla cactus, sotol, and agave continue to provide a desert flavor in this interesting montane community. In the pine belt, Broad-tailed Hummingbird, Western Wood-Pewee, Hepatic Tanager, and Black-headed Grosbeak are common summer residents, while Townsend's Solitaire, Western Bluebird, Brown Creeper, and White-breasted Nuthatch often are seen in winter. At any season, roving bands of Bushtits and Mountain Chickadees may be encountered, sometimes with a Plain Titmouse or two, and Canyon Wrens may be found in the rock outcroppings along the trail. Golden Eagles are likely (one of two pairs nest there), as are White-throated Swifts and Violet-green Swallows in summer.

At its highest point, the trail skirts true pine forest. Rufous-sided Towhees replace Canyons, and resident Hairy Woodpeckers appear. In summer, a good place for Cordilleran (Western) Flycatcher, Solitary Vireo, and Grace's Warbler (uncommon) is in the general vicinity of a primitive camp which marks the half-way point on the trail (marked by a sign). Most of the year, there are several small water crossings (often dry in mid-summer) along the upper reaches of the trail. Watch near these streambeds -- especially the first one after the mid-way point -- for Virginia's Warbler, an uncommon summer resident. Steller's Jays and Cassin's Finches visit the higher areas during some winters, along with other montane species. Migration brings numerous warblers, including Townsend's and Black-throated Gray.

Above the Visitors' Center, there is a 1.5-mile trail to Dripping Springs, deeper in the mountains and with more oak, juniper and hackberry. It is an easy two-to-three-hour round trip. Signs will remind one to stay on the trail, as this is a sensitive area with a unique flora. Birds to be expected at the higher elevations are Rock and Canyon wrens, Mountain Chickadee, Scrub Jay, Plain Titmouse, Rufous-sided Towhee, and Black-chinned Sparrow. Summer residents include Western Wood-Pewee, Cordilleran Flycatcher, Violet-green Swallow, Bewick's Wren, Hermit Thrush, Solitary Vireo, Hepatic Tanager, and Black-headed Grosbeak. In winter one may see White-breasted Nuthatch, Brown Creeper, Western Bluebird, Townsend's Solitaire, and large numbers of Chipping Sparrows and Dark-eyed Juncos. Golden Eagle and Prairie Falcon are possible year-round.

Please report any unusual birds to the naturalist at the A. B. Cox Visitors' Center. Unusual sightings at Caballo, Percha, or Leasburg dams should be reported to the Bureau of Reclamation, Rio Grande Project, 700 E. San Antonio Street, El Paso, Texas.

FORT STANTON - BONITA LAKE

At Lincoln, northwest of Roswell on US 380, check the historic old cemetery south of town in spring and summer for migrant and nesting flycatchers, vireos and warblers. Scrub, Pinyon and Steller's jays can be found year-round, along with Western and Mountain bluebirds and numerous raptors. From the Lincoln Courthouse on the north side of town, continue northwest on US 380 for 4.2 miles to the Salazar Canyon turnoff. The picnic area at the turnoff is worth checking; it adjoins the Rio Bonito (see note below). Salazar Canyon, several miles east on a dirt road, is also productive.

From the Salazar turnoff, follow US 380 again for 1.8 miles to a small well-house on the right side of the highway. Walking past the well-house toward the river, note the 10-acre "exclosure" on the left, where cattle have been fenced out by the BLM so that native grasses can return. In spring and summer this area should produce Red-naped Sapsucker, most swallows except Cave Swallow, Common Yellowthroat, Yellow-breasted Chat, plus hummingbirds, flycatchers, wrens, warblers and orioles.

From the exclosure, follow US 380 for 2.3 miles and take the Fort Stanton turnoff. Park near the bridge just before entering Fort Stanton and walk up- or down-river. Waterfowl, raptors, woodpeckers and jays are common year-round. Warm weather brings phoebes, flycatchers, Hermit Thrush, warblers and towhees. Montezuma Quail can sometimes be seen along the roads or in oak scrub near south-facing canyons.

Fort Stanton is State-owned, and permission should be obtained from the administrator for more extensive birding; however, the BLM campground several miles west of the fort is open to the public. The road is rough but serviceable, and birding is excellent at the campground and waterfall just up-river. American Dippers have been seen above the fall, usually in warm weather, and Virginia's and Grace's warblers breed here.

Return to US 380 and continue four miles to Capitan, checking the small park in town for goldfinches and other seedeaters. To explore Bonita Lake, take NM 48 southwest from Capitan toward Ruidoso and watch for the Lake signs. Before reaching the lake proper, walk up Philadelphia Canyon (identified by signs) for Acorn and other woodpeckers, jays, nuthatches (Red-breasted, White-breasted and Pygmy are all possible) and Red Crossbills. Most of these birds retreat to higher elevations in summer.

A large public campground beyond the lake attracts thousands of hummingbirds in the summer as campers provide many feeders. An occasional Magnificent Hummingbird appears among the Black-chinned, Broad-tailed and Rufous. Purple Martins nest in the older trees along the Rio Bonito. Other birds include woodpeckers, jays, chickadees, warblers and towhees.

NOTE: The spelling of Bonita-Bonito is confusing: it is Bonita Lake and Rio Bonito.

ALAMOGORDO

Birding in the parks and arid fringes of the city itself may prove rewarding to anyone without time for the following regional trips. Resident town birds include White-winged and Inca doves, Ladder-backed Woodpecker, Say's Phoebe, Great-tailed Grackle, House Finch and Lesser Goldfinch. Greater Roadrunner, Cactus Wren, Loggerhead Shrike, Canyon Towhee, Rufous-crowned and Black-throated sparrows are found in desert habitat at the edge of the city. In summer one should also see Western Kingbird, Violet-green Swallow, Scott's and Northern (Bullock's) orioles in the parks and residential areas. Cliff Swallows nest on the New Mexico State University (Alamogordo Branch) buildings while Black-chinned Sparrows breed in scrub near the campus. Additional migrants include Black-chinned, Broad-tailed (mostly spring) and Rufous (mid-to-late summer) hummingbirds as well as Hepatic, Summer and Western tanagers, warblers and other passerines. Yellow-rumped Warbler, Brewer's Blackbird and Dark-eyed Junco congregate in the parks in winter, Scrub Jays and flocks of Robins (plus an occasional Mountain Chickadee) descend from the mountains, and Northern Harriers patrol the open areas.

DOG CANYON

From Alamogordo drive south on US 54 (El Paso Road) for about 10 miles and turn left at the Oliver Lee State Park exit. In the three miles from there to the park (fee required) there are numerous side roads leading into the desert or one may also bird along the main route. Resident species in the area include Red-tailed Hawk, Greater Roadrunner, Verdin, Cactus, Rock and Bewick's wrens, Curve-billed and Crissal thrashers, Pyrrhuloxia, Canyon and Rufous-sided towhees, and Black-chinned and Rufous-crowned sparrows. Additional breeding birds are Swainson's Hawk, Western Kingbird, Northern Mockingbird, Blue Grosbeak, Eastern and Western meadowlarks and Black-chinned Hummingbird. In winter look for Green-tailed Towhee, Western Meadowlark and White-crowned Sparrow. In Dog Canyon, which is within the park, the stream and riparian vegetation support additional species such as Northern Flicker, Ladder-backed Woodpecker and summering Black-chinned Hummingbird, Violet-green Swallow, Blue-gray Gnatcatcher, and Scott's and Northern orioles. Along the canyon walls be alert for Golden Eagle; also expect Canyon Wren year-round and White-throated Swifts in the breeding season.

HOLLOMAN LAKES

Take US 70 southwest from Alamogordo about 11 miles and exit to the right (north) 0.6 mile past mile marker 204 to enter the BLM Holloman Lakes Wildlife Refuge, a series of effluent ponds attractive to many shorebirds and waterfowl, especially during migration. Over 30 species have been recorded here, but fluctuating water levels greatly affect the numbers of birds. When full, the ponds may harbor Pied-billed and Eared grebes, Great Blue Heron, Black-necked Stilt, American Avocet, large flocks of Wilson's Phalarope, as well as many species of sandpipers and Red-winged and Yellow-headed blackbirds in migration. Wintering waterfowl include large numbers of Mallard, Northern Shoveler, Gadwall and Ruddy Duck and less numerous Cinnamon Teal, Lesser Scaup and Bufflehead. American Pipit and Marsh Wren are found around the pond edges in winter; Barn and Great Horned owls have been seen in the fringing tamarisks.

HIGH ROLLS

Drive north on US 70/54/82 to the junction where 82 branches east, and take the latter for 9 miles to High Rolls (6,750 feet). Park at the east side of the High Rolls Country Store, on the left side of the highway, and walk a short distance north along the road beside the parking area. The orchards and pinyon-juniper woodland offer a variety of birds including Phainopepla and Black-throated Gray Warbler in summer. The fruiting cherry orchards attract large flocks of Band-tailed Pigeons in season. Return to the highway, cross to Westside Road (marked by a sign), descend the slope to the bridge and walk along Fresnel Creek. In summer, one may expect Western Wood-Pewee, Ash-throated Flycatcher, Western and Hepatic tanagers, and Black-headed and Evening grosbeaks. Resident are Scrub Jay, Mountain Chickadee, Plain Titmouse and White-breasted Nuthatch.

Continuing along US 82 for about 0.5 mile, turn right on A-62 (FS-63) to Karr Canyon Picnic Grounds, 4 miles distant. In May, breeding Red-faced Warblers (a small isolated population) are often seen near the water and in the mixed conifer forest on steep canyon sides within 0.25 to 0.5 mile of the picnic site. Yellow-rumped, Black-throated Gray and Grace's warblers also breed in the area and Orange-crowned, Yellow and Wilson's warblers are present in migration. Other summering species include Cordilleran Flycatcher, Western Wood-Pewee, Ruby-crowned Kinglet and Western Tanager, while Mountain Chickadee is resident. This area is closed in winter.

Return to US 82 and continue about 0.75 mile up the mountain to A-67, a paved road on the right (south) leading to Haynes Canyon. On the left side is an orchard which may have nesting Warbling Vireo; on the right is a row of elms attractive to American Goldfinch and Pine Siskin in spring and Lesser Goldfinch in summer. Yellow-breasted Chat breeds in the thickets along Fresnel Creek, which crosses under the road.

HORNBUCKLE HILL - TIMBERON

Proceed north from Alamogordo on US 54/70/82 for 2 miles, taking 82 east through High Rolls to Cloudcroft. In 16 miles one climbs over 4,000 feet, from desert to mixed conifer forest. Area roads are usually good but may be hazardous after heavy rain or snow. At the edge of Cloudcroft, turn right (south) on NM 130 for 2 miles and then make another right on a good, paved, unnumbered road with a sign indicating "To Sunspot." Numerous pullouts allow the visitor access to the forest, at an average elevation of 8,600 feet. After 15 miles, look for route 537 to Timberon; this dirt road turns off to the left. Six miles farther, turn right on FR 90 or C-3. Approximately a mile ahead, at the top of Hornbuckle Hill, is a splendid overlook where one may see Wild Turkey, White-throated Swift, nuthatches, and Mountain Chickadee. Continuing down the steep hill for 2.5 miles, park near a large water tank and walk into the pinyon-juniper woodland (7,600 feet). Several species of swallows, Western and Cassin's kingbirds, Bushtit, Solitary Vireo, Black-throated Gray Warbler and Western Tanager are to be expected in summer. Wild Turkey is possible in early morning year-round, and in spring and summer, Band-tailed Pigeon, Say's Phoebe, Scrub Jay and Rufous-sided Towhee are common. In early fall, migrant Wilson's, Townsend's, MacGillivray's and Yellow-rumped warblers are likely. About 2.5 miles farther along this road on the right is a second tank. Species here in spring and summer include Hairy, Downy and Acorn woodpeckers, Black-headed and Evening grosbeaks, with a chance for Red-naped Sapsucker, Western and

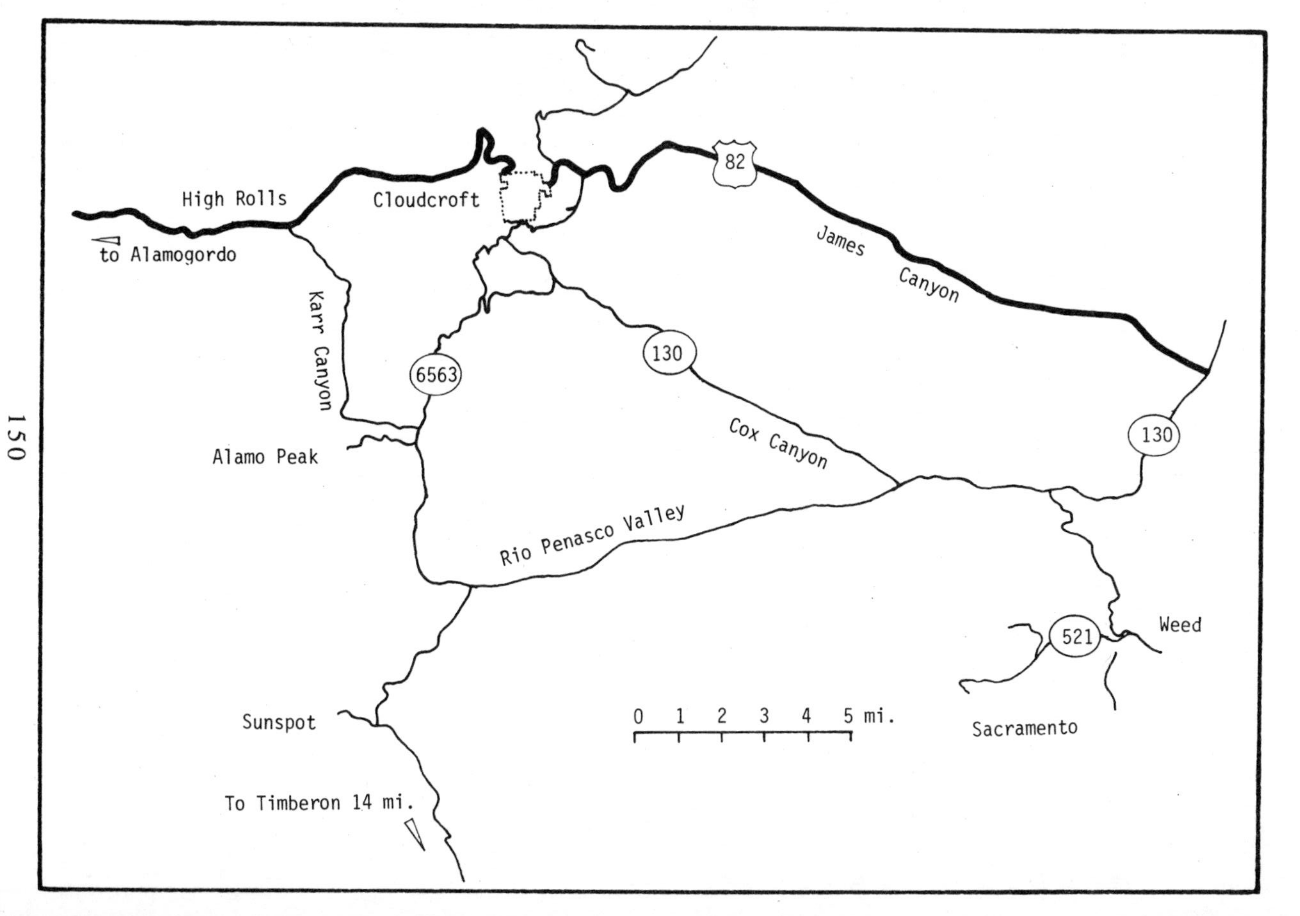
High Rolls
Cloudcroft
82
to Alamogordo
James Canyon
Karr Canyon
6563
130
Cox Canyon
130
Alamo Peak
Rio Penasco Valley
521
Weed
Sunspot
0 1 2 3 4 5 mi.
Sacramento
To Timberon 14 mi.

(sometimes) Mountain bluebirds, Cassin's Finch and Red Crossbill. Allow about 7 hours for the round trip from Alamogordo. The route is not recommended in winter or wet weather when the road may be impassable

To visit Timberon, which has many of the same species as the Hornbuckle Hill route, stay on 537 instead of turning off on FR 90, continuing another 8 miles to the town. Since most of the land in this area is privately owned, one must be content to observe from the roadsides.

COX CANYON - PEÑASCO VALLEY

This is a loop through mixed conifer forest from 7,000-9,000 feet with many of the typical species of the habitat. However, a marsh and meadows along the route provide greater diversity. From the west side of Cloudcroft, take NM 130 south for 13 miles through Cox Canyon, watching for Wild Turkey at meadow edges, Cassin's Kingbird, Violet-green Swallow and Western Bluebird on wires and fences. Steller's Jay, Mountain Chickadee and Pygmy Nuthatch reside in the adjacent forest. Leave the blacktop and turn right (southwest) on FR 164 (C-17). This is not advised for winter travel and for the next 10 miles the land is mostly private, so birding must be confined to roadside viewing. A marsh near the turnoff of C-17 may have Sora and Virginia rails and other wetland species. Continue west through the Rio Peñasco Valley (avoiding the road to Wills Canyon); a small stream on the left borders lush mountain meadows below heavily timbered slopes. Mountain and Western bluebirds and Violet-green Swallows are widespread as are Steller's Jays and Green-tailed Towhees. MacGillivray's and Wilson's warblers may be found in the meadows and in brushy wooded areas are Bushtit, Olive-sided Flycatcher and Western Wood-Pewee. Other summer residents are Band-tailed Pigeon, House Wren, Western Tanager, Chipping Sparrow, Dark-eyed Junco and Pine Siskin. Red-tailed, Cooper's and Sharp-shinned hawks also may be seen. At the 26-mile mark, C-17 rejoins paved FR 64 between Sunspot (left) and Cloudcroft (right). This loop makes a good 3-to 4-hour birding trip.

LA LUZ CANYON - WOFFORD LOOKOUT

To reach La Luz, drive north from Alamogordo 2 miles on highway 54/70/82 to NM 545, turn right and proceed through the village to a three-way stop. Mileages given below are from La Luz Plaza, on the left at this intersection. Go north from the plaza, follow the paved road across a bridge and to the northeast on highway A-59 along La Luz Creek. From 0.8 to 2.8 miles, there are several stopping points between road and creek. Typical species in season are Red-tailed Hawk, Gambel's Quail, Greater Roadrunner, Bewick's Wren, Black-headed Grosbeak, and Black-throated Sparrow. At mile 4.9 bear right on A-70 (gravel) and continue along the creek. Across the first cattle guard (mile 5.6) is a convenient place to stop for Gambel's and Scaled quail, Ash-throated Flycatcher (summer), Scrub Jay, Verdin, Curve-billed Thrasher, and Pyrrhuloxia. At mile 8.6, where A-70 turns right, continue straight on FR 168 and pause at mile 9.0 at a small turnout on the right to seek Indigo Bunting in the spring, Townsend's Solitaire in winter. At mile 9.3 a small roadway to the right leads to a swampy area; birds often seen here in summer include Scrub Jay, Crissal and Curve-billed thrashers, Red-winged Blackbird, Common Yellowthroat, Yellow-breasted Chat, plus other warblers and Chipping Sparrow in spring. A large cherry orchard on the right (miles 10.5-11.0) attracts large numbers of Band-tailed Pigeons feeding on the ripening fruit in season.

At about mile 11.0, the road becomes FR 162 as it enters Lincoln National Forest. The grade rises steeply and, in wet or snowy conditions, can be traveled only by 4-wheel-drive vehicles, becoming impassable at times. The forest here changes from pinyon-juniper to ponderosa pine-Gambel's oak and Douglas-fir with patches of aspen. Wild Turkey is recorded here on Christmas counts, while Mountain Chickadee, Plain Titmouse, Bushtit, Steller's Jay, and White-breasted and Red-breasted nuthatches may be present at any season. An area of little underbrush on the south side of the road near mile 15 is a good site for migrant passerines. Turn left at mile 16 on a steep winding road to Wofford Lookout (mile 18.4). Birding can be rewarding on the 10 acres of forest (mostly ponderosa pine and Douglas-fir) around the fenced tower. Hermit Thrush, Green-tailed Towhee, and various warblers are likely during migration; Broad-tailed Hummingbird breeds and Hairy Woodpecker, Steller's Jay, Mountain Chickadee, nuthatches and Dark-eyed Junco are resident. The round-trip from Alamogordo requires about 5 hours.

LOOP WEST OF TULAROSA

A shorter (one to two hours) trip on all-weather roads in mixed desert scrub/irrigated fields/pecan orchards may be taken any time of year, but there is generally no access to this private land away from the roadside. Although one may wander along any of the roads, a suggested route is as follows. Leave highway 54/70 in Tularosa, turning west on Higuera Street at the Tastee Freeze restaurant. Proceed 0.5 mile to an old cotton gin, turn right (north) for one block, then left (west) on West First Street, cross a railroad track, turn right (north) one block, then left (west) on County Road B-6. At 2.5 miles turn left (south) on CR B-5 which becomes Pecos Road after about 3 miles. When it intersects La Luz Avenue, one may turn north and return to the cotton gin. Swainson's Hawk summers here and Harris's Hawk is known to nest in the area. Burrowing Owl (along dikes and on fence posts), Greater Roadrunner, Crissal Thrasher, and Pyrrhuloxia are resident species of interest. Autumn brings thousands of Brewer's and Red-winged blackbirds to the milo fields, Scrub Jays to the pecan orchards, and large flocks of Turkey Vultures prior to their migration in late September. In spring and fall, Lark Buntings and Yellow-headed Blackbirds pass through, and when irrigation is in progress, the fields may attract Cattle Egret, White-faced Ibis, and Long-billed Curlew. Winter raptors include Northern Harrier, Golden Eagle, Ferruginous Hawk and Prairie Falcon; American Pipits and large flocks of White-crowned Sparrows and Dark-eyed Juncos also may be found at that season.

Long-billed Curlew

Lesser Prairie-Chicken

SOUTHEAST

Sherry Bixler, David Cleary, William Howe,
Dustin Huntington, Steve West

EDDY COUNTY

Eddy is one of the most varied of New Mexico's 33 counties, with riparian floodplains, grassland-shinnery oak stands (primarily east of the Pecos River and in the Hope area), suburban/urban areas, limestone and gypsum foothills (mainly west of the Pecos River), and the Guadalupe Mountains. This habitat variety, an elevation range from 2,925 feet (the lowest point in New Mexico) to 7,775 feet in the Guadalupe, its location in eastern New Mexico, and a history of bird observations dating from 1855 combine to explain the county's list of over 370 species.

Centrally located is Carlsbad, the county seat and largest community, which provides a good starting point for visiting many sections of the county. The best birding areas in Carlsbad itself are along the Pecos River (especially at Lake Carlsbad), in the older sections of town (the center around the Carlsbad Municipal Library), and along the north edge in the area called La Huerta. Three miles north of Carlsbad, the Living Desert Museum provides exhibits of desert animals and cacti and is an excellent place for birding; the slopes east of the exhibits support kingbirds, wrens, thrashers, Blue Grosbeak, towhees, and sparrows. Call 887-5516 for hours.

Lake Carlsbad is good for concentrations of blackbirds, especially Yellow-headed Blackbirds (thousands are sometimes present in September), and Great-tailed Grackles. The winter population at Lake Carlsbad occasionally numbers 500 individuals. Local specialties in central Carlsbad include White-winged Dove, Chimney Swift (usually in small numbers from May through late July), and Blue Jay (also in La Huerta). La Huerta is reached by driving north along Canal Street across the Pecos River. This residential area has an abundance of trees and fruiting shrubs and is particularly good in winter. During irruption years, large numbers of corvids (Scrub, Steller's and Blue jays and Clark's Nutcracker) may be found, along with Northern (Yellow-shafted) Flicker and several species of finch.

BRANTLEY LAKE

The 1990 completion of Brantley Dam, approximately 15 miles north of Carlsbad, created a new lake on the Pecos River, with a surface area varying from 300 to 3,000 acres, depending on amounts of water stored. Birding data on this area have yet to be accumulated, but many of the birds previously found at Lake McMillan (now a dry lake bed most of the year) will be found at Brantley. Large flocks of White Pelicans use the lake along with waterfowl,

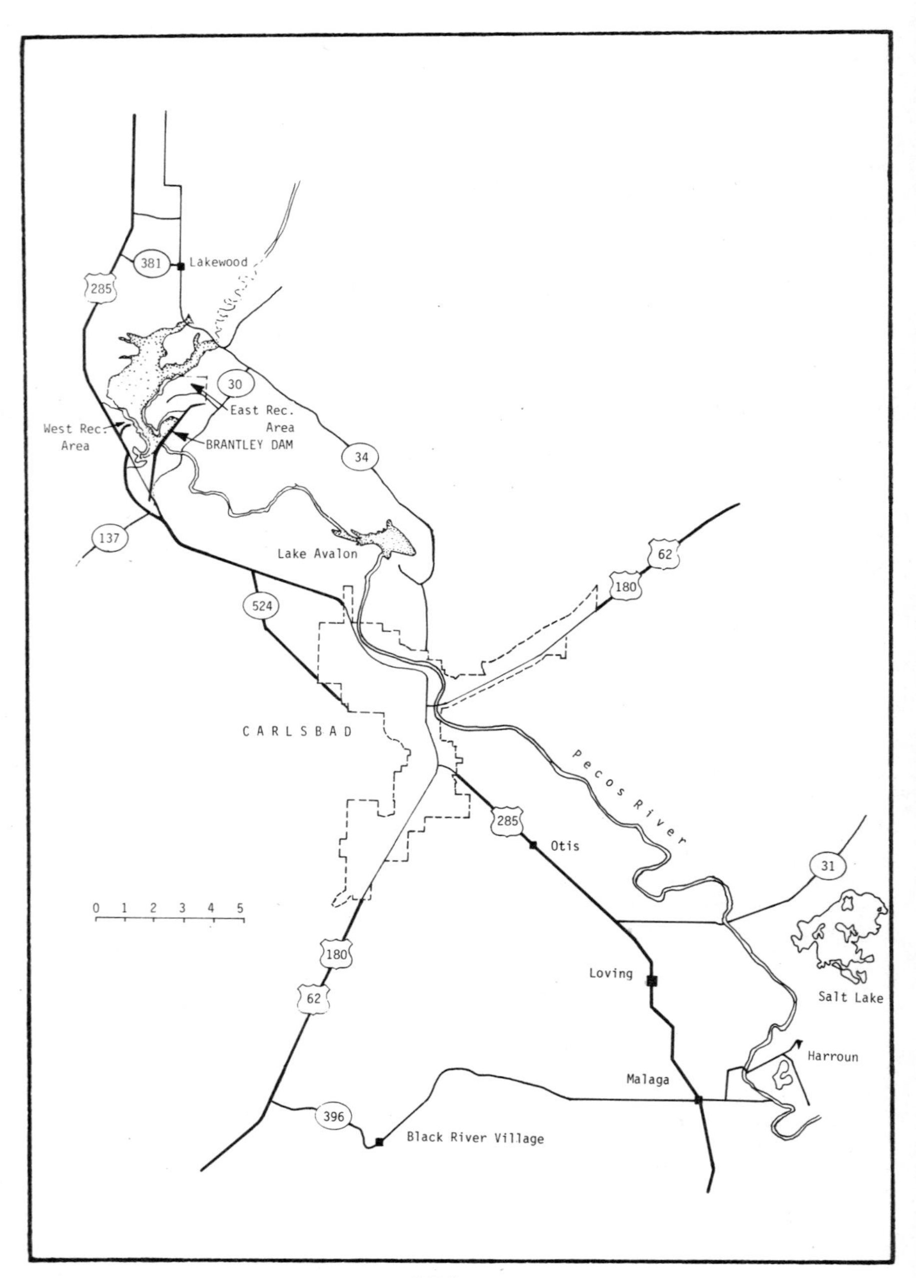
381
Lakewood
285
30
East Rec.
Area
West Rec.
Area
BRANTLEY DAM
34
137
Lake Avalon
62
180
524
CARLSBAD
Pecos River
285
Otis
31
0 1 2 3 4 5
180
62
Loving
Salt Lake
Harroun
Malaga
396
Black River Village

shorebirds, gulls and terns. Common Loons are almost always present in winter. The best birding at present seems to be along the northwest shore. Brantley State Park has picnic and campground facilities; there is a day-use fee. For more information, call the Park office at 505-457-2384.

It is hoped that Brantley Lake will prove as attractive to rarities as erstwhile Lake McMillan. These have included Oldsquaw, White-winged Scoter, Lesser Golden Plover, Whimbrel, Red Phalarope, Pomarine and Parasitic jaegers, Laughing, California and Sabine's gulls, Black-legged Kittiwake and Caspian Tern. Though smaller, Lake Avalon, north of the La Huerta area of Carlsbad, also attracts most of the birds found in this area.

PECOS VALLEY

The extensive salt-cedar growth along the Pecos River north of Brantley Lake lures large numbers of migrants in spring and fall and supports breeding populations of Yellow-billed Cuckoo, Crissal Thrasher, Yellow-breasted Chat, Blue Grosbeak, Indigo and Painted buntings, and Rufous-sided Towhee. Cassin's Sparrow is common in the adjacent grasslands.

To reach suitable sites, drive north from Brantley Lake's north entrance approximately seven miles on US 285 to its intersection with County Road 381. Turn right to Lakewood and then north 3.5 miles, watching for Burrowing Owl and Pyrrhuloxia on the way. Turn right north of the second right-angle bend in the road which changes from blacktop to dirt after a few hundred feet and continues through the salt-cedar to the Pecos River. Various paths and old river channels lead from this road and all are worth exploring, though less so in winter.

HARROUN LAKE

From Carlsbad, a productive one-day trip is to the areas east and south of town. Loving is 10 miles southeast of Carlsbad on US 285; from there, Harroun Lake can be reached by driving 5 miles south to Malaga, then east for about 4 miles. This lake attracts many of the species found at Brantley Lake but is more isolated and the birds less disturbed. A gravel road encircles the lake, but caution is advised, as some sections are often washed out. Rattlesnakes are also found here. Dickcissels are occasionally seen in the farming areas around Loving-Malaga, Cassin's Sparrows are common in grassland-mesquite areas, and Harris's Hawks are also likely.

LAGUNA GRANDE

The series of salt lakes known as Laguna Grande is 5 miles northeast of Loving on NM 128. They attract large numbers of migrating shorebirds, and during summer they support a large rookery of Black-crowned Night-Herons,

Harris's Hawk

Snowy and Cattle egrets, and usually at least one pair of Little Blue Herons. (Tricolored Heron nested here in 1981.) The best vantage point to observe the herons as they fly to and from their nests is by parking along the highway, 2 miles east of the junction with NM 31. All species that inhabit the rookery fly over this point. DO NOT ENTER THE ROOKERY UNDER ANY CIRCUMSTANCES, as disturbance can easily result in bird mortality. Banding visits are carefully controlled and monitored to minimize disturbance of this rare site.

All lakes in the area attract birds year-round, including wintering ducks. The best spot for shorebirds is at the first lake, about 1.5 miles from the junction of NM 31 and 128, where the low waters lap at the edges of the highway. Black-necked Stilts, American Avocets and Snowy Plovers also breed here, but again PLEASE do not enter the nesting area.

CARLSBAD CAVERNS

About 20 miles south of Carlsbad on US 180/62 is Whites City and the entrance to Carlsbad Caverns National Park. Proceed west along NM 7 for 7 miles to the Visitor Center and entrance to Carlsbad Caverns. Cave Swallows are abundant at the cave entrance except in winter. Also in the area are Canyon and Rock wrens, Varied Bunting (local), and Black-throated, Rufous-crowned and Black-chinned sparrows. The same species are present along the approach to the caverns as the road winds through Walnut Canyon.

Varied Buntings may be found all along the bottom of the canyon, with probably the best areas for this rare species being upper Walnut Canyon (reached along the loop road which starts just west of the Visitor Center) and at the base of the hill which one must ascend in order to reach the Visitor Center. Watch for the occasional Golden Eagle and, most winters, an abundance of Sage Thrashers. Green-tailed, Rufous-sided and Canyon (Brown) towhees are present in fall, winter and spring.

A bird list for Carlsbad Caverns National Park can be obtained by writing to the Park Naturalist, Drawer T, Carlsbad Caverns National Park, Carlsbad, New Mexico 88220, or from the Park office.

BLACK RIVER VILLAGE

Three miles north of Whites City, County Road 396, which leads to Black River Village 4 miles distant, is worth investigating, especially in spring and early summer when local fields are flooded. Observing from the road may be very productive, with herons, egrets, and many species of waterfowl and shorebirds including Common Snipe and American (Water) Pipit wherever standing water occurs. Migrants are also found here along with most of the blackbirds.

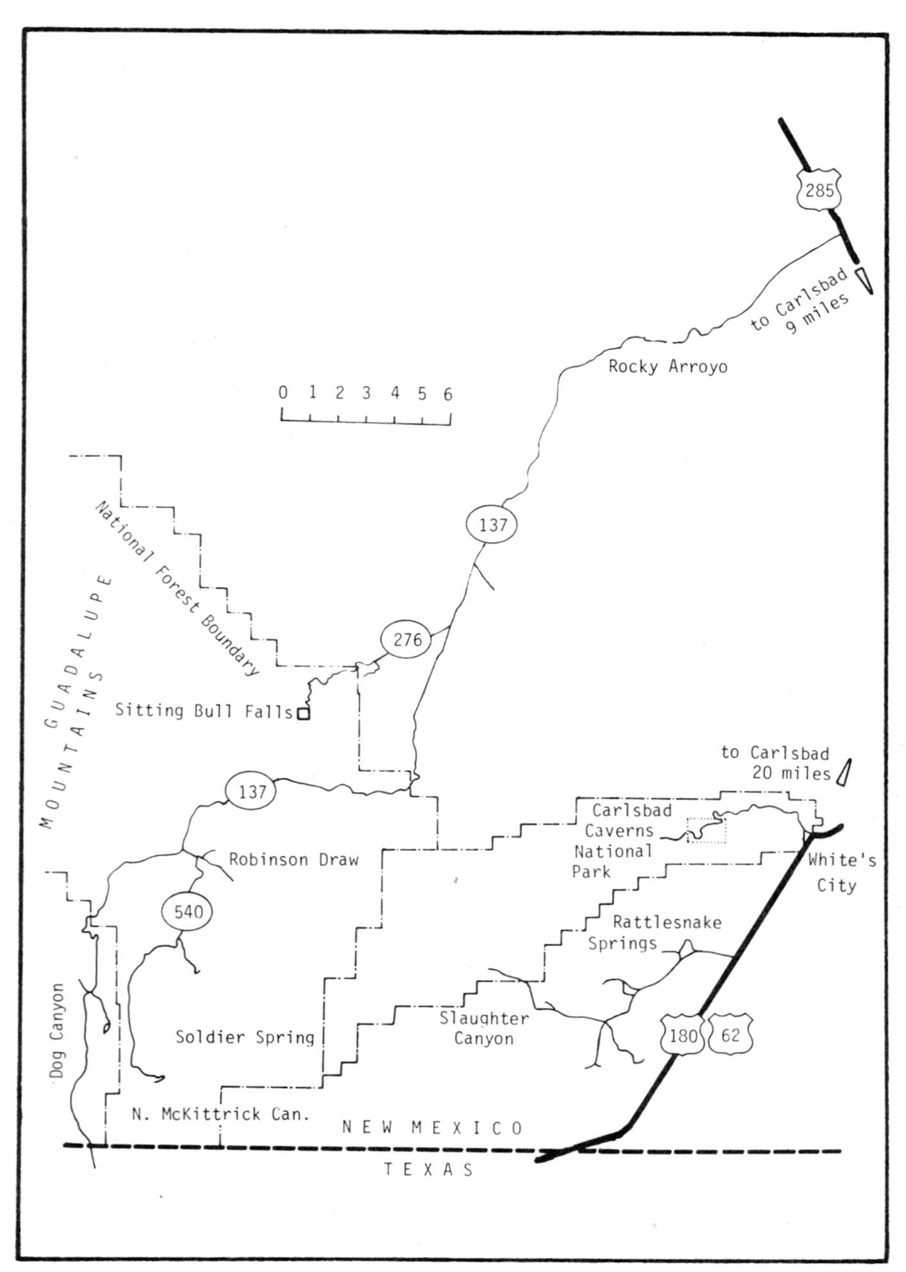
285
to Carlsbad
9 miles
Rocky Arroyo
0 1 2 3 4 5 6
137
National Forest Boundary
GUADALUPE
MOUNTAINS
276
Sitting Bull Falls
to Carlsbad
20 miles
137
Carlsbad
Caverns
National
Park
Robinson Draw
White's
City
540
Rattlesnake
Springs
Dog Canyon
Soldier Spring
Slaughter
Canyon
180
62
N. McKittrick Can.
NEW MEXICO
TEXAS

RATTLESNAKE SPRINGS

One of the best spots in southeastern New Mexico for a wide variety of bird species is Rattlesnake Springs, a small park with diversity of habitat, permanent water, and protection. It is reached from Carlsbad by driving south for five miles beyond Whites City, then turning west at the Park sign and continuing about 3 miles farther. Along this stretch, watch for a variety of sparrows and, in winter and spring, Western and Mountain bluebirds. Common Poorwills can sometimes be heard near the stream on summer evenings.

Despite its small size, nearly 300 species have been recorded at the Springs, including a large number of vagrants. During summer, breeding species include Mourning and White-winged doves, Yellow-billed Cuckoo, Lesser Nighthawk, Ladder-backed Woodpecker, Vermilion Flycatcher, Cave Swallow, Chihuahuan Raven, Cactus Wren, Eastern Bluebird (in willows along the creek), Curve-billed and Crissal thrashers, Bell's Vireo (also in many shrubby dry streambeds in this part of the county), Summer Tanager, Pyrrhuloxia, Varied (local), Painted and Indigo buntings, and Cassin's Sparrow (in nearby dry grassy areas). Winter birds often include White-throated Sparrows, rare elsewhere in the area.

Rattlesnake Springs is unique in New Mexico in having four species of oriole during summer. Scott's Oriole frequents dry canyons adjacent to the springs and occasionally visits there. Orchard and Northern (Bullock's) breed commonly, and Hooded Oriole is an uncommon but regular breeder.

The former Washington Ranch northeast of Rattlesnake Springs is now a school, and birding around the ponds and buildings can be productive. Please obtain permission at the office and remember that all land around the Springs is privately owned.

Nearby Slaughter Canyon provides a few species that may have been missed elsewhere. To go there, continue driving south on the paved road rather than turning into Rattlesnake Springs. About ten miles farther, after the road changes to gravel, there is a parking area near the numerous limestone caves which are the first known breeding sites of Cave Swallow in New Mexico. Other summer species include Red-tailed Hawk, White-throated Swift and Pyrrhuloxia. The Gray Vireo is common in some years and is best found in trees on the floor of the canyon.

GUADALUPE MOUNTAINS

About 9 miles north of Carlsbad, NM 137 turns west off US 285 into an area of limestone foothills populated during summer by Swainson's Hawk, Horned Lark, Eastern Meadowlark and an occasional Golden Eagle. Ten miles from

US 285 is Rocky Arroyo which provides different habitats from those of the surrounding dry hills. During summer, Poorwill, White-winged Dove (uncommon), Blue Grosbeak, and Painted Bunting (uncommon) are found here.

At 31 miles from US 285 turn right (west) on NM 409 to Sitting Bull Falls. The lure of water and adjacent vegetation at this scenic picnic site make it an effective "migrant trap," attracting such species as Dickcissel, Rose-breasted Grosbeak, and Indigo Bunting. Breeding in this area are Golden Eagle, Red-tailed Hawk, White-throated Swift, Canyon and Rock wrens, Canyon Towhee, Rufous-crowned, Black-chinned and Black-throated sparrows and, near the waterfall, Black Phoebe. Several other species can be found in the surrounding hills, including an occasional Gray Vireo.

Return to NM 137 and proceed 6 miles farther to the boundary of the Lincoln National Forest and its mountains covered with oak, juniper, and scattered stands of maple and ponderosa pine. Continuing south on this paved road, one comes to a fork at a collection of mailboxes. The left (east) road leads to several productive spots, and after about 2 miles, pines become increasingly conspicuous. Robinson Draw (1.4 miles from the mailboxes) is often good for Wild Turkey.

Along this road, there are vista points on the right (west) overlooking Dog Canyon, from which birds of prey (particularly Golden Eagles) often are visible. At the end of this road, one may park and take a one-mile foot-trail to Soldier Spring. This area has many summering species, including Band-tailed Pigeon, Broad-tailed Hummingbird, Hairy Woodpecker, Gray Flycatcher, Western Bluebird, Solitary Vireo, Yellow-rumped (Audubon's) and Black-throated Gray warblers, Hepatic Tanager, Rufous-sided Towhee, and Black-chinned Sparrow; Red Crossbill is irregular here.

One may also follow a poor dirt road from the parking area to the head of North McKittrick Canyon. The birds are similar to those at Soldier Spring, but the walking is easier and the campsites better. In addition, Spotted Owl and Whip-poor-will are frequently heard at night.

ARTESIA

Artesia lies about 36 miles north of Carlsbad on US 285 and occasionally has breeding Blue Jays and Common Grackles. Its best "migrant traps" are the Artesia cemetery on the south side of town and east of US 285, and a small woodlot east of town. To reach the latter from US 285, go east on Main Street (US 82) for approximately 1 mile and turn left toward a relatively large patch of trees 0.5 mile north. Although unpretentious, it has produced many unusual birds, including Broad-winged Hawk, Williamson's Sapsucker, Least Flycatcher, Red-eyed Vireo, Tennessee and Black-throated Blue warblers, and

Ovenbird. From the woods, one may continue east to the Pecos River where a walk along the banks may be profitable.

During significant snowfalls, flocks of longspurs and Horned Larks congregate along the roadsides near Artesia. One particularly productive loop from the city extends west for 34 miles on US 82, through Hope, turning right on NM 13 and eventually returning to Carlsbad via NM 360 and US 62-180.

The power poles along US 285 are used as perches by raptors of several species from autumn through spring. Frequent here are Golden Eagle, Rough-legged and Ferruginous hawks, and Prairie Falcon, with occasional Merlins and rarely Harlan's race of Red-tailed Hawk.

ROSWELL

Upon entering Roswell, 40 miles north of Artesia on US 285, stop at South Park Cemetery on the left. The extensive plantings here attract numerous migrants, plus wintering birds such as sapsuckers, all three species of bluebirds, and Townsend's Solitaire. Many warblers and sparrows which are difficult to find elsewhere in the area appear here with some regularity.

The city of Roswell itself has breeding Blue Jays and Common Grackles and one of the westernmost populations of breeding Mississippi Kites. These do not nest in a single colony as they often do elsewhere; look for them along the Spring River Corridor and at scattered locations throughout the residential area.

One of the best sites in Roswell for migrants is the grove of trees bordering the municipal golf course at the corner of Fourth and Nevada. In recent years, Cassin's Kingbirds have paused here in spring, along with Hermit and Swainson's thrushes, mixed flocks of vireos, a dozen species of warbler (including Northern Waterthrush), Indigo Bunting, Western Tanager, and several species of sparrow. Burrowing Owls nest in several places, and all three species of bluebird can be found in winter, along with woodpeckers, Northern (Red-shafted) Flicker, Blue Jay, Townsend's Solitaire, and Cedar Waxwing. A new lake being constructed on the east end of the golf course may provide more good habitat.

Chimney Swifts are regularly seen in April and September at the New Mexico Military Institute campus on North Main. Inca Doves have been increasing in the area, especially at the Rose Garden in Cahoon Park just west of Union and Riverside.

Near the pond at the Roswell Zoo, wintering ducks and geese are common. Walk the south bank of Spring River east of the zoo in spring and summer for Green-backed Heron, waterfowl (including an occasional Wood Duck near

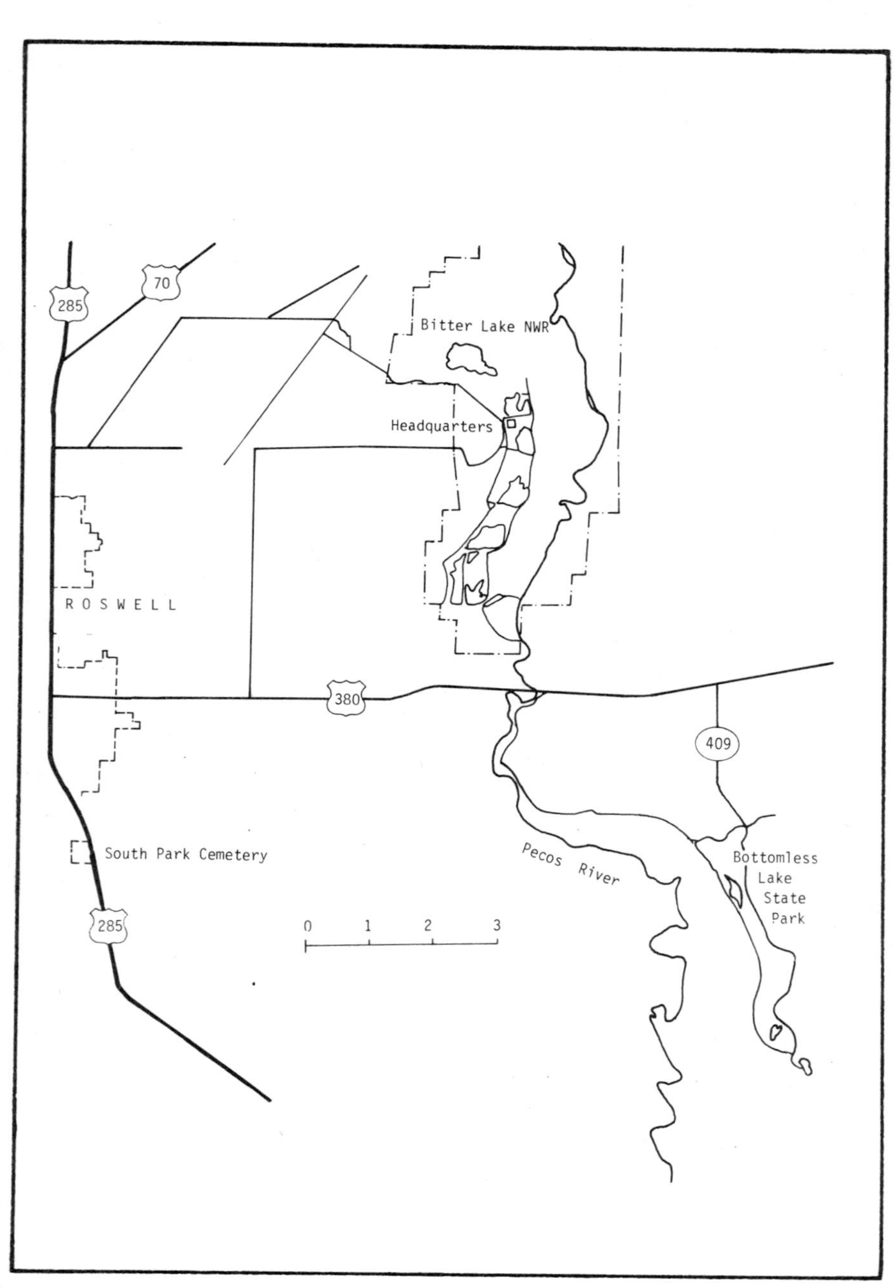
285
70
Bitter Lake NWR
Headquarters
R O S W E L L
380
409
South Park Cemetery
Pecos River
Bottomless Lake State Park
285
0 1 2 3

the oxbows north of the river), and Swamp Sparrow. Also, Rose-breasted Grosbeaks have been recorded in spring.

Take US 380 east from Roswell about 5 miles to the Pecos River. Sprague's Pipits have been reported in fall in the area southeast of the bridge (take the first road south after crossing the river).

To reach Bottomless Lakes State Park, follow US 380 east about 5 miles farther. Take NM 409 south, passing small lakes and mudflats which attract waterfowl year-round. Other birds found in winter are jays and juncos, with nesting Rough-winged, Cliff, and Barn swallows in spring and summer.

A recently acquired portion of Bitter Lake National Wildlife Refuge (described below) is the wetlands overflow area southeast of Bottomless Lakes; it serves as an alternate roost for Sandhill Cranes and Snow Geese in winter. Directions may be obtained from Refuge or Park headquarters.

BITTER LAKE NATIONAL WILDLIFE REFUGE

Back on US 380, return west about 8 miles to Red Bridge Road and the sign indicating the refuge to the north. Follow this road, turning east to the refuge on reaching East Pine Lodge Road. Checklists are available at the office or from a booth at the entrance.

This refuge is one of the best places in the Pecos Valley to see large numbers of waterfowl and shorebirds. Several species of ducks breed here, and thousands of Sandhill Cranes, geese, and ducks are present in winter. In recent years, the numbers of Ross's Geese in the large flocks of Snow Geese have risen to 40 per cent.

Most shorebird species recorded in New Mexico have appeared here, as have such rarities as Little Blue and Tricolored herons, Roseate Spoonbill, Surf and White-winged scoters and Oldsquaw. Numerous gulls and terns migrate through the refuge, with occasional jaegers, Laughing and Sabine's gulls, and Common Tern. A small colony of Least Terns make this the only regular breeding locality for the species in the State. Nesting platforms and decoys may be given a trial in 1992, as such methods have increased Least Tern populations in other states.

The refuge contains a series of ponds, most of them man-made. Distribution of species utilizing these varies with changes in water levels, but the southeasternmost marshes are good in season for herons, egrets, American Bittern, White-faced Ibis, waterfowl, Virginia Rail and Sora.

In fall and winter, Sage Thrashers and Pyrrhuloxias join the resident Curve-billed and Crissal thrashers. Seasonal sparrows include Vesper, Savannah,

Song, Lark, Sage, Cassin's, Chipping, White-crowned and Swamp, with occasional Tree, Brewer's, Harris's and Fox.

Migrants found around the headquarters have included Ash-throated and Vermilion flycatchers, Ruby-crowned Kinglet, Western Tanager and Rose-breasted Grosbeak. Also numerous are vireos, warblers and buntings. Spring counts usually tally over 100 species including Scaled Quail, occasional Bobwhite, Yellow-billed Cuckoo, most swallow species, Bewick's, Marsh and Rock wrens, and Blue Grosbeak. Northern Goshawk, Merlin, Peregrine Falcon and even a Black-shouldered Kite have been reported in recent years.

Recently added to refuge holdings is a farm south of US 380 (not normally open to the public) and bordering the Pecos River on its eastern boundary. Various crops are being tested here for their use as forage, and Greater White-fronted Geese have already 'discovered' this haven.

LESSER PRAIRIE-CHICKEN LOCALITIES

Lesser Prairie-Chickens are found in various areas in southeast New Mexico, their westernmost range, and they are easiest to find on their booming grounds in March and April. It is best to check with the Bureau of Land Management in Roswell for directions to the most current viewing areas, as some lek locations change from one year to the next. (Bureau of Land Management, P.O. Box 1397, Roswell, NM 88201; phone 505-624-1790.)

One consistently good site may be investigated by going east on US 380 out of Roswell for 42 miles to a roadside rest area on the south side of the road. To the north of the rest area, a dirt road leads to several leks. Since visitors' cars need to be in place <u>before dawn</u>, the area should be scouted ahead of time or exact directions obtained from the B.L.M. Once parked near a lek, birders MUST REMAIN INSIDE THEIR CARS and avoid making loud noises. IF UNDISTURBED, the prairie-chickens will display and boom quite near the vehicles.

Once the prairie-chickens disperse, a walk through the area can produce Burrowing Owls and Cassin's Sparrows. The rest area itself is one of the westernmost reliable nesting sites for Scissor-tailed Flycatcher. At present, the only large stand of trees for miles is found here, although enlargement and improvement of the facility is planned and some trees may be removed. Yellow-billed Cuckoo, Cactus Wren and Northern Oriole presumably breed in and south of the rest area. Numerous migrant species appear in season.

SELECTED SPECIES INDEX

(Several common species are not included in the index)